Walking Backwards
(Up an Apostle's Nose)

Alison Chandler
Walking Backwards
(Up an Apostle's Nose)

First published in the UK in 2019

Text © Alison Chandler, 2019

ISBN 978 1 78972 400 4

Typesetting and cover design by Laura Kincaid,
tenthousand publishing services
www.tenthousand.co.uk

Cover illustration 'Dandelion' © Alison Chandler, 2018

Printed by Amazon

CONTENTS

AUTHOR'S NOTE

This memoir is my truth captured at three crossroads in my life.

Spain has been at many other such places in my life but in late October 2015 I walked into Santiago de Compostela, an atheist on the last stretch of the pilgrim's road, knowing my life was changed – not only whatever remained of time ahead but my life already lived. I was walking backwards.

Almost exactly a year later the registrar at Aberdeen Royal Infirmary told me that I was going into emergency surgery for two abdominal tumours and more. The news came from nowhere. My immediate thought was, *I'm glad I walked on the Camino*. It hasn't been cancer or religion that has changed my life but that walk through north-west Spain. My story is not about malignant cells or my cauterised nostrils. The journey tale that follows had been written by the time I was turned inside out in November 2016. In illness words failed me. I closed my laptop and picked up a paintbrush instead. I drew myself back down the golden road. Step by step through the year ahead. With intravenous chemo in my arm and a bag for a colon. Brush stroke by brush stroke. Step by step. Past the wolves. I didn't expect it to be this Way.

I returned to the Camino in October 2018 with a new friend – one of the first people to buy one of my paintings. She has her own story but was with me in my choice of a way ahead: to walk the Way I had set out on in 2015 – a calm Camino. To walk at my own pace respecting the detail on the Wayside. To make a nothing out of the secrets that haunted me. To be part of the magical life of the city in the Field of Stars that I had run to in my dreams for forty years. To go beyond the confines of Christian pilgrimage to where the story of Europe ends. To find out if the magic of 2015 can persist in my life now that I have persisted so very far beyond that first Camino. To show myself I can really live – not just survive – and consider how to walk through the last years of our mother's life. I nearly went to where-we-are-all-going-next a bit quicker than her.

On return from Santiago in the last days of October 2018 I finished this book, 20,000 words of which had tumbled out of me in four days from 28 October 2015. The most recent pathways are in italics. As the title suggests, the story references older history but I do not claim to be a historian. I haven't deliberately changed any factual information but neither have I been writing a dissertation. Inevitably other real people are captured in these pages and none of them asked to be. Nor is this their truth. I have changed their names to acknowledge that I may have strayed from the stories they would choose to write. I am grateful to every single one of them for taking steps with me. I am well aware too that there are many miles that readers may have travelled that I have not walked… yet.

PROLOGUE

28 September 1977

She got up tousle-headed, last night's kohl eyeliner smudged.

'When is the flight?' Miguel asked.

She re-read – misread – the plane ticket on the table by the door.

'It's at 2.30.'

They went back to his bed for a bit. The fountain kept playing.

He made tostados, she damped down her permed curls and he put on his banker's suit with the wide-legged trousers.

She blew all but her last three pesetas on travel snacks. They'd been devalued. No point in changing them back. She had one day left on her visitor's passport and a year of her Hispanic Studies degree to complete. Her summer course in Santiago was over. No point in looking back.

He kissed her at Santiago airport, leaving a slight cologne scent in her nostrils and drove back to sort out the rest of his life. Adultery was still an imprisonable offence in Spain. Divorce was still illegal. Democracy was still eighteen months ahead.

Arriving at 13.30 she missed the weekly 12.30 plane to Edinburgh for which she had had a badly printed ticket. She talked herself onto the next flight out to Madrid by the skin of her teeth. Another near miss with life.

St James the Greater waited on his hill above the wet woods for the next load of sinners to come walking. There were hundreds of thousands on their Way.

CHAPTER ONE

PEBBLES AND PASSPORTS

16 October 2015

One pretty manicured finger up an Apostle's nose. Wasn't what I had expected on Camino. It got me thinking. It got me writing.

Now, four days home, thirty-eight years since the last time I flew out of Galicia, they begin to fade – the sun-brown hill-glowing faces, the deep-voiced songs, the scents of eucalyptus, fennel and freshly showered Spanish man, the pains in knee and foot and calf, the anger. The duendes: the Spanish spirits. And I must let them melt into my dreams and my subconscious. The memories will sink into the mould in which my life is shaped as every visit to Spain has done since 1971 when its dictatorship was growing old, boys were blinded by graffiti, policemen dropped their trousers in the shadows and I was barely a teenager. And, after four days home, I really must stop crying. I am not normally much of a weeper but right now feel bewitched, haunted, under a spell. I can't sleep it off, and I can't wash it off along with the sweat and grime of walking. It seems that the only option, when every moment of every day has been like a line of poetry, to see what was real and what was elf-stroke, is to look back. As you read this, years from now, I am far off down the track ahead, round a bend in the road, seeing things differently. But this story is still my truth as I sit in my grey room, my family sleeping, surrounded by papers dug from the past and dragged from the distance.

In every sense, I have been up high and down steep in the far Atlantic corner of Spain. My days were long and very full of living, on the Camino to Santiago this late October. From starry icy mornings to dreamy nights, I have been in the company of so very many strangers. Some were dead. Some were in my head. Some on paper in my pack. An unimaginable river of humans like autumn leaves caught in different currents, fallen from different trees, whirlpooling together or tumbling past each other. I thought that what would scare me on this adventure would be the dogs, huge wolf guards chained in farmyards or waiting at crossroads or slipping sleekly by against the flow of human traffic. Passing them by is huge for me – it is fear of dog attacks in other pilgrimage tales that has kept me from going on Camino for thirty-eight years. But my company of strangers looked out for me and the hounds haven't come back in my dreams since I've been home, and I can let them fade, shadowless into the impenetrable indigo gloom of Galician forest.

The rest though, the kisses on the back of my hand, the multilingual love singing on the road, the golden mists and plump vegetable patches, the shining flagstones, the reminders of revolutions past, the clouds of incense, the half-remembered poems, the emerald trout streams, the warmth of chocolate-pool eyes, the once-forbidden flutes and accordions, tambourines and bagpipes – can't I capture all these? Net them in words, click save and have them for ever? Perhaps fishing carefully for the right English words to write these stories of love and fear, land and memory, intellect and blood, I can make my heart and mind as strong as my body feels at the end of 116 Spanish kilometres. Because right now I miraculously have no blisters on my feet, but my heart aches, long-forgotten hormones are pumping and my Achilles heel is stinging. People used to go on pilgrimage to earn indulgences. It would be good if mine this autumn had not been entirely one of the self. Perhaps I can bring back from my medieval pilgrimage something of value to twenty-first-century living. Spain and I have been on some great adventures since 1971: there is a lot more than seventy-six miles of memory to share. They tell you, on Camino, that to ease the strain it can help to walk backwards a while, using different muscles. Let me try.

Where to start? Where does Camino begin? This is a frequently asked and very big question. There are hundreds of medieval starting points around Europe marked with a scallop shell. You can start in Cologne in Germany at the shrine to the Three Kings. You could start at Vézelay in France where the second Crusade was called and where Mary Magdalene was said to have been buried. You could start at Reading where a piece of St James' skeleton was taken. A route from the East, the Camino de Levante comes from the port of Valencia on the Spanish Mediterranean. The Camì Sant Jaume comes up from Catalunya in the opposite but for me equally loved corner of Spain. Many pilgrims from America try to fit in all the top three pilgrimages – Jerusalem, Rome and Santiago – while this side of the Pond. You can fly or sail to many modern cities through which the Way passes. Most people walk the Camino stage by stage, not all in one go, and we were walking only the last stage, from Sarria: 116km from the end.

Another answer to this Big Question is, of course, that you begin at your own front door. But which? And when? It might be that for you, like me, the starting point is not in the normal everyday life you live now but at some different place or time which seems, somehow, to connect you with the why or the when or the how or the with whom you are on this journey. That's where your journey to Santiago de Compostela begins. You might have to look far back to find it, far back into religious faith perhaps, or politics, a book or a film or a conversation with someone like me who has been and come back full of it. You may be inspired by dim memories of lessons where our heroes and heroines intertwined with Spain's. You may begin by looking back into a person you yourself used to be, decades ago. You may, like many ancient pilgrims, be going to fulfil a promise to someone else, lighting or holding a candle for someone you have lost. For many, the point these days seems to be complete before you go – to have already banked the sponsorship for a good cause. For others, it is to go as far and as fast as possible – the fitness of your body being the be all and end all. It wasn't for me.

When and where does Camino end? An even Bigger Question. Camino is pilgrimage to the shrine to St James the Apostle, son of Zebedee, fisherman and friend of Jesus. It is traditional to leave your rucksack and go and hug his statue in the cathedral and to kneel before the silver casket where he lies (some of him, perhaps) deep below Santiago de Compostela. For many, for more than a thousand years, that has been the literally awesome climax, with your bowed head only inches from one of the holiest twelve, with the huge thurible swinging incense high above your head to drown your sweaty pilgrim stench. But the word *camino* just means the way, the road, and there are many paths on which you can choose to journey onwards.

This is mine, this making of this story. This pilgrim's tale has many surreal threads to follow through strange days and wicked Spanish nights. It is a legend which, though full of the facts of a physical journey, is at the same time necessarily also a memoir of a nation close to my heart for a lifetime. It is also a love story, maybe two, maybe three. It is a testament to many women's lives. Many of them were me and the voices of others that I carried in my head as I walked. This writing is my way of going on from far behind my stepping-out point one October morning in 2015 to far ahead to where we are all going next.

*

At Montrose station my husband and daughter waved me off on my very big adventure, short legged and grey haired. We have been to the other side of the world and back together. It was October 2015 and I had not travelled alone for over thirty years. I got on the train to Glasgow and, as arranged, joined a group of strangers for the first leg of my journey. I was extraordinarily scarily excited, had been for weeks, my heart racing. My tongue raced with it. No train journey went faster. We had a lot of bonding to do. We didn't have long enough. Of the ten I was to walk with, I had met none but Linda more than briefly before this journey. Most worked for the charity we had fundraised for. None of them knew my story.

Pilgrims to Santiago de Compostela traditionally set off with pebbles, small weights to carry on their journey, adding to the drag of backpack and load of hopes gathered from home, and as they go they leave a pebble on a milestone along the way – with each milestone another burden shed and another step taken towards the future. You see someone ahead leave their pebble and go quietly on alone. You never know their story. You pass many more pebbles left by pilgrims who are invisible to you, gone ahead, far beyond the bends of the road. You never know whether the person you meet or walk with later has left that stone or, if they did, what it meant to them.

Some people I walked with were quietly carrying huge weights with them, of fear or grief or doubt. We walked for a common cause, with just a few days taken from our normal lives. Not everyone's tales got told. In a group of ten, some walked at a different pace and I was not always there when a story was there to be heard. Some outpourings – of matters as huge and ever-present as birth and death – touched us all. Our eleventh intended pilgrim became only an invisible member of the team, spoken of but never seen, a lost companion for Midge, her friend in our group. She never joined us in Spain at all but set off, called desperately in the other direction, to her son, his wife and their baby, born far too early at the troubled other side of Europe. We others didn't know her but her story still came with us.

There are lots of absent people on Camino, people who your fellow walkers never see. We all brought our mothers with us, that is inevitable – mothers we strive to emulate, mothers we are scared to age to be, mothers we don't want to be, mothers we want to leave behind. Ghosts of fathers too walked with us – fathers we would make proud, fathers we would make worried, fathers who wouldn't understand half of it.

Our oldest pilgrim Linda walked with us back to light a candle for her husband, tragically lost, the man who had founded the cause we walked for. She walked fast and with a determination fuelled by horrors I cannot imagine and looked beautiful every step of the way. Deedee walked apart from the man who had taken care of her comfortable life for forty years since she was a child and he was already not. Midge walked through what she knew were the last few days of her father-in-law's life. Our youngest companions, Grace and Alicia, walked towards other crossroads in their lives that those of us with long marriages, full attics and saggy bodies left behind a long time ago.

I was walking back to 1977 to being nineteen and a student for a summer in Santiago. I trailed poets with me in my head and in my pack. I carried with me in my money belt a small, perfectly heart-shaped pebble found on the beach outside my door by my nineteen-year-old daughter. It kept disappearing in pockets as I passed each milestone: not a burden but a reminder of who I am now, of my Scottish home and my responsibility to return to it. It came in handy. Maybe there were other things that hampered me too, stubborn weights that eventually wiggled themselves out of an unnoticed hole in a pocket as I stumbled along.

24 October 2018
Beside a rock pool at the end of the world – or perhaps tumbled into
it now – is a beautiful fused-glass pebble of many bright colours:
yellow of lichen, blue for the Atlantic, black for the pool's depths, red
for pain. Another burden from home that had doggedly walked with
me into another age to find its place on my Camino. I am outliving
my mother who taught us rock pooling.

What was and what is.

What has been and what might have been.

What will be and what is being.

I am not sure I know the difference anymore as I try to capture my memories on these pages now that I am home.

What that I have been sure of for thirty-eight years was I as certain of last week as I walked? What do I know that I am now, here, home, in a higgledy-piggledy fishing village snuggled on the North Sea coast? What legacy is there under the skin of my liberated Scottish adulthood of a while spent where Spanish fascists ruled the shadows? What if anything have I left behind in Spain apart from a book under a pillow, a water flask beside the road and a lipstick on a bathroom shelf? It's confusing. It's tense.

I have only been home four days. I am very tired.

Whatever Camino is for you – trip down memory lane, religious pilgrimage, history lesson, a fundraising challenge, a ridding of burdens, a life transition, a weaving of threads – it is not a medieval penance. It is a stunningly beautiful journey through the lushest, most myth-wreathed and bountiful part of Spain.

The humans on the stretch of Camino that we walked make a multicoloured ribbon winding alongside, over and under the grey highway of normal twenty-first-century Galicia. There are tight Day-Glo cyclists, warm pastel fleeces and silly songs twisted to reflect our jolly determination in Walking Back to Happiness. There is changing into pretty skirts and putting on lipstick in the evenings after a shower, and feeling pink and proud after the rain and the road. There is lustful noting of tight-fit bodies that pass you and greedily consuming delicious creamy coffees and fruity pastries in enchanting raftered cafes converted from thick-stoned barns. There is nothing ugly (or if there is it simply slides by unremembered, covered by conversation).

There are no children except a school trip in a fast blind swarm, eyes only for each other. Otherwise, no one under nineteen, lots over sixty and we are largely responsible for just putting one foot in front of another without thinking much about where we are going. No one asks, 'Are we nearly there yet?' No one whinges or chides. We reassure those who need it that it would be just fine to quit and get a taxi to the next hotel if you have to. It is your Camino. I am not the only one who has left a husband at home and is walking out as a single woman for a while. Humour can be adult – we passed a medieval out-door brothel just off the track – and flirting is common on the road. We all loved Derek, our sole male companion, and shared his company with his wife Fiona.

Though my group joined the Camino over the Gallego (that is Galician) border into the final region of Spain, with only six days' walking ahead of us, others we met had walked from France and were full of conquest and belief. They seemed not to look down on us short-term pilgrims but drank from our energy and told us that it refreshed their own. All along the Way, pilgrims' greetings were morsels of encouragement and comradeship. The rhythm of walking quickens with passing song, which comes up behind you, catches you and carries you up the track a while before the next bend sweeps it on.

This stretch of the pilgrim's road can be a tangle too, with complicated crossroads and hairpin bends and choices to be made, and in October there are many silent stretches. On wet days, the mists come and wrap themselves around you like ghosts seeking comfort, and even on fine mornings wisps snake around the valleys like shining dragons. Glittering snippets of gold leaf sprinkle the calm, soft wood-smoky air as they fall. You are stimulated, energised, disturbed. From the corner of your eye you perceive and, if you are lucky, capture the deepest, oldest, richest stories that flutter down to you through the still, ancient air. There is magic in it, slipping through the years, twisting out from between the trees, ready to enchant you if you open yourself up to it. I opened myself very wide indeed.

The mornings and afternoons on the road to Santiago are marked by the stamping of each pilgrim's 'passport' at churches, town halls, cafe-bars and stalls along the Way. The rules of the cathedral say you must collect those stamps at least twice a day. Not to be always in bars. They evidence that we have done Camino the hard way – on foot, bike or horseback – the spiritual or religious way – and will earn us a Compostela – a certificate in Latin from the cathedral at the end.

The illuminated paper testifies that we have woven our way along at least 100km of the Camino Francés from where it crosses the Pyrenees as hundreds of thousands do each year and have done (in greater or lesser numbers) since the AD 800s. We have taken the rough tracks carpeted in chestnuts and acorns and crossed streams on huge boulders of granite – step-stones for giants. We have visited tiny chapels and elegant town halls and teetered over wide rivers on rickety planks high above eel traps and bridges built by Romans and every empire that came past here since.[1]

---

1. https://www.youtube.com/watch?v=blK3IF51B0M

Europe, they say, was formed on the pilgrim's road to Compostela and we are still forming it, with Dutch and Germans, English and Danes and also with Americans, Canadians, Japanese, South Africans, Costa Ricans and Brazilians, as well as the noisy Scots and Spaniards. We bring our prejudices, our certainties, our principles, our different egos and we stamp them out with our feet and onto our pilgrims' passports and wonder what is important. I am still wondering now that I am home. I have only been back in Scotland for four days and feel still as if I have been walking for a lifetime. My head is full of heroines and lovers. Turn with me and look backwards and you will see them too.

Perhaps it is no more than now-ebbing hormones but I feel the Camino in me every day now, though I am lying in chilly Scotland with the yellow road far behind me. It is still streaming so energetically through my twist of veins that I know that whatever it brought into my life will continue with me through this grey winter and beyond.

On some days, the sense of it is stronger and more real than on others, and as I go about settling back into humdrum Scottish life, something of the experience still pulses as my heart beats, remembering the rhythm of my boots on the road. Invisible to others, the overwhelming hugeness of this presence in my life throbs like knucklebones on stretched animal hide, the Celtic drum which guides the sad melodies of Galicia. It isn't memory yet. It is still part of my living. This middle-aged Camino experience has not been a light nor romantic holiday. It has plumbed me back into a current of history that swept me along with it thirty-eight years ago as Spain put behind herself the last of Western Europe's dictators. Back then I walked beside Spaniards a while – and sometimes ran or hid with them when flames flew and jackboots shone and sometimes lay and listened to whispering fears in the night. It wasn't history. It was intimate and personal. I witnessed it close up and deep inside.

My Camino comes step by step along long roads from deeper history too, following half-forgotten maps in my mind, trails of study, through centuries of Spain and Portugal and their empires and those of their invaders from north and south, by way of a degree from Scotland and a summer at the ancient university of Santiago de Compostela. For years my teenage head had spun and my heart had danced behind cold Presbyterian walls with the love of the Hispanic soul: ancient and modern, gypsy and gaucho, modernist and medieval, revolutionary and priest, laid bare in the poetry and prose of the Peninsula.

For most Brits, Spain is a familiar holiday land full of unsophisticated seaside pleasures, where bureaucracy gives up at the edge of the swimming pool and modern politics melt uselessly like abandoned splats of ice cream on a beach promenade. That the history of the world from Baghdad to Cuba, Patagonia to Los Angeles, Carthage to the Philippines, pivoted on this peninsula has been forgotten by most. No one remembers, as they enjoy a bit of rumpy pumpy in the Balearics, that they are acting out the nation's name – the land of the rabbits, which according to the Carthaginians had overrun this jut of Europe long before we Brits did.

Here St Andrew was shipwrecked, carnival was first created and zombies invented, but few folk know beyond Galicia's borders. To me, though, the golden grandeur and dishonourable tragedies of Hispania's empires are very real. They touched and inspired many things that I have loved. It is the patron saint of all that empire: Sant Iago, Jacobus, Jaume, St James – whatever your people call him – that draws us in passion or otherwise to his cathedral in Spain's most secret corner.

Here England's sweet Laurie Lee first stepped out onto Spanish soil and slept in the hills with the wolves above Vigo.

Till I walked out this October morning I couldn't remember how much of all that I had forgotten. I have forgotten an awful lot more besides. Life took me in different directions and I have never exploited what I studied of Hispania in order to earn a living, keeping it practised and sharp in my mind. I learnt other lessons and made a career of them instead. Over the years, Spain sank out of my day-to-day consciousness and into the layers of who I now am.

On this Camino, though, I was stripped down like the coats of coloured paints peeling off Sarria's walls as we arrived. I searched out of the minibus window for the land I once knew: warm terracotta red, sea blue, earth yellow, misty green beneath a layer or two of half-hearted whitewash. Terrible wonderful Spain. Hemingway said it was the only country.

Nearer my own sweaty surface, Camino this October would tempt me to revisit – to reach out and let my lips touch – a bitter-sweet, cologne-scented, tinsel-sparkling ribbon of 1970s teenage passions. Those first young love affairs competed for my attention with studies of the great Hispanic poets, or were conducted in Spain itself. Spanish became the language not only of my studies but of my deepest teenage angsts and headiest conquests, my dreamiest days and for years my most extravagant and treasured excesses. It was the language that I heard in my dreams and in which I expressed myself when I wanted to be more globally poetic and less provincial Scot. Its poetry gave me certainties on which to build a life. To have the Spanish language in my ears again, before my eyes, on my lips this autumn was to be tempted again to plunge in and drown myself in Spain. In Castilian Spanish, when you really like something, you say '*me encanta*' (it enchants me) as if it is not something you personally choose for yourself – 'I love' – but something that happens to you. Spain enchants me and I fall easily under its spell. It is a serious affair.

Perhaps this tingling that I still feel in the air surrounding me, pricking in my toes, humming in my ears, is some basic instinct that is trying to tell me about who I am walking beside and how I can best walk beside them. All the world's myths are there on Camino to entrance you if you let them.

On the track through the forest perhaps it was the mythological circle of snake who let a coil curl out of the shadows like a twisted tree root in the mud, caught my damaged ankle and reminded me of endless love, the inevitable cycle of life and quite importantly that there's no place like home.[2] My mind wandered very far indeed last week as I walked off round the bend, watched by dogs.

Perhaps this weird feeling of otherworldliness that I cannot leave behind is revealing some truth. Perhaps the experience of my steps on the Way of St James has opened me to something even more ancient and universal than the monotheism the Apostle brought us. Perhaps deep down there is something fundamentally true in the myths that forever sustained ordinary people in their villages, before and later without the priests. They took and stored their golden grain on pillars where village vermin couldn't pilfer, but it is harder to steal women's stories whispered round a village washing pool. Perhaps I met the universal archetypes of wizard in a music shop and witch in a roadside store, hero and daemon in the sparking Iberian night.

The intention behind my Spanish pilgrimage was none of that. It was meant to let me take breath from the normality of life and indulge myself in long-treasured memories of Santiago. I do not believe in the myth of St James nor wish to make an alternative creed of daft paganism. I set off just wanting to consider what that was essential to a nineteen-year-old literature student in 1977 is still real now to a middle-aged mum? What has slipped out of my pocket and can be abandoned as a self-indulgent silliness? What needs to be searched for or

2. http://www.mcfarlandpub.com/excerpts/0-7864-1953-9.Chapter2.pdf
   https://www.theosophical.org/publications/1555

replaced? What is alive now of what was absolutely vital to her then?

- to never be pinned down by a piece of paper
- to never have to do what was expected; to never have to anything
- to never lie about myself just because it made others comfortable
- to never be mistaken for one of the baddies or those that they fed off
- to always make a point of my principles – particularly if someone was listening
- to live my own – my very own – truth however much it slapped me in the face
- to know stuff and be awfully awfully clever
- to explore every hot, damp, pungent corner of life as it opened in front of me, whatever lurked there, and call it freedom
- to make something poetic if it killed me
- to not be the village, the school, the clan, the class, the gender, the church or cult – but still belong somewhere
- to feel words on my tongue that shaped feelings that our mothers and fathers surely never felt – salty, sweaty, acid, fermenting European feelings that brewed so easily in a Galician cauldron at the end of the world, beyond the Pyrenees and before Africa
- to have secrets and to tell secrets and never have them cross the Bay of Biscay northwards and come back to haunt me

Back in 1977, I flew into Santiago, running from Scotland with my waggy tail between my legs from another near miss with life – a Free Bird who would not change for anyone. Now in 2015 I was walking back – slow slow slow – and wondering what point I was making and whether it would be a climax that I would mark with a piece of paper written in Latin. I have a drawer full of bits of paper: degrees and diplomas which never pinned me down and poetry I wrote back then, much of it in Spanish, perhaps to hide it from the grey minds around me. I have much of it spread on my lap now as I write. Its self-indulgent 1970s melancholia hides a basically happy soul. How much have I really changed since 1977?

***

October 2018
How much have I been changed since 2015?

***

I certainly have not been running away this time. To walk back to Santiago de Compostela in 2015 was a comfortable decision. It didn't start with any profound spirituality, just a deep-seated love of all things Spanish and some old dreams. My newly made and even more newly widowed friend Linda announced on Facebook in February that she was going and I could adventure with her, and she promised to look out for feral or otherwise fearsome Spanish farmyard dogs. She was doing it as a fundraiser for the charity which she had helped her husband Rick to set up and the opportunity was there for me, all organised, if I could raise the money and get fit enough. It was a cause I believed in: I am someone who was born and lived under a very lucky if wandering star and I know it.

Other folks with different abilities need people like my fellow sponsored walkers to raise the funds and provide the services which give them the life of quality and choice and freedom that many take for granted. I could walk back, and by raising the money I could give back. I bloody well could get fit enough – I *should* get fit enough, five years older than my dad when he had his first heart attack. I fell just before Christmas and lay a while on the frozen tarmac with a damaged ankle till saved by friends. I did a lot of lying down afterwards and my ankle kept hurting. I could give in or see what exercise would do.

I took the Easter holidays to work that out before signing on the bottom line. My husband wouldn't stop me nor want to come with his dodgy knee. I think he is comfy where he is. It is time for our daughter to find her own direction. So far, she has lived cooler, more poker faced than I, exposing her soul less. Walking with her unique spirit through the last years of her childhood has reminded me of what mattered to me once upon a time. Having got her safely to this point, there is a clear 'what next?', 'who am I now?' for me.

There were many lonely, risky inner-city times when I ran with wolves and it seemed I'd never settle with loving man and lovely child in the embrace of a small community. But I have and it is good and I can walk back to it – to them – with ease.

What about an awfully big adventure, some new adjectives and a bit of being exquisitely mad again? My father is long gone and my mother has lived strong to eighty-eight, and I can have decades ahead of me, like her, not really wanting to go far. So why not in the meantime, not knowing what lies ahead, do the thing highest on my bucket list for the longest time and return to Santiago. It wouldn't be naively, for the first time in thirty-eight years (my husband and I have been back as 1980s city-breakers to stay in the five-star Parador). But this time it would be the proper way, walking back along the rough tracks with my pilgrim's passport and pebble and messages of encouragement and support from friends and family. I would step out and take what came to me, mile after mile, day by day, not thinking ahead but waiting to see what rises up from the ground beneath my feet.

*

All along my Way there were other voices in my head apart from my own and my companions. Before I left, and recognising my challenge, my mum sent me the words of John Bunyan's hymn 'To Be a Pilgrim' – 'Who would true valour see, let him come hither...' I sang it as I walked. The English hymnal version sung at Margaret Thatcher's funeral doesn't mention the hobgoblins (perhaps too close to the bone) but they were very much apparent on my own pilgrimage.

The world has turned many times since fearful pilgrims started walking from front doors and meeting places to all the places which had acquired, somehow, the magic-bearing bits and bobs of some dead Palestinian, Greek or Roman. Onto the roads to Santiago, they came from all the compass points of Christianity to visit the relics of St James the Apostle and the closest they could come to their God before they took their sins for judgement.

Now we share our passions on Facebook. If others 'like' what we say that makes all OK and not a sin at all. The world has turned many times since that 1986 five-star break with my husband to Santiago and in those years since I married him and he became our daughter's father and we keep each other safe and life is good.

Though we both did plenty growing up in Spain – his in the nightclubs of Ibiza – we are otherwise like chalk and cheese. We won each other's trust hard a long time ago by stripping recklessly down to the rawest of truths which will remain wordless here, cached safely under the floorboards. In the early years, we examined loyalty and possession, vulnerability and trust in all their dimensions and took each other to ravines with the crumbliest edges in the process.

Being the end of the post-pill/pre-AIDS, illegally high 1980s, we looked over into an abyss where icebergs floated, and ad agencies warned of the unspeakable and poorly understood epidemic sweeping the world. People we knew were sunk just because they were not as lucky as we, not because we had been wiser or behaved much better. We had all loved hard and hot and loosely in the decades before and were proud of the stupid lessons learned. Guilt was a useless emotion. We accepted no one's morality without experimentation. Indulgence was not a sin but a right. We lost people without looking back just because we had loped off in different directions. Some got dead – not just AIDS but murder, suicide, cancer, alcohol, age. Some got bald. Some got babies earlier than we did. Some got on planes for other continents. Some got suburban. Some stayed put and it was us who left on a jet plane. Then, later, with the wonders of the World Wide Web, we refound some who had meant much to us just by popping a name into a search and clicking – easy peasy.

So it was that this grey, saggy woman could set off on Camino, with a pack on her back once again. She could wave from a train window to a tall blue-eyed husband and daughter, in trust and honesty, with a laugh and a joke, and step out and maybe meet Miguel, the Spanish boy she had loved and left thirty-eight years before at the airport of Santiago de Compostela, refound on Facebook in one bored moment a year or so ago. He and I had shared a paragraph of quick reminiscence then settled back to occasionally clicking 'like' on a funny picture and no more contact than that. But since I was going to Santiago it made sense to drop him a light note – might it be good to meet? Perhaps? Not important but…

By the time I flew out from Glasgow at 5.00 this October morning of 2015, we had a kind of loose plan – he, Miguel, and I. We would meet for one long evening of catching up on my arrival at the end of the Camino to Santiago where we had met in 1977, in an oak-smoky bar of low beams and sparkling mirrors and cider poured over a shoulder to fall frothy into its glass. It was on Day 1 of my journey little more than a dare, a giggle I shared with the group. 'Ooh, does your husband know?' (He did.) 'Ooh, we'll have to watch you with ten sets of chaperones' eyes!'

Santiago in 1977 before democracy had settled in had, though, been much more than about one summer of love. Walking back to it was not about re-finding one boy. It might be that the thought of reminiscing with someone who also remembered those times may have added a swing to my step as I set off from Sarria on the first day, light pack on my back, walking poles at the ready. My thoughts, though, were more of a week walking my middle-aged body on Spanish soil than one evening with any boy.

In every one of Galicia's many streams and rivers there are whirlpools where a fallen leaf, with no strength against the current, can be caught and confused outside the intended flow. Sometimes it may slide against another for momentary comfort before detaching and going on in the right and inevitable direction. The fingers of chestnut leaves clutch each other a while. Tiny birch leaves play follow-my-leader in tight spirals.

My Camino was not going to be so straightforward or comfortable as I had set off imagining. I had forgotten most of what Spain is to me, who I am, its hugeness in my little story, which is part of an immense story. It told itself to me as I walked, breath hot, unfolding like the warm rolling land ahead, gritty like the track, rollicking like the music of Tuna, the minstrels of Santiago University that Miguel took me to hear, snuggled on a cold cathedral step. With roots back to 1495, you can hear in their schmaltzy songs the whole Gallego diaspora – the music men took with them to blend into the music of the USA, the Caribbean and Latin America. More than anywhere else in Spain, Galicia lost its men to the sea and distant lands. Their songs are full of longing for home or are serenades of girls who lived behind railed balconies, embroidering fantasies. Medieval students entertained people in return for food. The Tuna still wear a long cape covered in multicolored ribbons thrown down from the girls he has charmed. They charm me still in 2015.

October 2018
They charm me still in 2018.

There was other forbidden music singing faintly in my memory as we flew in over Galicia's hills of yellow gorse and broom and sparkling hulks of granite mountaintop. The scents of the Peninsula twitched my nostrils at the airport as our goblin-faced driver loaded our bags into the minibus to Sarria and I inhaled my first breaths of Spain in a long time. Spain was different and proud of it; Spain was still the same as I remembered.

CHAPTER TWO

ON MY FEET AGAIN

4 November 2016

I wait for the trolley bed and the figures dressed in green scrubs to lift me onto it and whisk me gently away, round the bend in the road. I walked on the Camino. I do not believe in hell and know I am not going there. I have lived my life fully, left my mark and am free. I am unconscious.

---

8 November 2016

They used to say there were no atheists in the WW1 trenches. How many in oncology wards? Lying here shell-shocked I contemplate my own trip over the top. Not inevitable but no more in my control than it was for the Tommies. Will I find religion before I go? I lie stock still, empty my mind and wait.

What comes to me is the utter certainty that there is nothing. Death is death. There will be nothing more. It is a peaceful, empowering and fortifying confirmation.

---

8 November 2016
Cold breath in through the nostrils.

Suck the pain from its most intense point. Where there was gangrenous perforation and now there is a crevasse. Drag and tease out the needling, knifing, slicing garrotte. Up through belly, chest, throat, sinuses. Pull it in multiple strands up until they fill my nostrils and my breasts ache with effort.

Hold it. Hold it. Hold it!

Now! Lift back of head from pillow. Bring elbow back. An inch. At the peak of movement breathe out. Air hot. Power burn. Squeeze out every slick of vapour till again my chest aches.

DON'T STOP. Quick! Catch the next strand. Go straight from the bottom of the out-breath with the body starving and stretching for air and suck again. Hard!

My neck tires. I need the support of the other elbow but it is on my right side.

Suck the pain out of one fraction more of the right side of my belly. And at the crucial point inch the elbow back. Don't let the breathing speed up. Don't!

Instead breathe the urge up, up, up and out of flaring nostrils. Eyes shut. Mouth shut. Everything channelling from gut to nose, gut to nose, gut to nose so that pain does not, cannot, reach my brain. Pain need not exist.

Repeat.

It will take many moves until both elbows are back and my shoulders leave the mattress.

Never stop.

Not the most minute gap between the perfect point of breath and the movement.

Now! Out-breath IN-breath.

Now I must move my right leg to take my weight. Now it is at the wrong side of the pain. Any movement must pass from toe through abdomen to brain and I must catch it before it picks up pain.

As I breathe in I am netting it in filaments as strong as spider thread. I start at my big toe. Thinking my breath down to where the nail is in-growing. It will take many breaths before I have wrapped all the way to the hip in steely thread.

I pull my leg across the sheet an inch or two, my breathing bypassing the sliced muscles in my belly. It is exhausting and coats my nostrils in ice burn, but it doesn't hurt.

If I were to let go between in-breath, hold and whistling out-breath through clenched teeth... then... Well, let's not.

Nearly there. Practice perfects.

I go through this process many times in the night. By morning a venture to the lavatory means only a dozen movements before my legs have scissored their way till my knees reach the edge of the bed.

Right leg, right a bit, left leg, right a bit.

Now my knees bend my feet towards the hospital floor. My weight sinks into my forearms and the base of my hands. My breath is the engine. I can feel it in — must share it between — the pad of every fingertip. It must be powered through every junction or the whole net, so carefully strung up to hold my body, will unravel back to my burning belly, where it will fill my head with screaming.

Nearly there. Now the movements must come on both the breathing in and breathing out. Twice as exhausting. Now there is gravity to contend with. As feet reach cold floor my flesh is stretched to its full five-foot length and my neck and back ache. There is nothing for it. I have to bend at the waist.

I have to bend at the waist, flex my calf muscles, pull on my thigh muscles, lever with my arm muscles, grip with my toe muscles, stretch with my neck muscles, hold it all together with my back muscles. I have, instead of splitting like a sack full of mouldy potatoes, to stand.

Bend is a big word.

Each letter is a breath in and a breath out, and the tiny movements must flow smoothly so that none of the pain escapes but is held there... I must flex.

Flex, pull, lever, grip, stretch, hold, bend are all big words when each is spelt out in raw flesh.

Suck the pain up from where it surfaces like a lava flow and push the foot into the floor. Grip with the calf and thrust with the thigh so the buttocks leave the bed and the arms rise up, bringing hands and fingertips to float up up up like feathers, and I am standing, arms lifting from my sides like wings and it feels like flying because I feel no pain, no pain, no pain.

Arms out from my sides, fingers feeling the air between them, sweat cold on my back, cotton brushing against my thighs, I can put one foot forward.

November 2016–October 2018

I could put one foot forward but there were many backwards steps. Healing took three months, not three weeks, before I could let the poison treatment find its way through my veins. There could be no thinking ahead. There was a lot of lying down. There was a choice to give in. There were months of not knowing or thinking about what half a day would bring.

Something woke and rose in me day by day by day as thirty-eight years became forty-one and nineteen years old became sixty-one. Something strengthened and quickened inside me and flowed down my arm and into my paintbrush while chemotherapy ran in through the other arm. It has turned into an iconography all of my own – a language of pebbles and pathways, waves and wolves, apples and oranges, red fish and salamanders, maps and footsteps and wild cherries. A language that I could speak in when I couldn't write a single word or take a step forward.

CHAPTER THREE

METAPHOR AND
MILES AHEAD

Meeting Miguel again was just to be a sweet sigh. There had been a lot of summer loving, a lot of Spain and the warm breath of quite a few more golden Spanish boys on my white throat before one in Santiago in 1977 and others after. In 1971, I had flown in with a gaggle of school chums and silly teachers to a grotty Costa resort half filled with boys from the roughest end of Glasgow and us from the poshest school in Dundee. While our tipsy gym teacher danced with a pair of paper knickers on her head, and the slum-pale Weegie lads dug holes through the plaster work to see into our bathroom, my thirteen-year-old friends and I were charmed by the more emotionally literate and golden-skinned continental boys.

We stuck transfers to our tight brown tummies and flirted our way onto free shots on the dodgems and sang 'Witch Queen of New Orleans' and 'House of the Rising Sun'. We ignored the sweaty men who flashed open their long black coats at us to show rows of watches and pockets of cigarettes, cheap cheap cheap.

My periods started, my vision wobbled and I fainted in the baking courtyard of a mountain monastery. Spain brought me round with the screech of swifts and the nostril-searing scent of frankincense and myrrh wafted by flustering nuns. We took the warm awakening of our libidos back to Dundee High and into goings out with aspiring rock stars from our own community and that got us through a year or so.

I wrote to one of the Easterhouse Academy boys on return but sent my steamy letter to the wrong address, my rather religious Glaswegian aunt's, causing much of a rumpus. I wrote sad poetry and drew drifty girls in sunny skirts wandering through flowering meadows that hid their undrawable feet.

In the next few years, pen-pal friendship with a rich Catalana from Barcelona introduced the delicate, tragic, confident manner of loving that is graciously donated by Spanish girls to their men. They were, in comparison to me, so cool as they sailed down the Ramblas to a stream of compliments that slid off their perfectly postured brown backs without acknowledgement.

We Scots lassies would, back then, have rewarded and encouraged the attention with giggles, grateful that someone had noticed that we were women now. Our Spanish friends had been precious lacy princesses to their fathers and uncles all their lives. They knew they had a God-given right to be flattered.

Spanish has a special word for that too: '*piropear*' – to shower someone with compliments. They had no need to acknowledge the light littering of it. They sensed no insult. They sailed past the ten-a-penny macho flatterers in a cloud of sweet chastity. Their only choices – whore or Madonna – were stark. They made a clear, cold, cologne-scented statement about which they were.

The Ramblas back then belonged still to old Spain not Europe. Tourists were visitors. We didn't feel or act like we owned the place. We had no right to remain. There were no post-Olympic gaggles of girly hen and staggering stag parties easily jetted in from Britain's industrial north to be tempted by endlessly living statues. Nor were there canvas-covered stalls with clever arty-crafty hippy niceties snipped from silver or stained on silk to sell to world citizens on city breaks. Any hippies around and about were heading for the ferry to Ibiza and far too far out for entrepreneurism.

The Ramblas belonged to perfumed old ladies in navy cardigans and loose grey tailored and lined shift dresses out to buy bunches of lilies and gladioli from the lines of flower stalls. Only a few now survive. Gone are the cages of songbirds, lizards, marmosets and mongooses for sale next to the flower-sellers, for a lady to keep on a cool marble terrace and talk to as she watered her pot plants high up behind a beautifully wrought iron balcony. From up here she has watched anarchists and communists, republicans and fascists, nuns and nancy-boys and whiled away the years without a husband, dead on one or another elegantly unmentioned side in the Civil War. The door to her apartment has five different kinds of lock and bolt and even the peephole has its own small cage of iron. She lives like a queen in a medieval castle.

The Boqueria covered market is still a genuine Catalan joy in the twenty-first century but the stall-holders and housewives have to push to get past the silly tourists with no use for nor even recognition of the ice-cold red fish or nuts or cured meats. Then, on my earliest adventures in fascist Spain, a tourist had to watch out for flying plums if a price war broke out between one busty Catalan costermonger and a competitor across the passage.

'*Me cago en la leche de la madre que te parió!*' one wifey shouted as I ducked beneath a hail of overripe fruit. 'I shit in the milk of the mother that bore you!'

Ah the richness of Spanish civilisation, always so concerned with the barbarism of others in its distant Empire and blind to its own. When the navy was in the docks down beyond where Columbus's column stands, the boulevards seemed as if the

Gran Teatre del Liceu had been turned inside out. Dazzling white officers with flashing dress swords on their slim thighs grandly entered the stage beneath the sun-flashing plain trees. Their olive-skinned heads could not have been lifted higher in any grand operatic performance nor military parade than by their pride in the gorgeous jewel that each carried on their arm. Her black hair crinkling in the warm breeze, her scarlet lips and black-lined almond eyes proclaimed him her own; the frill to her white skirts and the wine-red carnation in her hair asserting that so was all of Spain. Smart moustachioed young businessmen enjoying a cool drink, old white-capped men wasting the heat of the day, gypsy beggars all watched the show and agreed: Spanish women, their women, ruled the world with their smooth hips and demure smiles.

Walking beside my friends and amongst their compatriots, not mine, I was beginning to learn the power of sex. I was beginning to learn the trap of gender.

October 2018

The restrained, elegant dignity of Spanish sexuality affects me still. Beneath my spectacles and grey hair, I still respond to the theoretical passion which penetrates from a sparkling and quizzical gaze. In that direct, honest and calmly held appreciation of the sexually opposed other, there is an especially Spanish, elegant and arrogant grace. It quietly asks why should I not? Why should you not?

The power that the other person brings to the moment is respected, whether that is the power to becalm or the power to submit and, in so doing, challenge. What is sought is strength not fragility, spirit not breaking. There is solemnity and awe for the beautiful opportunity which the meeting offers. It has a wonder and a heat unknown in the north but bound up tighter than to the east.

It is there in special shining salons where long-lost friends who once were lovers share ample wine, warm proximity, sweet shellfish on their fingers and the conclusions of people who have given birth to others. Spanish sexuality is neither what passes for seduction by blunt brutal Scot nor by smarmy English charmer. While Spain becomes less different and more European, its always caged and wild heart is still evident. Though maybe a difference now less apparent to Westernised locals used to looking over the Pyrenees, it still tickles the nostrils of Hispanophiles who bury their noses in study of such things.

At home, there was a race to grow up, push our tits out, get drunk, get down and dirty on the dance floor to 'Je T'aime' and 'Let's Spend the Night Together', get felt up in the dark of the basement, lying on purple crushed velvet lit only by a candle in a Mateus rosé bottle with Mike Oldfield's *Tubular Bells* enchanting us. We were free – with every chance of good school grades, a driving licence, a pill to pop to keep babies away and a place at university to keep us out of work.

By the summer of 1975, virginity was hanging round our necks like an albatross. My Catalana and her sisters spent a Scottish summer with me and wrinkled their pretty noses when my mother served them sweet and juicy corn on the cob: what did we take them for? Farm animals to be stuffed with maize?

They were surprised to find no skinny maid picked up their dropped clothes nor polished their shoes and were even more surprised to read Franco's truths in my mum's *Guardian*. Opposition to his regime had been mounting in the last year. Even actors were striking. Universities were clamouring for democracy. The Basques were under martial law and the nation was in crisis. None of that was being reported to the middle-class teenagers who would inherit what was left.

My Catalan pen pal taught my friends and me the glorious masochistic (sadistic?) and very Spanish pleasure of deciding that love was impossible and could not be requited. No European nation is more interested in pain than the Spaniards – whether Inquisitors or self-flagellating members of Opus Dei, arena bullfighters or street bull-runners, painters or Holy Week paraders of bleeding Christs, bloody revolutionaries or blood-drained convents. Spaniards, so very unlike other Europeans, have taught themselves to make something beautiful even out of death. Passion is pain. To hurt, to lose, to bleed is to love, is to live. Ah the delirious delight of it in a long, light Scottish summer night, 1975 the hottest year we had ever known.

One of my school friends mourned the loss of that cool Catalana for a lifetime when she went back to Barcelona and married well. Of such is poetry made. Those long-ago friend-ships, though they waxed and waned for decades, endure perhaps because we stripped down so very bare, in our three-triangles-and-a-bit-of-string bikinis, exposed ourselves so very poetically. Many of those good-time boys and girls, now stalwarts of Scottish society, have been my Camino sponsors in 2015 and I took nostalgia for them with me.

October 2018
My paintings now hang on their walls. They stare alike at the butterflies I met at the end of the world on Camino 2018.

Anyhow, somehow, tragically agonising chastity held on by a thread and I reached university intact. And so it was that my own bursting into womanly blossom coincided with immer-sion in the greatest of love poetry – from Andalucían Federico

García Lorca and Chilean Pablo Neruda to many more revolutionary Hispanic souls – and no comfortably off Scottish boy was ever likely to match up to that. Spain, blood and love; pain, poetry and politics; honour, integrity and sentimentality would be for ever intertwined. George Orwell, Hemingway and Laurie Lee all taught me how to see inside the corners of Spain from the outside.

In grey Scottish adolescence, headmistresses prowled our discos in black cloaks with a leather tawse still up the sleeve in case we dared to experience pleasure. University, on the other hand, was a place of freedom where no grey adult dictated how long lust might last and wild ideas were all permissible if we could back them up with academic reference. Occasionally a nice warm-blooded boy crossed my cider-fuelled path on a cold October Edinburgh night. Once a London Sephardic Jew – ancestors thrown out of Spain centuries ago – sat naked at the end of my student bed in the dawn and played Leonard Cohen's words 'I loved you in the morning' on acoustic guitar and welcomed me tenderly to adulthood. My foot cramped in ecstasy. But virginity was ours to give in the British 1970s, and he and I were under no obligation to stay together. In those years I said goodbye with never a backwards look – out of sight out of mind. I am learning to again.

On middle-aged Camino, while your head looks and your nose points determinedly forward towards the shrine of St James, your mind, freed from the paraphernalia of the twenty-first century does wander and you can find yourselves seeing things forgotten or spun with time. For miles, there are no homely points of reference – forests are exotic, language parochial, constellations unfamiliar in the predawn, high moors utterly silent except for your own tired feet scrunching and your own breath heaving. Broadband is not medieval and your smartphone is tucked away and dumb. As a result of the unfettered swirling of thoughts and hormones, the older pilgrims that you pass may sometimes look a little dizzy. I am sure I did. I nearly tripped many times.

'Tragedy as metaphor – discuss' was the first essay I had to write at university and I felt inadequately equipped by life to do so. Metaphor I was fine with. Still am. I hadn't had much of the other by 2015.

October 2018
Have had some since.

Life did not, after all, begin for me in tortured fascist Spain in the 1970s. I am a baby boomer from the you-never-had-it-so-good late 1950s born to intellectual middle-class parents in a Scottish village where my father and my father's father belonged, near a town where we were someone to some folk. I had had a childhood surrounded by people who read the freest press in the world, who lectured, wrote and painted their way out of European horrors of the 1930s and 1940s as atheists determined to look optimistically forward. The Cold War raged in comfortable intellectual debate around my parents' dinner table. While the dictator Franco was safely propped up by NATO to keep the Commies at bay, the Costas had begun to spread to give pale Scots a taste of Viva España and a chance to turn lobster red.

Meanwhile near Dundee, and in case global thermonuclear war were to break out, I had held a nightly roll call of my teddies before snuggling up for the night in my father-architect-built bungalow. Spies had been handsome men on fun TV shows with names like UNCLE, Saint, Bond, Smiley. Onion Johnnies had come cycling, laden with exotic golden vegetables woven into ropes over their shoulders and handlebars, from poor distant Brittany for Dad to crack jokes with, showing off his French. When the wild geese arrived so had crazy Uncle Mac to shoot them, fresh from carousing with Robert Graves in Spain and with hilarious imitations of flamenco singers crying for the love of their donkey.

We had collected the pretty papers off hand-wrapped Andalucían tangerines and stuck them into scrapbooks for geography projects. We had learnt French from age seven at a good fee-paying school where we did the full life sentence – four years old to seventeen in the same dirt-grey uniform, with chalk-dusty black-cloaked teachers and lists of dead people from imperial wars covering the wood-panelled halls. We had holidayed in cool and sensible Scandinavia and the Alps, had walls full of books and original art and my parents had known everything about the world.

Being clever and knowing stuff was all important, and sharing facts was the family hobby, while others had darts or football. They had three newspapers daily from a variety of national and local perspectives, and Dad had advised and sometimes written for the BBC: we were apparently unburdened by dogma or prejudice of any sort. I was frightened by nothing but the Alsatians that I had to pass each time I left home.

Mum had worked and written as an expert on the cruel history of Scottish women's lives. She had talked of burning her bra while keeping my sister's pram in the hall.[3] My father and his frustrated friends had stepped around it to talk of artistic and intellectual glories that most would never reach from grey Dundee. It was unthinkable that my older brother, baby sister and I would be without opinions on everything.

---

3. 'There is no more sombre enemy of good art than the pram in the hall' – Cyril Connolly

My Dad's heart attack and fear of the next, my sister's late arrival and fight for a space to be heard, my brother's already established role as know-it-all – all were prompts to my contrariness; none were going to limit my story. For my mother, it seemed to me back then, it had been fine and safe for those firmly held opinions to be fed by the pages of the *Guardian* or the sky-high walls of books rather than by first-hand experience. *Tragic*! thought I. How could anything be known for sure (I thought at seventeen) if I hadn't held it in my own pretty sticky hand?

I intended to accept no assumptions about the world. Discussing tragedy was not enough for me to find my own metaphors for life. Nothing was too low, no one was too ignorant, nowhere was too grim for me to delve into it for some new perspective for liberated global sisterhood. There was a tremendous opportunity for me, their older daughter, to see how far the boundaries really stretched, to set off on rebellious self-discovery and to search for rare and precious somethings that I could know more about than them. Those things had, by school's end, become bloody Hispania and my own damply liberated body as a battle ground where lessons on gender could be fought. The family spoke French. I had given it up and taken Spanish instead. It was one thing I was rather good at. My generation of women had, of course, invented the multiple female orgasm. I brought it to Spain. Single-handed.

For all my confident solo Spanish adventuring, it has turned out in late middle age, however, that I was little equipped for the hardest struggles of the trip back to Santiago. Neither dogs nor blisters bothered me, nor was I brought down by carrying my pack or lifting my heavy boots. It was for the twenty-first-century law of the group of women that I was ill-equipped.

I found myself inept at balancing my agenda with the established but to me alien rules of this organised cross-country expedition. That bookish family of mine had not been whole-hearted participants in team sports – I played unen-thusiastically with jolly hockey sticks and bullying off. We didn't care about goals. In a countryside childhood, I drifted poetically alone in neighbourhood woodland and sometimes dozed beneath a tree with a book of ancient fairy tales from around the Celtic world.

My friend Debbie and I did share and even make competition of our poetry – who could get most read out on the BBC schools programme or published in the school mag – but it was not really recognisably a group activity. Going to the posh school in town meant that I barely belonged to my grandfather's village. I walked through it every day with my Achilles heel aching: belonging was becoming an issue by age thirteen and home was in Apache country: the natives were not friendly to a high school uniform. My elocution lessons and violin case didn't help me blend in amongst paper-mill kids.

In teenage years, I never belonged to a rock band who could create music together, and no one can write these words for me to capture my Camino experience. Everyone owns their own journey and there's no team captain in self-actualisation apart from one's ego.

I was away from home at seventeen, studying odd stuff like medieval epic poetry and stories of fourteenth-century corpse brides, stuff that would come to me as I walked the same roads that they did last week. I found fifteenth-century Hispanic globetrotters to be surprisingly obsessed with native women's breasts in the Americas, though that may have just been my creepy tutor and his choice of texts. I travelled to Spain each summer alone and made friends from strangers, oblivious to gender, just as I chose.

Individualism not team dynamics was the key to life in the late twentieth century – my friends were like Lynyrd Skynrd's Free Birds, free from each other as well as from the rigours of school playing fields. My kind of students seldom bothered with the bras that our older sisterhood had burnt. We took control of our own wombs, our own vaginas and when we entered the job market we refused to tell employers of our thoughts on motherhood, though they always asked at interview in the 1970s. We were taught by *Cosmopolitan* to shout at men who groped us on the bus and they never victimised me long. I have easily ignored the extent to which others at my meeting tables have had different body parts from me. A boss a few years back got jailed for assaulting colleagues of mine but mysteriously avoided me.

My family tree for generations back is empty of group players but still full of achieving women – the key to the passing on of their DNA has not been the ability to be or follow lead wolf. My career has had more years spent creating from scratch, digging holes under fences, leading thought than it has been about carrying a team with me. I'm not the best at working – or walking – in a group. Whatever the background we come from, I just do not see the route to success that females must take as coming from pushing for a place in the pack as if we were man-powered. I find from this pilgrimage experience that it's not just that I am not fit. I *don't* fit.

Some of my fellow walkers on the Camino to Santiago de Compostela had very clever apps to count the distance and elevation so we could pat ourselves on the back for our achievements when we met for dinner in the evening, as if we had beaten something. Was that a whiff of testosterone in the air? Some wanted to get to the end of the trail as fast as possible. For some, the bonding of the pack, the making of new friends through the trials of the challenge, was the key experience. I was going deep and raw back through the decades from menopausal mum to silly summer schoolgirl and I found that could only be done on my own terms. I had not foreseen that as a problem when I signed up. I only glimpsed it on the train as I left my family behind.

There was, however quickly it emerged, a challenge there for the self-identifying leaders of our jolly walking group and for me: the terms on which Camino is undertaken change the ultimate direction of travel. As the great Spanish poet Antonio Machado says, '*Caminante no hay Camino*' – 'there are no roadways, roads you make as you explore'[4] – the steps you take decide the place where you will find the journey's climax. That is not necessarily as you stand and look up at the encrusted façade of the cathedral of Santiago de Compostela with your pack dumped at your feet. It may be when you look into that pack on return home and see whether you still have your integrity packed there amongst the dirty undies and handkerchiefs.

October 2018
Perhaps your journey will, like mine, come to its climax on a hospital trolley, but you will still push yourself off and out through the forest until the yellow land beneath your feet runs out and there is only a wide ocean of calm stretched out ahead of you and the window of a shellfisher's boat is dazzling gold in the sunrise.

Some of my group took hair straighteners on their journey to Santiago. I took along two books of favourite love poetry in Spanish saved from my student days. They steamed lustfully from my pack and came out with my nightie. I posted bits on Facebook before I crashed into fat sleep or in other quiet moments as I sat with a glass of cool white wine. It was an odd thing to do with no visible importance to the dynamics of our team, but it was important to me. Being a snorer, I had paid

---

4. http://www.poemhunter.com/poem/caminante-no-hay-camino/

extra for a single room so had no cosy roomie to comment on this odd behaviour. Now, with the books here on my lap, I find that I had marked a favourite page with sage and rosemary picked from the verge of the Camino.

The most fabulous Andalucían poet Federico García Lorca said that Chilean Pablo Neruda was 'one of those … who have their senses attuned to a world which is not ours and which few persons can perceive… Pablo Neruda's poetry rises up with … passion, tenderness, and sincerity'. I learnt to love them both in my teenage student years and had stuffed both in my pack. Neruda's 'Tonight I can Write (The Saddest Lines)' speaks to me in the indigo darkness: 'I no longer love her, that's certain, but maybe I love her / Love is so short. Forgetting is so long.' Camino tunes the pilgrim's senses.

No one's journey is the same, short or long. The wind that puffs up from the Atlantic over the Galician hillsides touches everyone's body with an early-morning chill, but our souls are on a journey of their own. A much-repeated truism is that we all walk our own Camino. We all kept saying it as we managed our group procession, but two or three Alpha women seemed not to really mean it. What was important to them – keeping fit, eating healthily, bonding as one pack – should, it was made clear, be paramount to us all. All decisions were already neatly made and all we had to do was follow.

It is unfair to rail against this (though it is my personality to rail against all rules). It was the pre-organisation that sold the trip to me back in the spring, removing the excuses of decades. When I set off to walk the Camino I thought the challenge would be in my body, walking forward for all those miles, avoiding dog bites. I was ready for the physical challenges and would not have minded coming home with more physical pain to recover from. It has not, however, been the effects of the physical struggle that I have found most long-lasting. It has been in being part of a body of strangers while walking backwards through thirty-eight years of my own true life. My path got unimaginably twisted. Four days home, it is not my body that is recovering. It is my sense of self: past, present and future. At times I felt totally alone. At times I felt less alone than I ever have.

At times I burned with joyful energy. I was soaring above the everyday, my self untethered from my working persona, floating on an exotic southern breeze scented with hot olive oil, newly cut pine wood and rain-soaked gravel. Words stopped for a while from being something I merely do business in. I had a powerful sense of belonging to all diverse multilingual humanity, male and female, young and old, strong and weak – a bright current of hopefulness shining through 1300 years of pilgrims' flow.

In small stone chapels those hundreds of thousands of Europeans, and I amongst them, were reminded of other roads – out of Egypt in promise, to Bethlehem in pregnancy, to Jerusalem in flight, to the Mount of Olives in fear. They will have drawn their brown pilgrims' cloaks around them, kneeling wrapped in their own exhaustion. I, exhausted too, was reminded of seeing bullet holes in warm Catalan church walls and the angry pain in a boy's eyes. Images of agonies and ecstasies painted by the Spanish greats or written by the great Civil War Hispanophiles swirled in my mind. These were as alive on my Camino as the delicious air which filled my nostrils and stretched my lungs.

On several mornings, we heard the booming voices of hunting hounds on a parallel path racing alongside us and reminding me of their nightmare teeth as we walked through their deep dark forest. The magpies laughed above us and the robins beckoned us on and on into the magic, out of the woods and into sleepy farm lanes. For me everything was poetry and, carrying too much weight, my feet sank deeper than the fittest and fastest fellow travellers. I was glad to let these new leaderenes slide on fast over the sometimes rough and pitted, sometimes sandy and yellow, sometimes smooth and grey surface of the road.

Now that I am home, the blood-red flush of autumn chestnut leaves is cooling and the dull pewter shine of a Scottish winter is gathering around me like a damp shawl, but perhaps if I keep writing I can somehow keep my place in the never-ending line of pilgrims walking on. I can try to apply the discipline of step by step to other goals which matter for me and for my daughter's world ahead, for my mother, sister, brother, husband. Right now though, here, after just four days back at home, I am still caught in a whirlpool of emotion. I am angry. I am serene. I am ecstatic. My heart is broken. I am disillusioned and triumphant. All I want is to go back on the yellow road through the fresh green and the golden light, alone, seeking Spain's strange secrets and travellers who carry what I treasure.

October 2018
Now the writing is over and I have stepped far beyond that first Camino. Achieved the greatest goal there is, found the greatest treasure. Left the litter and raised eyebrows behind. Following my nose, I calmly wonder where is my place in the line now? I admit I am avoiding the full stop.

As memories of cheery night times and sleepy dawns on Camino begin to fade and I try to make sense of my discoveries, I don't want to forget the fun and friendship of the road or pretend it didn't happen just because something else happened too. You don't make a success of a career and a marriage without some ability to function in a group and I like people more than my parents' books.

There was beauty to point out all around us and the joy of it passed from one open face to another. Eyes wide, smiles broad, it beautified us all. The best way through steep, panting, sweating climbs and grinding straights is to laugh. I was one of the jesters. In a foreign country there are many ridiculous moments of misunderstanding that tickle for a moment like dandelion fluff but don't get caught and brought home. All our life stories and relationships have an element of farce. So to keep the adrenalin pumping we laughed and danced and sang in celebration of the living of it. How many songs can you think of with 'walking' as their theme? There are enough to last a good few miles. For once I was not the only show-off. We did look out for each other and we did make bonds, and it has been a long time since my face has glowed with so much laughter and I have enjoyed the company of nine women and one man so much.

I can walk to and through places, like Galicia, that are deep, shining seams of treasure in my life with people who are open to a bit of digging, and it was good to join with fellow pilgrims for discovery and adventurous uncertainty and games with words. I can walk through places I don't care about and let their landmarks flick by.

I understand that for some of my companions this was that sort of hilltop-bagging walk for them. But looking from one edge of our group to the other, from mid-twenty-year-olds to late sixty-year-olds, widows to once-child-brides, I saw that even twenty-first-century pilgrimage through a country for whom I bear witness was not going to be all a comfortable thing.

You carry your weaknesses with you and your expectations. My Achilles heel is not the same as yours. What one European holds dear is incomprehensible to another. My history is not all yours. I don't belong in the same place as you. Your Camino, your Way, crosses over mine and sometimes you stamp on something unimportant to you but precious to me and probably vice versa.

My Camino experience, with all its tightly twisted sinews, was rubbed a little raw now and then before we got very far. I had wanted to leave the delicate controversies of my profession far behind in Scotland yet found that some were brought along for me on the road, tying me down to who I have been, adding a little of the friction of a tugging rope from the start. I was not equipped out here to defend decisions I had been no part of back home. And I had bought in to a fundraising expedition that I might have been expected to embrace wholeheartedly.

I found quite soon, to my chagrin, that I did not know what I had been buying. I had met every stated expectation. I had raised the money, done the photo shoots, talked to the press. In my ignorant and singular life, I had not learnt that this ladies' walking group expected us to do more and me to be me less. My self was stretched further than Camino strained my body. The path took me far and high and steep, and the exertion stripped off the layers of adult disguise that I had accumulated. I was left feeling naked. With Spain being what it has been to me, feeling tender and weak, it turned out that I could not avoid being penetrated deep. For others, this was just another West Highland Way or Kilimanjaro but not as hilly. I have no interest in these walks. They are not going in the right direction.

Everything about the Camino Francés was created by millions of people in conscious and intense spirituality. In the twenty-first century, you may expect twenty-first-century comforts and sometimes they (heated towel rails, Wi-Fi access, lifts) were not available. On a thousand-year-old Spanish pilgrimage it seemed just as reasonable to me to be sensitive to currents of history. There were values and priorities, though, which we were far from sharing.

My group's feet all touched the same path which had run through nations and centuries to reach here. It felt, though, that some feet hardly touched Spain at all, while I was laid bare by the graze of its rough rock – peasant-laid dykes, priest-commissioned crypts, pilgrim-trod gravel, dictator-planned concrete. My years of teenage self-discovery had been intertwined with the Peninsula's agonies of transition from fascism. Now my feelings for Spain, the physical challenges and group noise combined as a grating, blistering friction.

I did walk merrily with almost everyone in our party, and the companionship and sharing was good. It turned out that I chose to walk alone for nearly half of every day, and the group also learnt to value the opportunity for each to do so. I walked with others, met along the road, that I would have liked to walk with for longer. They are now out there in the wide world – Copenhagen, San Francisco, Johannesburg and Guildford – telling their tales, and maybe I and my fellow *peregrinas* are part of them. Loads were shared. Loads were not. It was not my way in 2015 to lightly ask questions of others for small talk. They can tell or not at their own time and place.

Questions between strangers seemed to me to come from a particular direction of interest to the asker. I left a little bit of my heart with Spanish friends in Santiago and Catalunya many times without looking back till now, and I don't expect to look back much at this British group. We followed the same current for a while but swam at different times with different strokes at different depths. I wanted to examine every shape of leaf and the formation of every word and the history of every stone cross. I wanted more time amongst Spaniards. Trawling for every drop from the so-long-awaited experience, I dragged a bit along the gravel riverbed and that proved uncomfortable at times. We joked about the next trip but I doubt I'll be walking back in such a group of strangers, beating the same broad highway. That was never my way. It is not where I find strength. It's not what moves me.

Perhaps, though, the very individual challenge that I experienced made my Camino – my Way – clearer by comparison.

Perhaps I was driven deeper into what was there for me to experience, round the next bend. I will be forever indebted to those who inadvertently nudged me in that direction, before it was too late. My difficulties in adapting to the general attitude of the group may mean I am discovering what is really needed by the individual. Poetry seems essential. Sauciness only momentarily amusing. Myth informative. History vital. Dogma unfulfilling. Love? Ah... love. Spanish, the language in which so many of my life lessons were taught, has many words for love.

Perhaps following my own strange path is a blessing. Maybe the rawness exposed me to more of the true experience of pilgrimage than could be expected in just one five-day stage of the route. Possibly my attention was concentrated more on the value of hidden threads all around me and details I carried inside, while I had thought Camino would be about the challenge for my body. Maybe I can see now, as I look backwards, that I still have a lot to learn. I look forward to it.

It can be hard, though, being a pilgrim without blind monotheistic faith with which to face the dangers ahead. Galicia is known throughout Spain as being full of powerful magic creatures.[5] None are on the side of the pilgrim. Fairies ride on the backs of weasels, and there are at least three different kinds of witches: *chuchonas* (the most frightening), *chupadoras* (the bloodsuckers) and the red-eyed *meigas*. Locals call on San Silvestre to come out from his hiding place in the woods and keep them safe.[6]

There are giant one-eyed *ollaperos* that eat human flesh, *saceos* that seduce, beautiful *mouras* that hide their treasure beneath the earth and *trasgos* that play tricks on the innocent.

---

5. https://www.youtube.com/watch?v=ee_iLexM55E
   https://en.wikipedia.org/wiki/Trasgu
6. https://en.wikipedia.org/wiki/Pope_Sylvester_Iss

To keep the old doubts at bay the ancient Christian *peregrinos* needed chapels in every village with sweet Madonnas beckoning them onwards. In order to learn the morning's lesson, we unbelievers have to find it ourselves, somewhere on the road, and then decide whether it's worth learning. To belong and also to be free – ah, there's the rub.

CHAPTER FOUR

MEIGAS AND MAGIC

Looking backwards as I write my tale, the real day-to-day of Camino is dropping away behind me. It is unbearable. I feel bereft. I don't have the money or I would be booking my return right now so that I would never lose contact with the beauty of it – the cockerel crows, the shining paving stones, the peeling blue-painted barn doors, the apple-cheeked farmers with caps moulded to their skulls, the sweet bagpipes echoing in a deep archway, the sharing of that experience every day in conversation or just in the glowing eyes of a stranger greeted on the road, passing by or sat on a log adjusting boots or taking a swig from a bottle.

We set off in the middle of October, flown into Santiago airport and out without seeing the city's spires. (Others oohed that they could see something and I hid to not see, holding my breath till I could look a week later with exhausted pilgrim's eyes.) We were minibussed to Sarria fast on the smooth, modern roller-coaster road which soared up and round the forested hills. Their comfortable carpeting lay endlessly around us and tucked down into valleys where old and new routes across north-west Spain criss-crossed the same living space. We caught sight of signs warning us of wild animals crossing and spied strangely shaped creatures with long staffs and massively humped backs beneath polythene capes, as we peered from the steamy bus window before arrival, after sundown, at the Hotel Mar de Plata. We were very far from the silver sea that I know.

For a week our dawns were at 8.00. I was an organised pilgrim, sorted and packed before 7.00, bags left in the lobby, and out into the darkness alone to sit on the step of an old stone cross of softened lines and dim granite sparkle and listen to the rustle of drying leaves as the weather, and I, thought of the sea and of changing.

I was conscious that it has been my husband's skills for thirty-three years that have kept us to timetable, documents intact, on every other journey and I had to prove that I could avoid screwing it up. I screwed up lots of times in Spain a lifetime ago and it changed my path dramatically, though I have a good life now, not to be nudged off course by a misread ticket, a mislaid passport or money belt.

Worldwide connectivity seems as essential to pilgrimage now as a bishop's permission did in earlier times and each leaving of a hotel room meant double-checking batteries charged and adaptors unplugged and packed. Otherwise I would walk in and out of Santiago without photographs, without contact with family, without the delight of sitting a while with Miguel in happy memory of thirty-eight years ago. In the end, I only lost a book, a lipstick and a water flask and nothing else but perhaps a few layers of who I have been since 1977.

Each of the six little towns we passed through, and many of the villages and hamlets in between, would have merited a day or so of exploring frescoes and bars full of barrels, and it would have been perfect to camp down in the pilgrims' inns wherever we wanted to lay our hat. However, we were on an organised challenge – cultural exploration was not an established objective, nor were we (thank St James) individual pilgrims doomed to carrying our own bags. A dim grey light would see the group of strangers leave a different community each morning and a lasso of pure gold sunrise would draw us out of the silent village through tunnels into the forests and across the roller-coaster farmland in between.

On the first and wettest day we counted dead salamander, black and yellow reptiles, otherworldly, like witches' toys, caught by a pilgrim's bike or foot. Ancient pilgrims would have recognised them as magic for their well-known ability to crawl from fires (though they were only hiding in a log), while locals know them to be the broken-hearted undead, making their way to the cliff-top chapel for St Andrew of Teijeiro.

The gardens of tiny stone hamlets were bursting with enormous pumpkins and the roadsides thick with herbs. Mist lay in stripes in the valleys or curled round the trees on distant slopes like wizard's pipe smoke. Between the cheery greetings of the other early-morning pilgrims and the booming of deep-throated mastiffs and Alsatians in the hidden farms at every compass point around us, there was a blanket of miles of silence. None of the machine noise that is constant to our working days. No sea noise that is constant to my home.

Small, brown, round-faced people swept their villages or herded their brown cows from lush meadow to squat, brown stone barns. They, and we, came down paths weirdly fenced by huge granite menhirs and vast, smooth, dead but still erect tree trunks tied together with rope as if by evil giants to stop them marching off behind us.

A woman in a sodden field gathered into a wide wicker basket bundles of knee-high phallic fungi. Hawks hovered and eagles stared down at all the life that crept and multiplied below. Big black beetles scuttered. Thousands of snail spirals challenged our clumsy feet. Golden butterflies, like offcuts of the morning sky, did what butterflies do.

Every village was discovered by crossing a one-arched bridge or descending a ladder of a path studded with exposed rock and scarred deep by rain. Often we had to dance across step-stones in the mud or cobbled, forded rivulets in the middle of nowhere. Many of the hamlets higgle-piggled round tiny crossroads marked by ancient oak trees with trunks as broad as a cottage with a bench below for watching the centuries creep by. Some places confused us in our tiredness and we wondered if we had come past here before, the natural rolling of the geology producing as it did many similar bends and dips through minor valleys.

Everything was buxom and fertile and the soil a deep bed beneath our feet. In these hidden places, it was easy to look backwards beyond St James to a place near the end of the world where the old gods had drawn other pilgrims over the heather and granite hills, into the woods and out, mindful of Rome's deities of a thousand groves and of a thousand streams,[7] with no grand cathedral to stop at. They followed the Milky Way it is said, on to the crashing ocean which separated Africa and Europe from something entirely else. This is the one place in the world where all roads do not lead to Rome. Nor do they lead to Jerusalem or Washington or Mecca, or Aberdeen or wherever else commands your work-a-day attention. In this emerald corner of the world there still hides an older magic, and you have space in your head so that it comes creeping in if you walk slowly enough.

I walked slowly enough.

Santiago de Compostela is the third most important pilgrimage site in Christendom and there are many religious pilgrims with rosaries and priests and candles to be lit in tiny chapels. The Apostle found his way to this corner of Hispania in the years following Jesus's death and his tomb was rediscovered in the AD 800s. He was not from then just a box of bones to pray to but an active if ghostly leader and protector who at

---

7. http://www.ccel.org/g/gibbon/decline/volume1/chap2.htm

the Battle of Clavijo in 844 appeared on a white horse to lead the charge against Islam as Santiago Matamoros – St James the Moor-slayer.

Some find it too much of a coincidence that the tenuous links between St James the Greater and Spain should be so strengthened in this distant, pale wet extremity of Europe just at the time when the brilliant infidels were putting out the lights of Visigothic Christianity across the Hispanic Peninsula. The possible foot stepping here of a first-century Palestinian Jew might seem unreal as we take the high, wet inland route to Santiago through secret, forgotten, hard-to-travel valleys. But the coastal waters and narrow straits from Judea to Cornwall, from the fjords of Norway to the rias of Galicia were easier roads than this rough track, and the sea routes were busy for centuries with trade in granite, tin, ideas, slaves and treasures.

Layers of myth and propaganda, faith and greed drew pirates, merchants and pilgrims to where Galicia juts out into the great slate-blue Atlantic. For seven hundred years or so Spain was pagan and Roman. For seven hundred years all of Spain was in the grip or finger-touch of Moslem and Arab. Here in the far northern kingdoms of Galicia and Asturias, rings of mountains kept blood pure and secrets sacred.

Some say none of the stories are true, all just the opium of the masses, no one's words having a monopoly on good or evil. Some folk walk the Camino flagellated and carrying giant crosses and sure faith. Plato, who I think was wiser, said, 'When it comes to the gods I am unable to discover whether they exist or not. For there are many things which stand in the way of this knowledge – the obscurity of the problem and the brevity of man's life.'[8]

---

8. http://www.iep.utm.edu/greekphi/

October 2018
Perhaps at the time Plato had not looked close up at the end of
his brief life. Perhaps if he had he might have found comfort and
strength in a clear answer to his question. I know I have.

I know too that in 2015 it felt as if I walked a week of my life
amongst people thinking, on some level, about living a good
life and wishing the same on others that they passed. And so it
continues to be.

There have been several times in my life when I have been
amongst a mass of people moving together in hope and determination and equality of gender, sexuality and ethnicity. Many
of the most powerful of those times have been in Spain as it
went through the transition from police state to constitutional
monarchy, but I have been small parts of other such movements
in my working life.

Folk from the Middle Eastern diaspora met in my office
foyer to support the so-called Arab spring just a few years ago.
I made it, through my work, so that community activists might
celebrate their place in my city in parade, and way back I did
my share of marching in strident protest against the nuclear age
and for women's choices. I feel a sense of belonging amongst
those optimistic egalitarian masses and so my Achilles heel
doesn't ache like it did in my childhood village. The bonds aren't
artificial or forced or jollied along as on a school sports field.
There is instead healthy, undogmatic chaos in the dusty air that
they kick up with determined feet – one two, one two. Each
equal. Each necessary. Each individually responsible. Anything
can happen amongst such folk. Our world can change. The
feeling this October of being part of such an immense march

of individual humans with their different starting points was intoxicating, spellbinding, and the memory of that unbounded community is one that will last powerfully beyond these four days home. To Spanish speakers all over the world, the words for people, village and community are all the same: '*mi pueblo*'. It is a language I am at home with.

The fears of medieval Europeans in their little church-dominated villages wherever the church of Rome reached, and their belief in the power of being close to the Apostle's relics, fuelled the Camino with hundreds of thousands of poor and rich sinners every year for centuries as Islam's hold slowly crumbled southwards. Spain geared up to cater for the worried faithful. The first tourist guide was written. Monasteries and inns were built and communities grew around them. Waymarkers were created, crafts produced from the seams of black jet underfoot, prayers written, tracks mapped out to wind round the rolling contours of the land. Crops were planted. Animals were reared. Pilgrims' meals prepared. Daughters married off carefully.

Some believers headed from their homes towards Rome or Jerusalem, Walsingham or Canterbury. The pilgrims on the various paths called Camino head to where a star had shown a poor shepherd the hidden sarcophagus of one of the special twelve who had been hugged by the Messiah, God on earth, one of us, the meek. Here he was just a step removed from you or me. In the twenty-first-century villages of Galicia, old men still tell us they pray for the pilgrims who pass, and you know their ancestors never forgot but prayed for us poor sinners across 1300 years, though for a while the paths across the land began to grow over and become silent as the centuries passed and traditions changed. In such places, it is easy to imagine that the world we see every ordinary day hides another under a layer or two of veil. Here on the Way of St James, where none of the days are ordinary for those who live or those who walk along it, something magical, something archetypal, is sensed below. Maybe all that praying draws it to the surface here. Or maybe all that praying keeps the power of it suppressed. Most of the time.

You don't have to follow dogma or join a congregation to unveil it. When the clouds roll back and the sun sets, the nights on Camino are the pure black of Santiago's jet jewellery and the stars are the clearest of guiding lights. When we slept it was deeply. We can't (can we?) be sure whether outside in the steep lanes the legendary Santa Compaña came out from their tombs led by candlelight,[9] hooded in white, shuffling in ghostly comradeship through these borderlands between consciousness and exhaustion and death. No light pollution in the sky or earthly distractions of the mind hides the fact of the universe's deep mysteries. I walked aware of the millions who had walked before me in that enchantment, eyes and skin glowing, feet burning, knees crumbling, and I felt grateful that their belief (whatever it was) had created this unspoiled but believable fairy land where the lichens festoon the trees in silver and the mosses drip like emeralds into ditches full of golden fruit. Glowing yellow apples dripping with mist catch the autumn sun and conjure up images of childhood, mother and the strength I carry inside. There was not one of us who was not touched at least lightly by its spell.

It turns out, to my amusement, that the famous Wife of Bath in Chaucer's tales of pilgrimage to Canterbury shares my first name. She is provocative, chatty and vivacious. She has gone on pilgrimage to Santiago and now, on her way across England, is a merrymaker, a tough and compulsive traveller and the type of medieval woman who was thought should be forbidden to go on pilgrimage at all. She has been married several times

---

9. https://en.wikipedia.org/wiki/Santa_Compa%C3%B1a

and dabbles in remedies of love. She also seems to share with me a feeling for a truer, freer, older Celtic magic which maybe Britain and Galicia shared. Neither of us should be mistaken for women on pilgrimage through devotion or belief.

This is not a plastic Disney-style sugar-sweet fairy tale I am telling – any more than was Chaucer. The twenty-first-century Camino has stretches on tarmacked roads splattered with fresh, wet cow dung. Modern bridges cross largely empty motorways. We are re-energising a modern local economy as we sleep in comfy laundered sheets and wake to refrigerated fruits and coffee percolators. The milestones are graffitied with pilgrims' messages. Once or twice teenagers pass with music audible. There are (thank St James) signs in one or two hamlets advertising much appreciated ice lollies, and most hotels do have Wi-Fi and heated towel rails.

The Gallegos and the Gauls of France have similar stories to tell but Galicia is not Parc Astérix. Nor is it Paradise. There is much talk of the Virgin but you don't have to be one and aren't promised any. Just as well. It is twenty-first-century Catholic Europe re-energised in the 1980s by a Polish Pope but, if you step out for the first time from Sarria, and many times a day from then on, you do step into something very like Tolkien's Middle Earth. It is pretty clear that it is recognition of an older, all-too-believable European folkloric mysticism (which, much later, inspired Tolkien) that gave St James cause to come. The wizards and the *meigas*, the elves and hobgoblins were already here in the Field of Stars and something had to be done about it.

So very many routes round our world cross each other here on this furthest corner of Europe, south to north, west to east. Perhaps the Apostle's scallop-shell symbol is what he rose with from the river mouth where his sarcophagus lay buried when he came back to save poor shellfishermen and kill the Moors or whatever story you wish to believe. It could be just an easy badge for a pilgrim to wear to prove his intent or achievement and to use on the road as ladle or bowl. Or maybe the shell reminds us of our open invitation to come further on by many converging roads down to the sea, past Santiago and on near Fisterra, at the furthest reaches of pagan Rome. There, on the sands of the famous Galician estuaries, Venus – carried from the spume on a scallop shell – met older mother gods and we women pilgrims can shed our clothes from the road and look for fertility by making love in the sand.

The story can get a bit gritty. Lost souls, like Brazilian novelist Paulo Coelho,[10] have spun confections of modern myth about Camino like so much litter, but each pilgrim carries their own fantasy, even me. There are many truths about the Camino to Santiago de Compostela, and even the less than ancient ones are strange and romantic enough as they are. It turns out, though, that Paolo was right about the challenge of walking slowly, which makes you see things differently.

There is much to wonder at as we walk, to distract us from the day-to-day of now. It swept me along. Knights Templar dedicated to Crusade to the Holy Lands were also dedicated to the protection of the pilgrim here in Spain and many female pilgrims were somewhat grateful for their chivalry and, when short of cash, their loopholes in the law against usury.[11] The Knights Templar connect the Way to narratives on the blood of Christ and of my own clan. They thread together magic knowledge from Arabia and the immortality of Scottish kings. What secrets they brought from Palestine to Camino were, in truth, lost forever when the Knights were arrested and put to death on that Friday the thirteenth in 1307. Unluckily, they hadn't stuck to the only accepted path of Christianity.

---

10. Coelho, Paulo, 2009, *The Pilgrimage* (London: HarperCollins Publishers)

11. http://www.lagiraudiere.com/pilgrimage_route_compostella.html

Those Templars who escaped were welcomed, though, to Scotland by Robert the Bruce and helped him make the English think again at Bannockburn.[12] They knew Bruce's friend Sinclair, of my clan, who travelled the North Atlantic and had his chapel at Roslyn[13] carved with American flowers before Columbus sailed the ocean blue. Their secrets are lost or buried or simply make-believe and I am not sorry.

Though many kinds of believers walk on pilgrimage for answers, and I have been amongst them, it seems to me that if every mystery of Camino were explained, it would be a less beguiling experience. It is the sense of hidden and unexplained in life which I find so liberating. The world's great experiences – attraction, orgasm, pregnancy, childbirth, motherhood, abiding married love, patriotism, solidarity, facing death, artistic creativity – are so full of mystery and so entirely incomprehensible that the rituals and rules made up by those who pretend to comprehend can, I believe, simply be ignored. Not mother goddesses nor wise women nor scientists nor philosophers, gurus or psychologists and certainly not knights errant nor celibate priests have all my answers. Accepting the mysterious in the early steps of your pilgrimage stops you agonising over what is not put there for you to understand. You can, without any particular creed, just step forward into another day of unseen trial and challenge and can do so trustingly. You know where you are going but not what it will be like. You accept, open up and become more full of life than you have been for years. Pilgrimage was once but is no longer a normal part of European life. Love, the greatest mystery of all, still is – and is also a journey, as I keep on discovering.

---

12. http://www.scotsman.com/news/how-crusading-templars-gave-bruce-the-edge-at-bannockburn-1-1363283
13. http://www.bbc.co.uk/religion/religions/christianity/places/rosslyn chapel_1.shtml

❈

October 2018
I walk through Camino's continuing mysteries with my heart calm
and trusting, more full of life, love and acceptance than I have ever
been.

By the end of the twelfth century, 100,000 pilgrims every year crossed the Pyrenees to walk through wild, bandit-ridden, knight-protected, Moor-tempting Spain towards Santiago. They came to ask for health, love, babies, boys and heaven. But sixteenth-century Protestantism stopped the flow from the north and we Anglo-Saxons began to forget this wet green corner of Christendom and the spirits of common European ancestors that lurk there in myth and mist. Catholic pilgrims continued to make their way as long as there was the physical evidence of the Apostle's relics there for them to reach, but only that long – it was the closeness of the bones of a man one step removed from the Messiah that mattered, the real connection to the Divine. The world kept turning and the economic value of relics kept growing across Europe.

In 1589 the English pirate Sir Francis Drake raided A Coruña for his Virgin Queen, just forty miles from Santiago. It was feared he would capture the Apostle's relics and take Spain's patron saint to England to fuel our own useful pilgrimage-supported economies in cathedral cities. It fell to María Pita,[14] Spain's answer to Joan of Arc, with a Gallega cry of '*Quen tena honra, que me siga*' ('Whoever has honour, follow me!') to lead her countrymen and women and force Drake's retreat.

---

14. https://en.wikipedia.org/wiki/Maria_Pita

To be sure that St James' honour and that of Spain was properly protected, the relics were hidden. Unfortunately it was done so effectively, and the secret kept so close, that no one could find them for 300 years. It's enough to makes some folk wonder what other holier relics might be hidden and similarly forgotten in Europe's sacred places.

Without the relics, and with the changing of beliefs, there was no reason for pilgrims to progress to this distant wolf- and robber-ridden place with so many challenges on the journey. The magic of the Apostle and his story slept dark and deep below the huge cathedral in a forgotten vault and the world kept turning obliviously. The deeper, older truths sank beneath the creeping ivy and the ploughed field. No one listened to the nut-brown people singing earth songs as the wind parted the grass and excited generations of skull-picking crows. Finally, excavation at the cathedral hundreds of year later in 1884 revealed the marble sarcophagus of relics with its Palestinian carvers' script labelling it for James.[15] With another puzzle piece of the Apostle's bones existing in Italy, the relics could be authenticated and replaced in the silver shrine that we, and hundreds of thousands of others, set out to reach in 2015.

In the light of the rich silver shining, interest in the Way of St James reawakened the imagination only slowly over a century in which potential travellers were caught up in a long series of hellish Spanish, European and world wars. When St James' Day on 25th July falls on a Sunday, as it did in 1948, it is a Holy Year and Santiago's shrine broadcasts wide to draw in the faithful or searching. That first post-World War Two Holy Year was one of the few in peace for a hundred years. The third most important of all of Christendom's pilgrimages was at last publicised beyond the great wall of the Pyrenees, and the

---

15. https://albertosolana.wordpress.com/la-aportacion-de-la-arqueologia/

magic of the experience began to come alive again for others to follow.

Then, in 1965, a group of 'Friends of the Camino' began to make the long journey to Santiago practically possible for more to follow. There was, until then, nowhere for weary, blistered pilgrims to stay apart from monastery cells or haylofts or, as I saw some do, in tents under apple trees. In 1965 the memory of Camino was alive and respected, but squat brown farmers had planted their wheat and maize over the long-abandoned pilgrimage route. It took the mammoth work of a Galician priest to mark the entire length of the Camino Francés from the Pyrenees to Santiago with the still ubiquitous yellow arrow using surplus paint that the Galician highway authority had going spare when Europe decreed their road lines should be white.

When I arrived in 1977, only twenty or thirty pilgrims a year came on pilgrimage along the Way and entered the waiting city on foot. No one I knew in the years that followed thought that my dreams of doing so were worth considering. No one thought the dogs worth chaining, though every now and then someone would write, and I would read, about terrifying encounters with them. Since another Holy Year in the 1980s and another Pope, John Paul, who came and spoke to a new generation about a new Europe without iron curtains and fascism, pilgrim numbers are back up to twelfth-century levels again. The dogs are getting used to us and the farmers seem to know the economic sense of chaining the ones that can't be trusted. Mostly. Now you can post on a web forum the location of the loose and scary ones and an Amigo of the Way will pop down and sort him out – bish bash bosh.

The World Wide Web, though, is a very new phenomenon. My life had to take many turns before I received – ping! – Linda's Facebook dog-free invitation to put my best foot forward out of my safe little corner of the world. I haven't looked back through the years for a long while but walking down this very particular and strangest of roads has turned out to involve checking what lurks behind me, sniffing at my heels.

There are still dangers and some pilgrims never come back. Like Emilio Estevez in his film *The Way*,[16] it is not unusual to get lost in bad weather on the Pyrenees crossing to Roncesvalles. I heard the other day of a lost Scottish soul who disappeared on our own gentler stretch of Camino this autumn, leaving no trace. I passed his image off down the social-media trail to Santiago in case he is lost in some ward or cell with the mysteries and witchery swirling in his head and clouding his road back home.

It could easily happen that you forget yourself on Camino. You pass little shrines from time to time to people turned invisible on the road but still making their presence felt. We don't have knights to protect us anymore (unless you count our companion Derek or Miguel just a phone call away). Nowadays, most deaths beyond the Pyrenees are prosaically from car accidents. My scallop shell, tied to my rucksack as a plea to protect this passing pilgrim, came undramatically from a smelly plastic crateful of bits of dead sea life round the back of our local Scottish fish house. Cleaned and painted with a cross of St James, it knocked against the aluminium water bottle at my back and reminded me tunefully of my twenty-first-century home. But there are still wolves in the Galician hills – 350 of them killing over 2,000 farm animals in recent years – and according to a local paper I was shown, boar tusks killed someone while we were there.[17] This is why the dogs are so huge, their barks so loud and the gates they guard so strong. Old magic does not feel entirely incompatible with 2015. It

16. http://theway-themovie.com/
17. http://www.iberianature.com/material/wild_nature_sites/wild_galicia/galicia_nature.htm

would be unsurprising to me if what I end up capturing here is not pure truth but another myth – I may have sinned by omission or imagination or self-indulgence. Forgive me please. The duendes, the Spanish spirits, still have me in their grip. I have only been home for four days.

October 2018
Wolf-like dogs have always stalked my nightmares and at the height of my real terrors leaped to my throat in a hospital ward, but last week a barefoot wolf prince in his tiny castle gifted me a pebble, a she wolf showed me the right road in the morning, I dined in a wolf's lair and a wolf-killer hugged me in a lingerie store and I feel the power is shifting.

All of my senses were attacked by the experience of Camino. My hands were grazed by ancient striations of honey- and cream-coloured stone in narrow alleys. My eyes struggled blindly in unlit forest-tunnel mornings or blinked in cool strobe of shade and strident midday sunbeam falling warm from vaults of embracing oaks. I snatched handfuls of herbs which lined the hedgerows for miles, crushed them in my hands and they scoured my nostrils as I drank their air – rosemary, bay, mint, fennel, eucalyptus and lavender – before stuffing them in my money belt.

I ate the ripe golden-yellow apples from mossy trees with bare branches like witches' fingers and collected the prickly chestnuts and bullet-hard acorns and brought them home. The paths have been trodden down into the ground, well below their natural level, by millions of scuffling exhausted feet and I, in awe of the human and natural history that I walked through, was pulled down into the infinite layers of pilgrim-trampled leaf mould and its intoxicating, warming mustiness. The history, the meaning, the vitality of the route was unignorable to me. Field level is often eye level on Camino, the perspective of a mouse – just as well I was seldom really alone on the road or I might, flopped in the V-shaped roots of a black dragon-skinned pine, have been absorbed into the moss and ivy.

I walked without religion, Christian or Pagan, and I wondered what I was walking to and felt myself very small as I followed Don Elias's yellow arrows. I still feel tiny and insignificant out here in the world that I have come home to, although here I am something to some people.

We trudged the last stretch of only one of the Caminos – the Camino Francés, which crosses through Charlemagne's Spanish gate at Roncesvalles.[18] We met very many who had been on the road far longer than us, on the English Way from the port of A Coruña, the safe North Way beyond the Picos de Europa where the Moors never reached and revolutions brewed, from amongst the other peoples of Portugal or Catalunya or Lorca's south. In the crowds at the Pilgrims' Mass in Santiago there will have been those who had come by each point of this peninsula at Africa's gate.

We only saw the hills of Galicia, neither the plains of Castile nor the mountains of Navarre which come before them on the way from east to west. Each has its tests. Past pilgrims say that in the mountainous ups and downs of the first third of the journey from France all your concentration is on your body and what it is made of – weak muscle, grating bone, thin skin. Then you find you learn how to walk and become calloused and feel strong and it is the straight flatness of the *mesetas* of old Spain and the tempting site of the evening's destination in a distant village on a church-topped outcrop that tortures you for the next part of the journey.

---

18. https://www.youtube.com/watch?v=blK3IF51B0M

You get bored and scratchy and see that your weaknesses are more than physical. The red demons find you out on the fiery stripe of blinding white road. Your true spirit wins the battle by the time the road rises again to meet you for the final third of the journey and you near Galicia's cool green village surprises and their hidden welcome just around a bend. Strong, hopeful, your spirit rises and Santiago's spires are there for the reaching. Now, in purged peace, you can contemplate Camino's end, whatever that may be for you. That journey, like all of the best of human challenges, takes (depending on how fast you walk and how much you stop) forty days and forty nights (or thirty-five days at fourteen miles a day). In my travelling party, we had only had six days to cram in something of the Camino experience. I plumbed myself in as quickly as possible to the spirit that was travelling amongst those already toughened pilgrims who had come the whole Way and had already been tested many times. I strained to keep up as they sped on with an encouraging call over their shoulder.

I was violently sick many times on the first night in Spain. Diarrhoea before the dawn in Sarria did not bode well. (Looking back now, simple and unaccustomed ill health that my mind was not practised in challenging took more out of me than I realised while I was being held up by adrenalin.) A breakfast of moist almond cake and chamomile tea did settle me though, and with determined first-day spirits and lots of photographing of our merry polythene caped band, we set off on Camino.

The morning was still not broken and the rain was pouring down. At least, unlike Scotland, the rain was vertical, not slapping in against our cheeks. Spain slept. We followed our guide Alicia first through a street or two of puddles and mediocre modernity then enchanting steep and narrow medieval town lanes with swinging inn signs depicting cloaked pilgrims. We saw that this road had been made for us and millions like us.

We stopped at the town hall to have our passport stamped for the first time and again at the Convento de la Merced on the edge of town where some of our party had to be told to be quiet. We saw that this was a sacred undertaking. We poked our noses into the pretty cobbled cloisters and into incensed and candlelit chapels then moved off past the neat and tidy white-walled graveyard and steeply down out into the rain-swept hills and dripping woods.

Lucy waited to hurry me across the first mossy, Roman footbridge – don't stop to look at the detail – and left a waking town behind us and hit our first up slope. We saw it wasn't intended to be easy.

---

19 October 2018

Downhill all the way. For seven months from November 2016 I was heading downhill all the way. Now tears brimmed and nostrils filled as the rutted road fell away from Sarria and memory came tumbling. The stream persisted in its different direction. We crossed and climbed the slithery bank where morning never reached. At the top of the climb I stopped for a drink from my water bottle and found a miniscule caterpillar dangling centimetres from the tip of my nose on a string from an oak tree. Until I focussed I mistook it for a soaring eagle.

Robin, my one companion on this new Camino, wondered with me at his little world and how we were so close to missing noticing it at all. How many other lives do we all pass by without a moment's respect? How much beauty is there right in front of us in the detail, devalued as we worry about the distant future that we cannot change? Inspired, it is five minutes before we moved on, walking slowly. I focus my mind on that tiny acorn caterpillar surrounded by the endless mysteries of the human Way whenever the world threatens to overwhelm me still.

Steep and rough and narrow we ascended with the air sucking from our lungs through mist-scoured nostrils with nowhere to step without crushing prickly sweet chestnuts beneath our feet. An elderly local in a flat brown cap and with square brown shoulders accompanied a bright young traveller, explaining the local life and use of the land, enjoying her pretty company and she his gravely dialect until he reached his home beside the path and said his merry *'Buen Camino'* and waved us off ahead. Tree roots looped and striped reams of rock scarred a chocolate-brown track only just wide enough for two, like a stairway into darkness. The first realisation came that this soaking-wet corner of Europe is a land of giants – giant oaks, giant chestnuts, giant eucalyptus, giant rock fence posts, giant rivers, giant stepping stones, giant pumpkins, cows and dogs.

The densely forested hills rolled more like steep, stormy Atlantic breakers rather than soft British farmland. The walk was physically more challenging than some of us had antici-pated – walking with fitness freaks means folk have different understandings of the word 'hill'. But if it goes up steeply for half an hour or more then down steeply for half an hour or more and hurts then that's a hill to me. OK? Frustration stopped me in my tracks. I'm a linguist. I know what hill means. It was supposed to be Spanish that was misunderstood.

To tell the truth the wet made even the flats hard going. All day the rain streamed down on our heads, on my sleeves where my hands stuck out to hold my walking poles, under our feet. Then through my husband's supposedly dry-as-a-bone hat, down the back of our necks, into our bras, up through the mud and into our boots. A little petulance squirted between my smiles. We soon had soggy knickers and there's nothing inspiring about that.

The red-breasts cheered us along though with liquid song and the crows laughed with us, and we found ourselves just a few souls amongst fellows. We saw that every human was heading in the same direction and that simple fact is not a normal experience. There is no to-ing and fro-ing of life on a road which exists for one purpose only. No one's face is coming towards you to be judged before you greet, or not. We are all walking beside each other, following or overtaking each other. Every passer-by called out '*Buen Camino!*' whatever that meant and we, thinking it little deeper than an American 'Have a nice day' cheerfully, doggedly called it back in human solidarity against the rain and the pain now relentlessly developing in feet, ankles, calves, knees, thighs, hips and backs.

The Spanish pilgrims replied to us with '*Igualmente*' – equally! May we all have our fair share of whatever is ahead of us, on the Way to Santiago and beyond. Equally, may we recognise that none of us can know what is round the next bend or change what the Camino is.

✺

October 2018
Ultreia et suseia – *above and beyond, further up and further on the pilgrims call or graffiti or signpost. Being in Latin we miss the significance for a journey that is meant to bring answers. Robin, who has never been to Spain before, and I, who have, are still and equally on our way further on.*

✺

You are never alone on Camino, even in October when the changeable weather keeps many of the thousands at home. Ahead there were others limping or hunched against their own personal challenge. Through the first day we began to get to know each other a little in our group – red-haired Stacey had flu and had just stopped smoking. She was not a walker, not a Hispanophile, not wearing the right footwear and was here only for the cause. She doubted every morning and every afternoon and noticed the signs nailed to a tree here and there advertising tempting local taxis. She limped and lugged and laughed her way along.

Blonde Lucy carried a life-saving syringe in case of nut allergy. Your burden is my burden on Camino. The idea that she might have to use it, as she had had to on other adventures, scared us stiff. I kept my supply of nutty snacks hidden to be sneaked out when alone.

Someone had to lead the group, looking out for the stopping points, making sure we didn't miss a yellow arrow and take the wrong track. Someone had to bring up the rear, leaving no one behind, moving at the pace of the slowest. Alicia, our guide, and Lucy shared these roles and showed those who paid attention how to stretch our complaining muscles. We gradually realised that in our combined backpacks we were a walking pharmacy – pills for irritable bowels and pads for friction blisters, pastilles for gratey throats, sun creams for pink skin and ointments for cold sores, tubes of liquid to aid digestion or to still runny tummies, painkillers for wobbly ankles. Some folk like Lucy and Alicia were taking responsibility and being paid to do so. Some kept watch for me as huge dogs loomed. Some strained at our leashes.

October 2018

Tramadol. Paracetamol. Ibuprofen. Dioralyte. OmniFiber. Half a suitcase full of ileostomy bags in case of leaks. Flannels in the knickers. The right scissors. The right seals. The right gauzes. The right barrier cream. The right adhesive powder. The right disposal bags. The wrong travel insurance for ongoing conditions. The responsibility for our health and safety all ours, taken voluntarily, no one watching, no one making choices for us. No one leading. Just millions of pilgrims who have walked ahead of us with their own imperfections and two women getting to know better what it is to walk beside one another through someone else's territory. The huge dogs slept as we walked by.

Morning and lunchtime stops were taken in enchantingly odd cafes like the Taverna Mercado Brasero and the Casa Cruceiro on the first day, made in ancient stone barns of huge granite blocks and blackened beams with massive trestle tables. Their kitchen counters and toilets were tucked into strangely shaped corners, up or down darkly hidden steps, squeezed beneath low roofs, cuddled up against whitewashed boulders. One high wall was decorated with a hundred straw hats. Another had an arrangement of ram skulls, behind which a silent old lady with less teeth than a dead sheep sat on a purple couch in a beam of sunlight from a tiny window. Giant rakes and cart wheels were stacked and cobwebbed. I didn't see if she had red eyes.

It was nearly Halloween back home and I bought a purple-dressed *meiga* doll on a broomstick for my daughter from a plump lady with slithery curls of black hair. One day's cafe had a rainbow roof of hanging neon T-shirts. Another a dolls-house-sized cabinet of scallop-shell mementoes for sale. A constant stream of grateful pilgrims flopped in; soaked up coffee and cinnamon *pain perdu* or Spanish omelette and chips, strewing the assorted dining chairs and benches with their rain-dripping bags or sweaty jackets, sharing their experiences – so fast you! So sore me!

---

10 October 2018
In a bend on the road to Portomarín is tucked Casa Morgade where a protected holly tree drips its bloody berries into a greened stone

trough and golden cows jangle their bells under the apple trees. Stuck in a moss-covered tumbledown wall amongst the brambles something glints: a strange little silver dagger-like implement, its handle towards me, juts from the greenery. Inside the house, under the wide slope of terracotta pantiles, a wood fire burns. Outside a chapel smaller than a garden shed, a family scrapes back the encroaching forest. At dinner, pilgrims from Finland and Korea, Switzerland and Maine, Ireland and California, Scotland and South Africa share Spain's surreal secrets gathered on the road. Their scoured eyes blaze clear. Wrought iron and warm stone guide feet to bed ready for the short walk into Portomarín tomorrow – but only for those with time to take it slow.

We were our leaders' burden as well as their companions. Ankles threatened to buckle, boots grated, feet fell heavily. Whenever we stopped the warmth of effort quickly disappeared into the chill of wet clothes. Overstretched muscles seized into agonising stiffness. The fastest walkers needed to move on from the rest stops by the time we slowest arrived but the leaders felt our group had to stick together on this first unfamiliar day. Thus those who needed to rest most rested least. The team was undynamic and its bonds new and weak. At the end of Day 1, we came down an agonising and very real hillside. In the driving drizzle, we crossed a frighteningly high bridge where the Atlantic wind grabbed my soaked hat from my miserably rain-splattered head and whipped my cheeks to remind me I was far from home.

The first signs of what would be the challenges of my Camino were emerging from the grey gloom as we reached Franco's rebuilt Portomarín at the end of that first challenging day. Dictators love civil engineering and Franco loved dams.

Far below where his concrete pillars strode across the wide valley from hillside to hillside, down at water level, were the remains of the bridges of other conquerors: Napoleon, Charlemagne and Rome crossed this crucial corner of Europe. Francisco Franco, a local Gallego boy, had inundated the valley with his vision and moved the inconvenience of the lives of peasants and their market square up to the windswept bleakness where we found it. Climbing the torture of a staircase up and through a brutal Roman arch at the end of the bridge was nearly thirty steps too far – with every army-cut block I had to overcome, my muscles cried out for a nice steep but natural hill. It had been a long, challenging forty-eight hours with little sleep and many miles covered since Montrose. We still had a steep wet and unwelcoming empty street before we reached our second Camino hotel, the Hotel Villajardin on the journey through Spain's very well-watered garden. I was not turned on by the idea of stretching exercises with the team on arrival.

The rain did eventually stop that evening and Spanish boys put a smile back on my face – out with their guitars, a natural extension to their bodies and part of the rise and fall of their chat in the huge church doorway. I was back in Spain, the home of the guitar. My heart sang. This was not the land of the Costas and expats, of holiday houses and international businesses, of nylon flamenco dresses and Aussies running with the bulls. This was a proud small town whose generations had seen many armies come tearing across their land and chopping up the stone which lay beneath it. These villagers had been scared by the hobgoblins and red-eyed spectres in the forests. They had been no match for Franco when civil war broke out. St James, in a brown cloak like theirs, with a walking staff like theirs, carved simply of uncarvable granite, there in their town square, was a plump comfort and a pride. I don't share their religion but I come from grey granite villages who value their own mercat cross or war memorial. My fellow *peregrina*, Lycra-bummed Deedee, climbed up St James' statue for a photo shoot and stuck her beautifully manicured finger up the Apostle's nose beside the church where the boys sang.

I turned my back as I heard her boast of it. It made me wince just as if my body had been penetrated so roughly. I shuddered with tired and cold. I drew into myself and my Spain – my gentlemanly, honourable Spain. It was just a silly moment. No one paid much attention.

But it felt like a sign of things to come. It disrespected so much that mattered to me, that mattered to me so much. It became symbolic of the strain I felt those first few days tied to this band of strangers. These were not my soul mates back home with whom I have travelled in many cultures, respecting many religions. Nor were they the Spaniards whose history I have studied, whose myths and legends I have come to love, whose friendships I treasure and whose patron saint this was. Even in medieval times it was ever true that 'some women travel on pilgrimages... in order to frolic and kick up their heels in jolly company', and there has long been a fear of 'how dangerous it is to lead young, nay attractive women (in whom levity and lust are inherent) into foreign parts... particularly inexperienced wives'.[19]

This Alpha A-team pilgrim and I were both in our late fifties though and were well travelled, not children, far from uneducated. Looking back, I understand Deedee was even less used to being without a watchful husband than I and had been to these parts before with him for jolly fun. Perhaps she thought she knew something. I thought she knew nothing worth knowing. Her actions alienated me, leaving me lonelier as a result. That night, stripping off my cold wet clothes, feeling the scrape against skin and the weakness where there should be muscle, catching sight of the white sag of belly and clammy breast, it felt a long way back to 1977.

19. Hopper, Sarah C., 2006, *Mothers, Mystics and Merrymakers: Medieval Women Pilgrims* (Stroud: The History Press)

11 October 2018
In Alberque Ultreia in Portomarín, night two comes with the sound
of many pilgrims bedding down in the dormitories, bonded through
the unimaginable kilometres from France that Robin and I haven't
walked. There never was a less lonely or alienated group of people in
the world. If I can do this 116km walk maybe I can join them myself
in their knowledge of the road across the Peninsula, a long way back.
For now, I lie content in my skin and smile to hear the dormitory
fall into silence. I am in good company.

I was not the oldest in our group but I was one of the least prepared. I had had six months since I signed up to walk on Camino and I had exercised more in that time than ever before. But I live my middle-aged life down beside the sea, not in the wild Highlands, and had walked mainly the flat haughs or gentle farmland of the Mearns of Scotland – Lewis Grassic Gibbon country, my own territory – at my own speed, stopping when I wanted to here or there, no one to keep up with, no goal to reach.

I had sat and rested in a wood alone and a family of roe deer, fit and brown, had come down to the stream beside me and leaped it silently with their golden muscled legs stretching in the dappled sunlight. I had slipped down into the grass by a Scottish barley field and watched a hawk swoop for a scuttling partridge as I took a drink from my bottle. I had seen brown trout shimmy beneath a footbridge while I leaned on the rail above. I had, step by step, stretched my ability to walk past dogs off leashes and not to be put off by them from paths I didn't know.

It had been a delight. It had filled me with pride at the beauty of Scotland, tanning my skin, shedding weight and gaining compliments. It had set me thinking about my Camino and what it would be. I wondered as I walked. From 1977 I had had a decade of troubling recurring dreams night after night, tortured with running back in my sleep through Santiago's shining streets, desperate to reach its glorious centre but never managing it. What magic had enchanted me that summer that had the power to penetrate so deep into the mould of my life, calling me back as if in urgency?

This year 2015 has been a great year – a creative, proud year. I have walked beside my daughter Hannah through her final exams at school and into college. Right up to the final days before I left for Galicia, presenting at a charity conference had boosted my self-belief. I felt valuable in a changing world. What I had learnt through the decades felt worth saying. The community projects I had developed were blossoming. I had won small accolades for my endeavours and made new friends. I was well led and by women. With the help of some learning from Carl Jung, I was more aware of how I walk beside others. I play my part in my village community. I hardly think these days of how I came to be here in my own grey Scotland rather than living out earlier dreams of glorious golden Spanish adventure that trickled between my careless fingers somewhere, way back. I stepped out into the Camino's bright light in excitement and positivism – ready to find out.

I had been this last summer to scorching Barcelona for a happy week with my old Catalan friend and my child, her god-daughter, and found the Spanish language tripping easily off my tongue in shops and bars and beaches and art galleries. I had seen my daughter dance in the rainbow stained-glass light of Gaudí's near-completed Sagrada Familia. I caught a tear in my eyes, having seen through decades past the famous towers as just one unloved and ridiculed façade – a miraculous but skeletal vision, unfleshed by Franco's other budgetary priorities – prisons, playas, petrol, Pentagon. I had set off from Montrose for Spain with pride in myself and in the eyes of my lovely dancing daughter and sweet husband Joe as they kissed me goodbye.

But in that aching first Camino night in Portomarín, I felt pathetic, stripped, in just one day's uphill struggle. The proud Hispanophile identity that I had packed with me, along with a dose of lefty feminism, felt weak in comparison to the jolly tight-bodied A-team ladies. My self felt like an insane nothing. My Camino felt like a nothing too. In the glare and noise of the cult of the beautiful body, it was hard for me to keep sight of the more subtle, secret, exquisite spirits of Spain that others had no time for. Tucked up in my chilly hotel bed feeling sorry for myself, I searched for them.

As my daughter has grown, the toddler that I taught to paint and draw and make has become an art student, surpassing me by far. Watching her express and create has reminded me of the girl I was, who came to Santiago to study Spanish culture, who treasured the art of the word, the preciousness of poems. As I walked in Scotland in preparation for this challenge and thought about my path ahead and what goals I wanted to set myself, I regretted letting poetry slip away behind me and thought that it might be something I would like to find in my life again at the end of Camino. Poetry beats to a more intimate rhythm of heart and breath and blood.

That cold night in Portomarín I dug in my pack for the books I carried with me and posted to Facebook some sad lines from Pablo Neruda, favourites from university a lifetime ago. I posted them and though in Spanish I still got two 'likes'. They felt like two small boosts of approval and gave me hope. One from childhood competitor for BBC airtime and fellow Hispanophile, Debbie, lost, with my love of poetry, somewhere back in the UK. The other from another Spanish speaker, Miguel, somewhere out there, much closer now yet thirty-eight years away. Outside the wind blew in from the huge Atlantic and the sad lonely stars came out, pinpricks in the black, and sparkled dimly on our planet as it floated on the everlasting Milky Way. No point thinking ahead.

❋

October 2018
Woods full of birdsong and meadows owned by cats. Magpies, jays and buzzards.

Robins, wrens and tits. Sparkling sand full of mica, spindly lilac crocuses with saffron beaks. Golden apples, golden butterflies, golden cows and golden sun. Mint and walnuts, pears and brambles. Drifting moisture in the air, each miniscule misty drop visible silver. Acorns and chestnuts and green grapefruit and figs and peppers like plastic toys. In a hamlet, a barn and off it, a warm shelter with a smouldering ashy hearth made of giant blocks of soft-cornered stone and a bench for pilgrims and a bird's nest in a cranny and a framed piece of old writing about sharing a smile with someone who cannot.

Narrow strips of field fenced by a man who had an axe but no sawmill so every post is a separate creation.

In many hamlets built around a farmstead, one roof slides gently from several storeys high down to our chest level and ends in an orange frill laced with stonecrop, moss and miniscule flowers. Below, boulders and the end of beams blend with age under veils of lichen and cobweb. Without division, the terracotta slope, in places held down by slabs of granite, stretches down yards of village street, encompassing barn and byre, sheds and stables, home and yard all under one warm roof.

A gateway halfway down is wide and high enough for the most harvest-laden of wagons and its door strong enough to keep out the most determined of bandits. If opened it displays all elements of life – bright white drying nappies and stacks of dusty tools awaiting usefulness; cats and mice and dogs and rats; swallows and flies and spiders and ants. Tractors large and rusting or small and plastic.

In one such yard there are tables laid out for us with free food – cinnamon-dusted egg-fried bread, apples and figs, slices of capsicum and tuna-filled pastries, cartons of fruit juice – worried over by a man with a sad, faraway look in his eyes and daemons in his pale skull.

In 2015, Day 2 on the road left the rain behind us and, as we strode determinedly out of Portomarín, we were rewarded by a high blue sky, a glowing golden dawn and the Camino alive with huge flocks of schoolchildren laughing and singing, eyes only for themselves and with cries of '*Buen Camino!*' that were sing-song and full of excess energy.

Climbing the first steep and uneven wooded path across the river on the edge of town, I struck up chat with a sparkly young American couple – Taylor and his girlfriend. I was glad not to be carrying their huge backpacks with rolled-up tent and groundsheet. Further on we met again on different days and we couldn't remember her name so called her 'Swift'. Taylor seemed to have been walking through Spain in one direction or another for ever and his eyes were like pools of chocolate swimming with optimistic dreams. Their love of Spain was bound up with their love of each other and of adventure in ways that I recognised. They knew roads through other parts of the country, some of which I had walked. They had stood looking out from the Alhambra over the rooftops of Granada, with the snowy Sierra behind them into which Boabdil, the last Moorish king, had been banished to live on a farm looking over to Africa. They had gazed over the plains of blue wood-smoking villages ahead of them and understood the sign which reads:

Dale limosna, mujer, porque no hay nada en la vida como la pena de ser ciego en Granada

Give him alms, woman, for there is nothing so terrible in
life as to be blind in Granada

They had walked over the Roman bridge into Cordoba and
seen the Christian ruination of the conquered mosque, its
delicate geometry dumped upon by a heap of horrid Catholic
baroque. They had sat beside the slow brown arrogance of
Seville's Guadalquivir and thought about the gold that had
been brought up river, and stored and squandered there,
leaving only poetry. They had walked along ravines at Ronda
and Úbeda, passing stables of princely stallions who flared their
nostrils and remembered Arabia. They were twenty-something
and blessed with the endless unfettered freedom that I had
known long ago, and their camaraderie talked me up a hill
before I knew it. Perhaps it would have been better to stick
with them that day, in cheery company, but they were younger
than me and I didn't want to hold them back, so I stopped for a
drink from my aluminium bottle and sent them on. Their pace
had separated me from the back of our group and the crowds
of kids separated me from our fastest so I walked on alone for
a good few miles.

The path and the main highway ran together for much of
this day and we were in higher, barer country, heathery and
rolling, vertically striped with dark pine peering down like thin
hungry giants on yesterday's cosy valleys far behind and below.
It was good that the sun was warm and lovely and the views
wonderful. So exposed and high it would have been a miserable
walk in wind and rain, though the road carried only the occa-
sional vehicle. For some hours, we either walked an unchanging
flat ridge-top existence or struggled with the steepest ups and
downs.

It was good to walk alone on roads lined with broom and
glittering birch, but there came a point where the sprits, the
Gallego duendes, were coming out to meet me, flickering in

the low dazzling light through the birch trees and skinny pines. The spells they tried to cast were too glum and full of *saudade*: the Galician and Portuguese sense of longing and nostalgia which cannot be translated. Their critiques nagged at me with reminders of years when I had left Spain behind and spectacularly misspent my young adulthood. They flickered out from beneath the white tree trunks and rowan berries and threatened to strip me too naked, out here without my soul mates. They lingered in the bracken by the roadside and offered me little bundles of guilt like unlucky heather in the fists of gypsies. I said no thanks. Too soon for the big questions. Only halfway through Day 2. Not the place here at the start of another steep climb. They wouldn't give up but neither would I. Step after step, just step after step.

CHAPTER FIVE

SCORCHED, SCRAPED AND STRAINED

In my notebook, I have snatched what I see. Rain on rust. Green lichen, grey lichen, white lichen splats. Acorns, acorn cups, minute beetle holes in acorn, the tiny little sticks that connect acorn cups to twigs, grains of stone.

Graffiti brings other voices to me: '*78.5k to go*', *Jules & Magna*', '*58k to go Campanilla*', '*Max und Bea*'.

Cypress trees, blue light into dark, wet step, ram-skull teeth and white tin plate, clay tiles, wrought-iron rakes.

Grooves, locks, hinges and handles. Peeling paint, shiny brass. Wood growth lines in huge planks.

'*Osky with us 21.7.14*', '*19k to go*', '*Frank and Michael 09/04/15*'.

Circles in the pool – black and brown and white. White water splash. Dry leaves in a corner nearly orange. Green moss. Iron swirl, gate closed. Bay hedge.

Peach pebble, white pebble, square pebble. Embedded stones, flecks in granite, facets where the rock was roughly cut.

'*Human rights are naked.*'

Utterly black hole high up, yellow arrow, white tunnel.

October 2018
'Life is short but broad.'

I stopped at a waymarker, had a swig from my bottle, and looked for the little heart-shaped pebble from my girl Hannah but could not find it. Not the place for this small comfort either, apparently. It was, it turns out, saving its reminder of home shores for challenges ahead. For the first of six or seven times on the journey I instead performed what became a strange little ritual.

At home in Scotland this spring, when not walking or working, I had handmade 100 soft red felt hearts, each unique, tiny strands of coloured wool fibre meticulously needled together. I had sold them to raise funds for our common cause, promising that each would be photographed on Camino and returned to Scotland. I had planned to keep them packed up until we arrived in the city and their pictures would be proof that I had done what I was sponsored to do. But the rain on the first day made me think what a miserable chore that might be if it bucketed down in Santiago and so, as a safeguard, I decided to take pictures of some each day at different (dry) locations that caught my eye.

This little decision added hugely to my Camino experience. Stopping in strange corners of the walk to lay out and photograph the hearts patiently one by one became meditative, like the lighting of a candle, or the saying of a rosary. It made me stop and see the tiny details of the curves of wrought-iron gates, the creeping of moss and lichen over an old church wall, a beetle hole in an acorn, the jigsaw puzzling of paving stones, the hundred tiny corners where I could prop or wedge a soft two-inch heart. It made me notice an arrow carved into the skin of an apple stuck on a stick wedged in pebbles and crawling with wasps and tiny ants – a very surreal alternative road sign. The ants were the first few arrivals of a line marching up the stick. The sun was high. The flesh of the apple was still white. The apple-carver must be just a few yards ahead of me, just around another bend. I loved the creator's mind without ever meeting whoever it belonged to.

Elsewhere I got down on my knees in the deep-scented wildflowers of the wayside and crouched at strange angles to make my little hearts seem big against the landscape. I had told my sponsors I was doing this thing because Robert the Bruce's heart was taken to Santiago and because I once lost my heart there to a local lover. Both the Bruce and I came back to Scotland. The tales that I told encouraged my Scottish donors to dig deeper in their pockets for the cause which justified my walking. It made those who backed me become part of my story and made me feel them with me as I stopped at shell-marked milestones: a lifeline of friendship back to Scotland where I belong. Where I belong.

So there I was fussing round my bags of felt hearts, feeling a trifle bewitched, doubtful and conflicted when up the path behind me – St James provides you with what you need on Camino – I heard a rough Glaswegian laugh. There came plump ginger Stacey, agonisingly lugging herself up yet another unexpected hill, in her already disintegrating footwear but with her skinny tattooed friend Eve. From that point, we three developed a happy camaraderie, a solidarity of the unfit and a comfortable pace for the steep mornings. Laughing through hardship is elevated to a fine art amongst Glaswegians and we celebrated each wee triumph and filled the Facebook photo albums with great cheery smiles. We became the Blister Sisters, a winning team! I had a purpose which was not about wallowing – we were there for the cause and the comradeship.

El Pueblo Unido Jamás Será Vencido! We would not be defeated by some mere hill.

Politics was tangled tight round me with threads of love and poetry and sex and religion and pain and land and health in my 1970s. In Spain, I felt I reached out and just about touched revolution only a finger stretch away, not in the pages of a broadsheet newspaper. Revolution came out and touched me too. For that first school trip to the Costas in 1973 teachers warned us to cover our newly curvy figures and to leave at home bikinis which were not part of Franco's Catholic fantasy of Spain. Later on, student nights in Edinburgh and Santiago spent exploring bodies had followed daytime tutorials academically analysing the love and protest poetry of assassinated Lorca or weird and wonderful García Márquez or surreal Buñuel. Looking out on medieval skylines, all of the Hispanic world was picked apart with professorial rigour.

Walking on Camino now I remembered how much I had forgotten of the Visigoths, the conquering and dismantling of the Spanish Empire across the Atlantic, the words of La Pasionaria, the revolutionary fishwife, and the 'Situation of Women in Spain Today'.

My sallow black-eyed tutor, as Spanish as a Spaniard though Edinburgh born and bred, stared into space from the David Hume Tower as he recited the fascist-bothering sexually charged poetry of Lorca, scared to look his female students in the eye in case we accused him of being seductive. One day I sat with him alone, fearlessly talking gypsy metaphor into the darkness without either of us ever noticing or thinking to turn on the light, lost in his ivory tower, twenty storeys above the wine-reeking gardens of the university. Lust was poetry. It was there for exploration. That beneath our clothes he was a man and I was a girl was academic. It never crossed my mind, which was filled, too, with other studies which put Spanish

culture and history in context: of Romanesque cathedrals, of
Western aesthetics and philosophy, of the fine art of Surrealist
nudes, of Philip's Armada and Elizabeth's anger, of Wellington
and the Peninsular War and poetry in English and medieval
Portuguese.

Meanwhile, as we tipped into the second half of the 1970s,
the regions of Spain – the Basques, Catalans, Asturians and
Gallegos – simmered.

It all wove into my heart like the multicoloured threads of the
hearts I needle-felted, carried and delicately positioned amongst
the stone and earth and growing green of the long road.

Trusted Catholic teenagers were freer to mix in Spain in
1974 than I was used to in schoolgirl Scotland. On a summer
visit that year to my pen pal in Catalunya, nice boys with families
known to her family took us, clinging on to their golden-brown
backs, on one-seat motocross bikes high up into the Pyrenees
to a mountain marked by a giant cross but named for an older
tradition of sacrificing cockerels to some forgotten god. We scat-
tered jewel-like bee-eaters as we passed and stopped to drink
from sweet mountain springs bursting from the earth beneath
birch roots. We munched crusty bread stuffed with *tortilla de
patatas*, poured thin wine down our throats from goat-skin *botas*
and looked down from cropped summits to wild horses in dun-
coloured valleys like stacks of egg boxes tumbling off to hidden
France. Later we wove the ribbons of rope sandals round our
ankles, joined hands and danced the *sardana* in village squares.
Secretly in evenings without grown-ups we played the sex poetry
of Leonard Cohen or the banned protest songs of exiled Lluís
Llach who sang in poetic code of the toppling of Franco and of
the long journeys of faithful Catalan freedom fighters.

I was with my Catalan pen pal and her wealthy friends
later that summer in the pine-scented foothills of the Pyrenees
when the whole of Catalunya said 'Franco is dying, tomorrow

revolution' and said it with fear of their fellow Spaniards. They had no faith that their compatriots in Catalunya itself, in the Basque country and distant anarchic Asturias or its neighbour Galicia – or indeed in other, right-leaning parts of the country – were capable of or interested in transitioning smoothly to democracy.

I met a medical student, much later, who had been in the hospital the old *caudillo* was taken to. They had cleared three floors of sick citizens to keep secret the preparations for his death eighteen months later. We had wondered together when he had really lost control, how long before the declaration of his death in November 1975 had the old general been kept ticking only artificially, apart from prying eyes while acceptable arrangements were put in place and I had drunk cava with families with surnames as old as the Catalan hills?

October 2018

In 1977 Spain passed a law to make itself forget. Still in 2018 Western Europe eulogises a dictator unthinkable in Germany or Italy but whose words and mass graves are barely discussed in Spain till now. Still his monument stands. Still his Foundation is funded and his children enjoy their titles. Still known torturers live beside the holes in the yellow earth that they and their neighbours filled with each other. This 2018 weekend a film of remembering is released to Spanish cinemas.

I was this October walking back through free Spain, not anywhere else in the world where you can bag a few hilltops and clock a few sponsored miles. Spain is different. It is nearly Africa, nearly Arabia, nearly South America and for ever poetry:

romantic or tragic. It was the treasure chest in which Islam kept safe the secrets of the classical world while Christianity went dark. It was the last police state in Western Europe, the country where in the cafe-bars of Catalunya, I met Franco's victims face-to-face and they were my generation, not distant history.

In 1976, I got a job outside Barcelona as au pair and English tutor for a family of four. I spent a summer speaking English in quick snatches on my Saturdays off and otherwise Spanish for three and a half months until I dreamed in it and it could last me a lifetime. Franco was buried but only months back. You could still smell his stench in the gypsy shanty towns that crowded Barcelona's railway lines and in the earnest discourse of students from professional Catalan families. The future was far from hopeful.

My new friends, met in Barcelona cafes on days off, were the boy whose girlfriend had lost her baby when the Guardia Civil had beaten her pregnant belly; the boy whose brother had been blinded by their taking his spray paint and emptying it into his eyes on the spot where he was caught writing political protest. At home Britain swayed gently between Harold Wilson and Ted Heath and none of my friends talked politics though we were free to do so.

Each Saturday in Barcelona three buses of civil guards parked on the Ramblas and swept down the boulevard, rifles in their hands looking for trouble. Each Saturday night queues formed outside the cinemas in Perpignan across the French border as Spaniards pined for pornography, illegal at home. The woman I worked for and lived with told me that no one wanted the new King Juan Carlos – it was a shame, he was nice, he would only last a few months. He was not enough of a dictator.

A sad, stiff housewife told me her husband's thick hair was so white because he had lain in a trench on the Teruel front in the Civil War beside his dying brother, who he had shot fighting for the other side. I had no idea how to respond. The little church near where we sat still had bullet holes from firing squads in the walls. Inside, the chaste saints bled like nowhere else in Europe. They'd done it for centuries and across continents. It did no good.

Now in 2015 I have been back walking across windy bridges through nowhere else in the world: not the adventure tourist treks nor the grouse moors of Scotland nor even the pilgrimages of England. I didn't want to do it fast or noisily. Knowing how very lucky I have been in the ways I have been allowed to walk through life, I could not do it lightly. I was not doing it selflessly. Others may have been exercising; I myself was on pilgrimage, going backwards through Spain. Having the language and going slow, I was lucky enough to be able to see deep into its tender places. And mine.

Back in 1976 as Catalunya simmered and Franco's memory putrefied with horrible reluctance, I was very much myself, alone, in the little Mediterranean village where I worked. The resort at Llavaneras had been built for young families. Their men worked on in steamy Barcelona, the most densely populated city in Europe, and commuted at weekends to join young wives, grandparents and primary-school children by the cheapest bit of sea for miles around. The Costas hadn't, just a few station stops from the city, become photogenic enough for foreigners. The hinterland was flat and bare and there was little beach between the water and the railway line that came down from France.

I tried walking inland to the prettier old village one day along beside the froggy ditches, but it was too far and too hot. The word got round fast that I was a foreigner in town and I was muttered about as I went by, down to the beach with the children every morning. There were flags to warn of sharks, they told me, and a Saturday helicopter dropped out a giant beach ball advertising the Corte Ingles store in town. Lads and dads raced out to catch it.

After lunch, every little girl from babyhood upwards was dressed in layers of stiff lace and petticoats and ribbons for the afternoon. Every little boy had his wiry black hair combed flat with gallons of cologne and had his tummy stuffed into long shorts and white shirts which mums and grannies and nannies like me spent their afternoon trying to keep clean of the yellow dirt of the park between the apartment blocks. I learnt enough Catalan to say no to Susi, the two-year-old. Though she spoke both Castilian Spanish (that I had learnt in school) and Catalan, her mother was stricter than her nursery-school nuns and it was Catalan that was spoken at home and in this quiet park.

I learnt how to say: 'on the stairs on your tricycle – no, Susi'; 'standing under the tap – no, Susi'; 'to the swimming pool alone – no, Susi'; 'with your fingers – no, Susi, with the fork'; 'be quiet and eat, Susi'.

Mrs Menta, my boss and hostess, was in her early thirties, had a husband and four children aged two, four, six and eight and was going blind. She was told when Susi was born that she would be blind by the time Susi was two. They were nearly right. Her husband explained this to me, day one of the summer, on the way from the airport.

He explained to me too that he works six days a week in Barcelona and doesn't see the children except on Sundays. Her medical bills aren't cheap. He told me that the children have just lost their grandfather. When told Grandpa had gone to heaven, María Luisa (aged 8) looked up to the night sky and said she could see his eyes twinkling. Quique (age 6) looked up too and turned to his sister with contempt and said, 'And how did he get up there? With a ladder?'

Mrs Menta's way of dealing with all of this, apart from hiring an au pair and English tutor for the summer, was to not embrace her children with wreaths of smiles while she could still see them. Instead, unsmiling, she took each chance to ram home the highest standards of discipline before she could no longer see their misdemeanours.

Susi's ribbons and lace were the starchiest in the village – I know; it was my job to iron them. If she was not silent for the two-hour siesta I laid her down for then she was shouted at not comforted. If Quique did not eat every morsel of his food he was punished, even if the foreigner was struggling to eat hers. Mrs Menta was still able to cook six dishes (on Sundays we ate out) and cooked them week in, week out. Five of them were inedible.

Monday's meal was slimy tinned tuna mush, covered in over-liquefied packet potato puree mush, covered in cheap oily supermarket mayonnaise mush. It made me gag. I would tear off and stuff in a lump of crusty bread (thankfully served with every Spanish meal), ladle in some mush, stuff in some more bread and chew as little as possible then swill down with a glass of palette-grating red wine (thankfully ever present).

I survived on the crusts I cut off Susi's *pan i tomat*. Sent out to the butchers where they chopped raw yellow chicken on a sun-hot slab and for hake at the fishmongers where the counter I was squashed against was icy, hunger got the better of me and I fainted clean unconscious into the ample bosom of a neighbour.

On Sundays heaven reigned. Down by the beach was the kind of cheap and basic cafe that in Britain would be poisonous and fetid and overcooked but in the hands of Mediterranean Europeans is a freshly fried or roasted wonderland. It has its equivalents in Greece, Italy and France (and I am sure all round that wonderful sea at the centre of the world) but this one was Catalan.

I cannot be sure of the order of dishes for it is a long time ago and there were so many. But that is what is so different in Spain from Scotland. Bread is a course, rubbed with garlic and salt and post-box-red tomatoes. Green beans are a course, sautéed with chopped cured ham and garlic and herbs amongst them. A whole roast chicken is a course – for one, small and yellow and tasting of the farmyard. That is after a steak as thin as a flannel. Which is after a plate of hake. There is always hake on the plate in Spain. It's the law.

There may have been soup along the way – either light and chickeny or substantially floating with beans and ham and spinach. There will have been the best chips in the world – not peeled, not straight, but thin and salty and golden from olive oil. There may have been spaghettis which are of course plural and just a vehicle for tomato sauce. And then, only then, the main course. Paella. Glowing like a sunset. Studded with the jewels of Spain – ruby peppers, emerald parsley, mother-of-pearl prawns and mussels on a shining golden bed of saffron rice. No wonder the only Spanish pudding worth bothering with is 'flan' – crème caramel to settle your tummy.

And at the table next to the sad little Menta family of four stiff children, all seeing Mama and exhausted father and me was another family of thirteen or more. Some were seated and more were held in arms, filling the little cafe with their perfect family love. In fact, there must have been at least three tables all pushed together end to end to accommodate the four generations or so of them.

This was not, to be clear, a special occasion – this was every Sunday throughout the summer. Amongst the noise and aromatic black tobacco smoke and general chaos of paper tablecloth changing, bread slicing and wine pouring, a few individuals caught my eye – a miniscule lady in black, not the only one, but the great one.

While her charcoal daughters were still buxom in their decades-long widowhood, she was a tiny currant beside the still rich juicy raisins of their gossipy judgemental cackle. She, *bisabuela* (a great-grandmother), was barely still on the planet but noticed, and was noticed by, everyone else. Should she have protested, they would have ceased. Her motherhood ruled. No one sat till she was comfortable and they were all engaged in the business of making her so – moving chairs, closing blinds, finding cushions, storing her accessories, pointing out this and that.

Her grandson, keeping an eye on her, making sure delicious morsels were offered to her, ruled for her. He was rounded and moustachioed and deep voiced like any Spanish man should be and of course slicked back with cologne. Details of etiquette and appetite did not concern him as long as they did not concern her. That his family loved each other and respected his grandma was his only concern. Pass on that squalling child. Don't annoy your demure virgin of a sister. Do what your great-aunt has instructed – for the love of the mother of God, boy! What is your problem? In three hours of luncheon these were his only legal pronouncements and everything else was laughter and cheek-squeezing and ordering of more of that wine that he loves or the bread his mother insists on or the little plate of snails that so delight his favourite niece.

Finally, and queen of the show, was his tiniest daughter or maybe granddaughter. It was impossible to know whose she was by birth because she was everyone's. She was a squirmy worm of a child. If she had been British, her parenthood would have been clear to see on the sweating grumpy brow of her mother, left to navigate the hunger, boredom, indigestion, tiredness of two-year-old tyranny. But this lacy brown berry with gold pierced earrings, gold around her chubby rolls of neck and gold round her stubby fists was the King of Spain's daughter, a little nutmeg demanding that everyone danced for her and they did. All of them.

She was passed from black bosom to lacy cleavage, skinny Nike to sweaty Adidas, aunt to nephew to mum to white-capped grandpa, and each were delighted to take her and feed her morsels and eat with one hand. No one of them ever had to do so too long. No one of them knew what too long meant. Someone else always wanted her, opened their arms for her so she never knew what it was to do without and demand too much and be rejected and think what that means. She might, if they were lucky (cross yourself quickly), never wonder what lay beyond the family. Her dried-up great-grandma had lived within it happily since she herself was a juicy brown berry who didn't even need a seat at the table.

And between these three stars of the weekly show were quiet skinny teenagers who felt loved by no one outside this table because of their acne and wet dreams. And maiden aunts who felt worthless in the village except to the bleeding saints and nuns this morning at mass. And the fat little princes in the stiff white shirts who only cared about chips and chocolate and knew one day they would be the ones in regency over the table as long as they respected their grandmas. And for all of the table full of them there was a love spread amongst the baskets of bread and bottles of oil that made me think. Perhaps it was not so stupid to think that just love could turn water into wine. Love could provide loaves and fishes equally to everyone without being just a chore to a sickly mother.

One day, worried about for weeks ahead, near the end of my stay, both Menta parents were gone before breakfast time and would not be back till the next day. I was in sole charge of maintaining Spanish domestic standards for a two-year-old rebel, a silent four-year-old waif, a sharp and cynical six-year-old, and a neurotic mumsy eight-year-old for twenty-four hours. I made some small adjustments. I let María Luisa make the beds and prepare all the meals. I did not expect Lisa nor Quique to be polite or friendly to anyone but let them carry on with whatever intellectual exercise engaged their clever brains. And I did not expect Susi to eat anything she did not want, fed her sweets to keep her going and did not ask her to keep her lacy dresses, neat white socks, cute little hair ribbons clean or dry. I didn't even take them out of the wardrobe. I put on pants and sandshoes and that is all and sent her out to play in her lovely olive-brown skin.

I think she had the best day of her life. She stood under the tap to fill her bucket. She splashed the yellow gravel into sticky mud and fixed it into her hair with chocolate biscuit. We washed it off together in the swimming pool. I had my employment terminated a little early as a result of this entirely inappropriate and revolutionary behaviour (reported to Mrs Menta by all the grannies in the village and María Luisa to her never-ending shame), but one little girl got the chance for a day to know what it is to be a Free Bird and I hope it stood her in good stead.

For an eighteen-year-old Scot who arrived with good schoolgirl Spanish there had not been much relief that summer except a sense of adventure and freedom just from being on the European mainland a stone's throw from Berber Africa. I watched coal-black Sub-Saharans pick fields of carnations and olive-skinned farmers dribble water from tin cans on allotments of tomatoes by dried-out concrete riverbeds. In the nearby city on Saturdays off, I found that if I sat with a notepad as well as a Coke and a fag and painted what I saw then the hours would go by and I wouldn't mind being alone, and the memories of what I saw and heard and smelt would be captured quick. Being a painter of sorts attracted company in the resort too – first small nosey children and then, if I was lucky, their older brothers or sisters, someone not too much younger than my eighteen years to chat with in the shade of a poplar tree. My Spanish fluency improved rapidly. I spoke English for maybe a few sentences a week if I met a Northern European on the Ramblas.

One day, a couple of months into the summer, I was leaning over the balcony in the village, looking down into the communal garden below, with a wee bit of time to myself while the children had siesta when I spotted a wondrous sight! A slim brown male back belonging to someone clearly beyond puberty and keeping fit. There was an up-to-date cut of curly black hair on top and one long brown leg and five brown toes stretched out in front. The rest I could not see for shrubbery.

I grabbed my pad and traveller's set of watercolours as bait and scrambled downstairs into the park. I straightened my scarlet dress over my teenage bum and sauntered over to the bench with a studiously dreamy expression on my face but not a glance in his direction, and set myself down all arty-like to capture the pretty village scene around me and perhaps a bit of male company. It worked, and he struck up conversation in lovely, deep warm Spanish and we were soon locked onto each other in something with potential for more than just companionship.

But oh when I deigned to turn to him, the tragedy of summer loving! His other leg was entirely in plaster: from the hip! He was stuck here with the old folks and kids because of a motorbike accident, and it took another month before we could scratch the itch which had been sparked by mutual art appreciation on that village bench.

Many turns of the world later, but years before this Camino, I popped his name into a search on the World Wide Web but he did not come back to me, despite my taking his virginity that summer on the deep hot sands of the Mediterranean once the children were asleep and I had explained to him what his hips were for. I had told him he looked like a Christ figure from the Byzantine paintings I was studying at university and he, convent educated, called me his María Magdalena, the Bible's whore. I understood it as a compliment.

One night after the children were in bed and I had slipped out to meet him in the dark, our loving was disturbed by torch beam sweep across the sands where we lay between upturned fishing boats. Scared, he swore. 'We must hide.' He had come out for sex without his ID card and this was the Guardia Civil, the foot soldiers of the Inquisition and even now of Franco's not-quite-dead state. I scoffed that being British I had no ID to bring, feeling I had nothing to fear with Her Majesty's protection. He whispered that the men with the torches and the flat-backed hats and guns would not stop to care and that I should shut up quickly and dig. We stuck our bare bottoms in the air and scrabbled like rabbits, burrowing under a boat and dragging our clothes in afterwards, then lay naked as the boots tramped by.

Spain's journey through fascism, not yet over, had come very close to my bare skin. My diary tells me that I saw it as preparation for the summer of 1977 when I would spend longer away from home.

Meanwhile, that summer of 1976 changed me for ever. Well, it changed my two front teeth anyhow and gave me a new sense of mortality.

After three months' work, I left the coast and the city behind and went to spend a week with my Catalan pen pal in the high villages of the Pyrenean foothills where I had motocrossed with her friends a couple of years before. This time we were more grown up and wilder. My Spanish was better and I revelled in being with people my own age, with more chance to speak my own language and with no responsibility. The nights were hotter and my pen pal and her friends could take me further – to lie in itchy haylofts on steep rutted slopes which smelt of sheep and wild horses and pine and fell away to sleeping convents far below. Pink Floyd futilely wished we were somewhere more progressive than still-far-from-democratic Spain and we drove fast with them loud in our ears round and round the steep egg-box valleys to reach the larger towns or higher passes. Helter-skeltering one afternoon in convoy we hit a line of mud across the road from where on one side the mountain wall rose vertically and on the other side dropped through a palisade of tree trunks sheer down to a distant lowland village.

For eons, Spain has been rubbing France up the wrong way, pushing up sharp ridges and folds of Pyrenees between the two. Hot winds blow over the peninsular bridge from Africa, lifting hundreds of red-leg-trailing storks in invisible merry-go-rounds in the skies over Andorra on the borders with true Europe. Storms crack over Catalunya to fall as floods in France and only a little of their water falls on these yellow mountain-sides. Just enough trickles down, dislodging the weakest and least-resistant grit and using it to grate away a little rut in which to rivulet, spiralling through the wild herbs and grasses, careering now down the cliff, gaining momentum, picking up more and more from the surface, turning brown now as it descends through more sheltered topsoil, pushing before it a soup of slippery mud.

It has been coming down here since long before man built a road and so ignores it, sliming across the tarmac to ooze down the other side in a never-ending slow motion in which pines don't have time to root themselves, building up a loose mass of soft grit and bundles of bramble coils in the gap created. I was supposed to be in the crowded car in front but had a cold and had wanted the breathing space of an empty back seat so swapped at the last minute before we set off. The lead driver saw the mud and swerved from it. Our driver close behind over-did the swerving, caught the mud, spun and shot off the mountainside at ninety degrees. We flew.

It's been a nice life, I thought as we went airborne out towards the opposite side of the valley.

Pity it's only been eighteen years long, I thought as I saw the terrible tree trunks fly close by. We nosedived and there was no tree trunk ahead to save or kill us. The only collision was my teeth against my lips and then against the seat in front. The brambles caught us and pulled us in amongst their safety net, catching our twist on the muddy slope. We stopped. Alive. Just a mouth full of bloody spaghetti flesh, a shocked and shaking scrabble up through thorny, gravely, slippery mountainside and a chipped and squinted tooth which I didn't get sorted till my second wedding.

I never forgot I was alive when in Spain, which, though just a stork flap from the rest of Europe, has more dangers and more blessings. Spain makes not just bull torture but even one-car teenage crashes poetic.

And mange. Leaning on a restaurant terrace wall one day, now-accustomed black tobacco cigarette in hand, I gazed into the geological wonder which is the Tremp valley, a round and shallow bowl of lowland shoved up high amongst the mountain ridges which came down to meet it like the points of a pentagon. Belly full of herbs and snails from the hillside, fresh trout netted from the waterfall pool nearby and stunned on a marble slab just before its cooking, I watched the tiny trucks of an army camp manoeuvring on a secretive hilltop far below. Again, and not for the last time, I was Spain's unseen witness.

An eagle floated by, spying on the little village lives. Resting my glass of earthy wine and bare brown arms on the stone, I could see down into its yellow eye and it, hunting, never recognised my superiority but mesmerised me still. Quite alone, my friends being still at long Spanish lunch, I exhaled blue smoke and felt myself float out into the giant bubble of blue Pyrenean space, into the air which had come stroking up over the Peninsula laden with desert and orange, wheat and rabbit hole, charcoal and sage. High above me, a tiny chapel peaked our ridge top, the highest point of the highest ridge of the valley.

I might have fallen but for a loud animal snort close behind me. It pulled me back to earth with the sudden knowledge that I was not, after all, safe and alone.

I whirled. Across the flagstones and just a yard behind me was a primitive and biblical stable which I hadn't noticed, tucked under the crag. Just a crude shelter roofed in bending branches and weedy thatch. In its tiny black square of shadow glowed a turquoise horse. Its long untamed tail sparkled. It tossed its crinkly, shining mane and snorted again. Blue sparkles filled the air around it. It flashed its dark eyes in the gloom, stamped a gleaming foot and flared its soft black nostrils. It breathed out stardust.

Dizzied, I needed a seat and hurried back into the white-washed dining room and the reassurance of my friends. The restaurateur clarified it was neither Pegasus nor a unicorn that I had encountered but an ordinary white horse rubbed all over with blue crystalline powder to treat mites. An ordinary part of village life. Spain has the power to infect my mind with poetry even on a microscopic level. It has enchanted stronger minds than mine, and I am the least of those who would fight to tell its tales.

I was in Spain when Hemingway's Civil War masterpiece *For Whom the Bell Tolls* was, as censorship was loosened, put on sale with a sticker saying 'First time in Spain' – first time you free Spaniards have been able to read your story told by one of the world's greatest storytellers and greatest Hispanophiles. Now Barcelona has a street named for George Orwell, who came and fought and wrote in homage to them, and Pamplona honours Hemingway who loved its gory glory and its men.

When I flew in for my summer course in Santiago, with Franco a bit more dead, Galicia's people were freer in 1977 than at any point before. But still not free. In my diary of the time I took a note of the graffiti sprayed on the walls by more brave boys looking for a better future:

'*Freedom is ours not the states.*'

'*Dissolution of the bodies of repression.*'

'*Referendum without freedom – don't vote.*'

'*25 of September against fascist assassins.*'

On that first visit to Santiago there was something optimistic and wild in the air and it had been easy to fall in love with Miguel, snuggled on a cathedral step, as the minstrels came serenading down the Santiago streets with their lutes and mandolins, flashing smiles and swinging black capes. We went together to Ortigueira for the first concert in the Gallego language since the Spanish Civil War.[20] Democracy not yet begun, but a generation of Celtic musicians had had enough.

This was the Spain I was walking back through last week. Every step of it mattered to me.

I was in Spain again, in a small Catalan market town, in 1978 when, with my own life pivoting, the telly in the living room called out the grandest of proclamations 'Día 6 de Diciembre, Día de la Constitución!' and the nation voted for the world they enjoy today. Franco had been dead three years but was still rolling restlessly in his grave.

I have a copy still, on my lap right now as I write, of the cartoon-strip pamphlet produced to teach a generation what free voting that day would involve because they did not know and did not trust each other and because no one had been interested, till now, in teaching their disenfranchised to read anything other than Catholic dogma.

This was the Spain whose lessons I was remembering, more with every mile walked on Camino.

Between and amongst Spain's great bends in the road to democracy came more of my own great crossroads. It was in Galicia that I learnt from a photo book about how fast a baby, wanted or not, grows in the womb.

It was to Spain I ran when a boy hit me and made me bleed.

I celebrated my twenty-first birthday in Catalunya with people I didn't know well enough to refuse my first taste of snails – fifty-six of them.

20. http://www.galiciaguide.com/Culture-gallego.html

It was in Catalunya that I received a marriage proposal by telegram. As this country that I loved so much chose to become free, I did the other thing and came home to marry a Scottish bass-playing IT and linguistics nerd who I thought knew how to love me.

October 2018
Of course it would be to Spain that I would head when I was done with thinking of dying.

I was carrying all of this and more with me a lifetime later, mythologized and fantasised over decades. Each came to me as I walked, in its own place on my journey, each story telling itself to me in its own good time. This Camino, as the end of my working life looms, may perhaps have led me to another crossroads. Perhaps by the end of this writing I will know where I am heading next – uphill or downhill.

At the moment, in these days of recovery and looking back, last week's path seems to have been a messy tangle of half beliefs and unclear memories. I cannot separate what was the challenge of the walking and what was the challenge of remembering Spain's pretty passions and priceless poets. Its forbidden bagpipes, its brave brigades and its bedside bibles were close neighbours of my own love stories and rubbed off on my sense of self. They all travelled with me this October, sank with my boot prints into the soft yellow gravel of the road and clung to me high on Franco's bridge across the Minho. There was a tension between belonging in this newly met group of Scottish women and of remembering a belonging with people with whom I shared another place and another time and much more of myself.

Walking beside each other got more difficult for a while on Day 2. The challenges of the everyday Scottish working week were brought out to be aired high on a boring stretch where the path ran alongside the road and modern commercial properties lay behind high fences beside us. We passed a battery chicken farm. It stank. Two fiery red personalities, Lucy's and mine, met and failed to accommodate each other's experiences and ambitions. My old boss had abused my colleagues physically, sexually and literally and her only professionally. It's not a comfy subject.

Feeling wrong-footed made me grumpy. Further on, I was presented with a different vision of our last evening in Santiago from the Hispanophile one that I had set my heart on in all the months and miles so far. I got grumpier still. My dreamed-of Compostelan night was, it seemed, to be one packed with artificial finishing-line hotel jollity with my new acquaintances. It was a stark contrast to my yearned-for convivial Spanish bar life where we pilgrims would have the best and most fitting reward. Deep dark benches would nestle heavy trestle tables. Sparkling mirrors would catch the flash of fleet-of-foot wait-ers. Barrels would let loose a score of precious tongue-teasing liquids. Local laughter and entertainment would arise naturally from the picking up of a guitar, the strolling by of a mandolin player, the glistening of poetic eyes, and we would luxuriate in the joy of lingering amongst the like-minds we had walked with from across a huge and turning world.

There was to be no time for that.

What was actually planned was team celebration as if at the end of a school sports day, contrived somewhere in an office in Scotland before we set one foot on the Way of St James. It seemed a small-spirited thing in the richness of Romanesque Santiago, the great city of learning and soul.

For a while I really did not want at all to be on this walk up exhausting hills that I was not allowed to call a hillwalk. I felt alone and, family being a long way behind, increasingly yearned to be with someone who understood me, perhaps someone nearby, who had accepted me thirty-eight years ago.

The second half of Day 2 I walked through real physical pain with our Gallega guide Alicia by my side – beautiful, young, super fit, intellectual, a brilliant leader and a sweetheart with a touch of iron and of fragility like a bird. Gallegos seem to come in two shapes – the round, flat-faced, earth-skinned, mousy-haired folk we greet in the villages and, like Alicia, the long-faced, olive-skinned, glossy corkscrew-locked ethereal beauties. She walked all season with people of all sorts and levels of fitness and what judgements she had of us she kept silent and cool.

The hills were bare and stark and steep on the downward slopes and I felt like my knees were going to separate from my body. Real doubt about what I was doing oozed from my flesh to my head. I would have struggled to put self-doubt aside without Alicia's particular skills in walking beside me. I expect she employed the same skills elsewhere in the straggle of our group from the fastest to the slowest. As we put the long miles behind us, she and I talked for hours in Spanish passion about being a woman, being a democrat, being a poetess and we marched the road by. Miles of high moor lay around us, scorched black by forest fire or maybe dragon breath with giant teeth of granite exposed at their peaks, and the sun was a hot, unblinking dragon's eye in an ice blue sky.

On straight high stretches the agonies to come are all too visible. The downs are the most painful. The climbs you can put your back into heroically and feel proud. The downs just seem to want to hurt you, tearing at your knees, burning your sinews, trying to remove them from your legs in multiple places.

Each day starts busy on Camino as everyone who has stayed the night in the same village sets off at dawn. I dread to think what it is like at the height of the pilgrimage season with 2,000 passing through each day.

As the sun gets higher in the sky, never too hot in October, so do the gaps between people. By our afternoons we slowest were on a long lonely road with, as always, its ups and downs. Now my fellow walkers were fewer and further between and I was amongst a different type – slower, older, fatter, heads further down, walking alone, silent, more likely to stop and add a pebble to a pile. It was good to have company on the long, long ascents and descents of that second day, and Alicia's professional skills distracted my mind from my pains. There was a place, I will admit, with high bare moors around me and the path ahead no broader than a sheep trail as it cut through a narrow gully, that I hit a wall of pain. As I looked down at the miles of sharp descent before me, from somewhere round my knees came the question 'Can I do this?' Just that one moment, in that very empty space with not a building or animal in sight, I did wonder.

October 2018
For a while it is cold, windy and grey. My calves ache, my thighs ache, my back aches, my shoulders ache and what is left of my insides aches indescribably. The fleeting thought 'Can I do this?' cannot be denied. But I know that a wall of pain is of limited dimensions and that my answers will always come from my head, not my body. I breathe in through my nose as long as I can and breathe out long and controlled till I pull up again from way down below my thighs. I wonder at what I can do.

Alicia, walking beside me, picked me up and got me discussing the Spain I had known that she, born ten years into democracy and its obligatory forgetting, had never been told about. She hooked my passion out from my memory as if pulling me up by my boot laces, and with the anger of it came enough adrenalin to keep my feet moving. She asked me if I had been scared that summer in Catalunya when the jackboots tramped down the Ramblas and across the beaches and I had to admit that I had been – deliciously, intoxicatingly so, with my British passport and lack of Catholic guilt. We talked about the dissertation I had written in 1978 on the 'Situation of Women Today', which I have on my lap now as I write. It had captured a moment.

Spain's villages were transitioning in that moment from an undisturbed medievalism in which a modern Catalan adulteress had been sentenced to stoning by her twentieth-century community. Moslem-fearing twenty-first-century Europe chooses not to know what Christians were doing half a generation ago, but some of us remember. A generation of village women took to the streets to protest and stop the punishment, bringing it to the attention of the world beyond their little deep-forgotten valley just the wrong side of the Pyrenees. Learning from Spartacus, they had paraded with home-made banners shouting '*Jo també soc adultera*'. For the first time as the 1970s grew old, the women in that community stood up and supported their neighbour and stood against the men, the church and the state in which adultery was a criminal offence.

As I did my best to keep pace with this gazelle of a girl, she slowed down for me and we walked beside each other through the miles. Alicia and I talked about divorce and contraception and abortion, all illegal in Franco's Spain, and the London clinics which filled with Catholic Spanish and Irish girls and about the secrets I had brought and found in Santiago, aged nineteen. We talked as we passed sawmills and truck stops about truth and reconciliation and European money and monarchy. We did not always agree. Spain had fallen out of love with their King Juan Carlos, sending him to abdication. But I remembered him as the guard of a fragile new democracy who I had seen filmed at the shrine of St James when his seat on the throne was new.

She talked as we walked down through sleepy farmyards and over squat bridges about Gallego culture. I surprised her by showing that 1977 had not been just a short summer of love but a deep one of immersion in the poetry of Rosalía de Castro and Celtic music and the sad Hispanic far-west soul to which my illicit still-married lover had introduced me.

Alicia and I passed abandoned concrete village laundry pools, barely tamed from the rough stone springs dripping from the moss beside them. I remembered my horror in the 1970s at seeing them still in use by loudly gossiping, head-scarved women, scrubbing their family's clothes on the sloping sides of a wide deep pool under a low roof. Spain's backwaters still lived in Biblical poverty till Brussels reached out to it. While now in 2015 we had to call 'car' to warn other walkers, I remembered in the late 1970s passing carts on solid unspoked wheels drawn by emaciated cows. Women back then walked into town with milk churns or tin basins of greens balanced on a twisted circle of newspaper on their heads, from which snaked long grey pigtails.

Down in the valleys Alicia talked of Medieval local girl Inês de Castro who broke the heart of a Portuguese prince and of Christopher Columbus, who may have been Gallego before he was Genoan, and I shared the vocabulary for naming the trees we passed – oak, chestnut, beech and birch, pine and fir, holly and ivy.

She showed us Venus's belly button – a round-leafed plant – and how it can be used to heal the skin of raw-rubbed pilgrims. She told us of how the first eucalyptus seed brought back to Europe by a Catholic missionary became another of Franco's great land-destroying feats, and how divided and deserted pockets of farmland which families called home for genera-tions become unpopulated forest. There are many methods of raping a land for wealth. Fascists know them all. These aliens don't sing the songs of the lands of the Celts as their branches weave through the astringent breeze. Growing from glowing, smoky-blue shrubs with heart-shaped leaves, their multi-coloured peeling pillars soon soar relentlessly towards heaven, draining the goodness from the earth below and threatening to explode with fire, and we pilgrims are tiny and bent, trudging in the darkness left behind, carrying our burdens.

In one hilltop village, Ventas de Narón, we found the tiniest and simplest of cool stone chapels, smaller than my living room, almost entirely bare except for one sweet image of Mary Magdalene for this was her *capilla*. At a large empty table in the musty stone darkness stood her guardian: a blind and smiley hobbit whose hand we had to guide to get a stamp on our pilgrims' passports. He still put it on upside down. What fun he had joking with us that he would stamp our foreheads instead and then ringing out the church bell with a rope above his tiny door to send us on our way.

Everywhere were dotted the classic Galician *hórreos*: terracotta-tiled, plank-walled grain stores with crosses on their eaves and lifted above the damp and vermin on two- or four-stone pillars at their corners, topped with overhanging slabs and reached by ladders. Most very much in use, some decorated with pots of geraniums, some abandoned and sagging back into the stone and wood of the land. Prouder than a small barn and more enchanting than a garden shed. Many of them proud historians of the richness of the north-western soil and the monasteries that fed off it. Faux *hórreos* posed as postboxes in the gardens of wealthy modern folk. Others without the same share of resources had built equally beautiful traditional solutions to storing whatever they had. Circular *piornos* – withy-woven huts like giant baskets with conical thatched roofs – stood on one stone pillar, safe, in village corners or farmyards. There were newer riches here too, built into neat bourgeois cubes of modern comfort, eaves frilled with neon-modern terracotta, funded by the neighbourliness of the old Spanish Empire just across the Atlantic.

As the road rose and fell ahead of me, weaving through the soothing green and in Alicia's clever company and the music of her language, my love of Spain flooded my mind and swamped the physical pain.

Spain's beauty is not, like France or England, in self-satisfied richness nor cosy biscuit-box prettiness. Like Scotland, it is a crueller, more barbaric beauty which even in its quiet corners lets its history flash out like a red petticoat from beneath its words and provides solidarity to those who also suffer (even if only from the torture of tearing muscle in aging legs).

In Scotland, we grew up talking freely to fathers and grand-fathers who, neatly medalled and uniformed, had all fought on the right side in just wars, liberating masses on lands across the sea. In the end they won, Mussolini dangled and Hitler buried himself. In Spain, in our fathers' lifetime, on village doorsteps, against warm church walls, brother had killed brother, neighbours knifed nuns, miners blew up monks, poets were disappeared and thousands – who just wanted to stop eating black bread and acorns and have a fair share of the wheat baskets – were exter-minated. The Nazis were invited in to pulverize the ancient oak of Guernica,[21] where Basque and Spanish kings swore loyalty, into nothing but great art. Hemingway and Orwell and Laurie Lee came and made great writing of it. Working Scotsmen from my home town came, died – freely, un-uniformed.

La Pasionaria, Dolores Ibárruri, whose parents could not afford to educate her, whose six children died because she could not afford to feed them or treat them, founded the World Committee of Women against War and Fascism. Her words: *'No pasarán'* – they shall not pass – became the famous battle

---

21. http://www.nabasque.org/old_nabo/Pages/gernika_tree.htm

cry against fascism as it rose across Europe and South America. She told other wives and mothers: 'It is better to be the widows of heroes than the wives of cowards!'

Some of those heroes came from my childhood and current home cities in Scotland. In her farewell address to the International Brigades, La Pasionaria said in Barcelona, in November 1938:

> It is very difficult to say … farewell to the heroes of the International Brigades … an infinite grief catches our throat … Mothers! Women! When the years pass by and the wounds of war are stanched; when the memory of the sad and bloody days dissipates in a present of liberty, of peace and of well-being; when the rancours have died out and pride in a free country is felt equally by all Spaniards, speak to your children. Tell them of these men of the International Brigades. Recount for them how, coming over seas and mountains, crossing frontiers bristling with bayonets, sought by raving dogs thirsting to tear their flesh, these men reached our country as crusaders for freedom, to fight and die for Spain's liberty and independence … We shall not forget you …

The fascists won. Franco died comfy cosy with his family around him when the twentieth century was old and I was nearly a grown-up. The anarchists never gave up. The miners of Asturias still march down from the Atlantic. No one asks what Daddy did in the Civil War. These truths lie under just one layer of scarred olive skin – terrible, grotesque, barbaric and tremendous like the land itself. No one has admitted shooting Lorca's words from out of his fine head.[22] He does not rest in peace. Civil War is not so easily buried beneath memorials.

---

22. http://www.wsws.org/en/articles/2003/10/lorc-o11.htmls

Alicia sees the transition to democracy that ex-king Juan Carlos oversaw as over, complete. The figurehead with a unifying crown no longer needed. I, though, am one of those with a longer memory. I have seen rights held dear in my own country thrown away within a generation. Bourbon Kings may very well not hold our answers, but I don't see truth or reconciliation here in Spain yet with civil-war heroes still hiding their secrets from each other's daughters. It's a long way from The Hague. Spain is still a tragic, bloody, fierce place which is serious about love and dances through pain. Compared to my country – not fought upon for centuries, Culloden its last battle – it certainly stirs the adrenalin. No wonder Madrid worries about Scottish independence and the ideas it might fertilize in secret corners of Spain.

The longer I was on the road, the more the Spanish language itself was part of my story. I loved the speaking of it, the debating of it, the passionate tremendous insistence of it, like machine-gun fire, like drums, like fireworks, like the serious business of midnight loving, and I was taken by it far from the regulations and expectations of normal working life.

The more exhausted I became, the more it became clear to me what my Camino must and must not be. My self, my ego, might crash against the groups dynamics like a roller hitting the cliffs of Fisterra down beyond Santiago, but what would be must be.

Thirty-eight years could not have as its climax a party of strangers at a hotel full of silly team clichés which had nothing to do with Galicia or Spain.

I could not spend only a snatched, drained hour speaking Spanish with an old Gallego friend in an old Gallego bar because of a mediocre tourist meal and laughter out of tune with the gentle, fierce, honourable spirituality of Compostela.

I could not join Deedee and the other Lycra ladies for afternoon shopping and be too tired for the gleaming wet, lamp-lit streets of Santiago at night.

And while the lovely, generous Stacey and friends would have welcomed my Gallego to their table, it had been made clear to me by Lucy as leader that groupthink made such hospitality beyond consideration, even when the fundraising challenge was done. Miguel was not one of us, though this was his country, which was deep inside me. Some were to be welcomed more *igualmente* than others.

I was sad that silly quizzes in the bar of Pensión Arenas Palas on the second evening of Camino had used up time that we could all have used to discover pretty Palas del Rei where our pilgrims' passports were stamped in the parish church of Santo Tirso. The back wall of the evening's dining area had looked out on sweet irrigated allotments – *huertas* – of capsicum, spinach and fig – and a crumpled countryman with a broad flat beret, a long white beard and dirty boots came in from the sunset and leaned comfortably against the bar. Real Spain village life was out there beyond our hotel windows. Still, getting-to-know-you time that early on in the adventure was, I had to admit, a good idea, and Stacey and I, Team Blister Sisters, won the silly quiz. I crossed my eyes to slide a chocolate down my nose and win that competition too. Could it be I who had been going the wrong way about this pilgrimage? I was certainly seeing things differently.

As our group parted for an early night I learnt, 'Tomorrow's going to be the day of the flags!' Lucy's jolly super-photogenic team activity for Day 3 was to be a littering of the woodland with armfuls of plastic and paper, brightly branded in the name of our common cause. We would prop them on milestones along the roadside. Hurray! Lovely pics for the Annual Report!

Once again, I was clearly not walking with soul mates. It was surreal to hear my tired voice attempt to stay calm as we waited for the lift up to our bedrooms.

'We can't do that!' I said, not for the first time or the last.

'Why not?' she said, painfully smiling. Once again, I had taken a contrary position like Mary Mary with her Catholic cockle shells.[23]

'You can't litter the Camino. You can't leave things'

'Other people do all the time!' she countered.

I caught my breath as the chasm between us widened. Looking from a different vantage point, she did not immediately see the gulf between this soon-to-be-soggy merchandise and the spirit of pilgrims' arrangements of precious tokens amongst mounds of pebbles.

'Yes,' I snapped, 'their dead grandma's rosary that they've carried from home, a sprig of heather they've picked, a carved apple, a grass-woven crucifix, a loved one's tiny stone heart. Not marketing materials! Not plastic!'

I was speaking my mother tongue but knew I was not walking with spirits that my own ancestors, never mind Miguel's or Alicia's, would understand. There was no more to be said.

There is a word I have used here already, both untranslatable and misunderstood, which begins in the ancient magic of the green woods and whose presence was felt by my namesake the Widow of Bath on her pilgrimage to Canterbury and by myself and others who look out for it on the road through Spain's greenest corner. It is the spirit experienced by the Celtic peoples of the British Isles and in Galicia and understood as elves, hobgoblins, leprechauns. Hispanophiles who have heard the word 'duende' understand it to be something like a Muse which provides the unique inspiration of the great gypsy guitarists of the hot dry south. Lorca, whose understanding of the true Spanish soul was incomparable, said: 'The duende … is a power, not a work. It is a struggle, not a thought. The duende climbs up inside you, from the soles of the feet.'

---

23. http://whatdoeshistorysay.blogspot.co.uk/2012/07/dark-history-behind-nursery-rhyme-mary.html

In the south, the duende is hot and red and passionate. Here in the north west he is cool, green and mischievous. Whereas in Lorca's Andalucía he may make you dance, stamp and sing – here in Celtic Galicia the duende is more likely to trip you up and make you wonder why you have come. Hobgoblins come in many disguises.

I am no modern pagan. But there was in this experience something I could only express in the language of myth and I wondered, as I walked, why that might be and thought of something else I had learned way back. Carl Jung, like Lorca, sees something that rises from the ground we walk on, something we use the language of folktale to make sense of when we contemplate creativity. He says: 'Before artistic work is born it is a force of nature ... The creative urge lives and grows ... like a tree.'

Jung talks of mythological figures that appear:

> wherever creative fantasy is freely expressed. In each of these images there is a little piece of human psychology and human fate, a remnant of the joys and sorrows that have been repeated countless times in our ancestral history ... The moment when this mythological situation reappears is always characterized by a peculiar emotional intensity. At such moments we are no longer individual, but the race; the voice of all mankind resounds in us.

Jung says too that:

> The normal man can follow the general trend without injury to himself; but the man who takes to the back streets ... because he cannot endure the broad highway will be the first to discover the psychic elements that are waiting to play their part in the life of the collective. Here the artist's relative lack of adaptation turns out to his advantage; it enables him to follow his own yearnings far from the

beaten path, and to discover what it is that would meet the unconscious needs of his age.

I am not aiming as I sit here writing this, with a laptop and a notepad on my knee and the great grey Scottish sea roaring outside, to achieve brilliance or great art. Something more than litter on the road I hope for. I cannot honestly pretend to have felt the special torment of the mysterious skeletal red duende of Spain's south, though I have been in a strange and tearful state of mind ever since I got home and at the end of my physical journey.

I do want to explore again, as I did when nineteen in an ivory tower with a fellow Hispanophile who could not look at me, what it is that is captured, netted, in the pen of the poets – the Lorcas, Nerudas, Chaucers and de Castros of this world. Like the aroma from the kitchen of a great cook catching the nose of a hungry beggar, the essence of something true wafted out to me from their words as I thought of them on the road. And as I fill a Scottish winter with this reading and writing, I know that the inspiration that climbed up from my footsteps through the Galician forest, up from the primordial, was very real and very powerful and more heated with passion on Camino than at home.

I don't want to let it go. I do not want to go onwards amongst normal women if the beaten path is littered with cultural carelessness. I want to have silence from the shrieky girly giggles and to hear something in the silence that my ancient ancestors would have understood and turned into poetry or psalm or hymn or nursery rhyme, even if, as women do, just to sing it over a cradle or round a laundry washing pool.

2017
Searching beyond my brainful of wolf images of fear, I turn to Lorca and Neruda and spend these days – when three days a fortnight

plugged into a ward of dying people is my norm – painting their poetry: their carnal, passionate, penetrating metaphor full of moonshine and smells of seaweed and Hispania.

I lay awake in that unheated night in Palas del Rei with noisy Spanish pilgrims next door and was tormented not by the duendes of the south but by ever-growing conflicts of finding my way on this confusing Camino.

I could refuse to be part of the touristy group hilarity in our hotel on the last night and go off alone to my own authentic Santiago experience. I would have to if I was to have my own Camino and be true to myself and my Spain and my place on the Way.

I could, through mile after mile, drag along, collecting and binning any plastic merchandise that my group left behind them. Whatever it was that spoke to me in the night: conscience, ego or duende – it was very clear to me about that. I could not walk on by.

I had jarred with the A-team that dinnertime on the pace they were skimming by. I felt alone out there on the edge of the group. I felt torn with how much more Lucy and Deedee and Midge, the Alpha ladies, would hate my alienating myself from the all-important team. I didn't want confrontation. Galicia has plenty mountains to climb. I didn't want to make any more out of molehills. I was very, very tired. I couldn't sleep.

Then, curled up beneath thin sheets in a narrow bed, I came up with a plan and thanked St James for the blessings of Euro-subsidised Wi-Fi. I could not change anyone else's journey ahead but I could take control of my own Camino. I could tip the scales. I could change my own plans.

There, in Palas del Rei, everything began to change from what I had intended when I boarded that train from Montrose.

The rest of my Camino would be an unimaginably different story from the original plot.

October 2018

A large yellow dog approaches. This is his track, not mine, a fact of which I am conscious but he brushes calmly past we pair of pilgrims and pees in the weeds beside us. And passes on.

In a hamlet, a man rounds the bend. He calls his large dog to his side. This is their track, not mine. The dog brushes calmly past the pilgrims and passes on.

The dogs are golden like the leaves and the butterflies and the bracken and the sandy road and the sunshine.

The Wolf's Castle has a paw print and a man's bare footprint in the stone of its doorstep. The tiny squint-walled shop on the outskirts of Palas del Rei is still and quiet on the edge of forest. Behind the counter a man with a long elegant face, silver-streaked black hair and beard and calm black eyes talks to me of dog language and wolf fear. He tells of walking from Austria to Santiago without shoes or collar on his dog, leaving no mark on the land. He hands out free pebbles and spirituality and makes and sells wolf-paw earrings which jangle from my earlobes as I type. Spain's – and life's – raving dogs are no longer 'thirsting to tear my flesh'.

CHAPTER SIX

MYSTERIES AND MEADOWS

What you need on Camino will be provided, they say. Miguel, my Gallego, had suggested that he met me at the airport or along the road before the end in Santiago. Back at home in Scotland, over the social-media airwaves, I had turned down the idea. Unsure if I was up to the challenge, I did not want to catch up with this handsome old lover while sweating and hobbling like a crone – no way! I would reach the city and meet him there, somehow, in the crowds of pilgrims, triumphant.

Now, though, I was here, far from anyone who loved my soul. I was envisaging Camino-end being just a big corny forced-smiley photo shoot. It seemed a deliciously tempting solution not to wait till journey's end to see the smiling eyes of someone male who had loved the real me and really wanted me by his side. By the power of European Wi-Fi, I messaged him to meet me to walk the last day together. We could, I suggested, have cheerful sunny hours beside each other, and how sweet and fun it would be to step into town with him beside me, arm in arm.

Sending the message gave me a spring in my step, and other people's ideas of Camino seemed less earth-shatteringly unacceptable. Waiting for his reply, I was looking onwards again and with more gusto and sociability. I didn't spot any abandoned flags.

Each morning on Camino started with a small mystery. We needed our guide to lead us back out of the dawning twenty-first century, down a narrow lane apart from the main highway with its welcoming bus shelters and tempting taxi ranks, and out again past the big dogs woofing in yards to meet the friendly little yellow arrows showing the right way. Right across the country, those roughly painted markers dance before the pilgrim, sometimes obvious, painted on the tarmac, sometimes small and high on a crumbling wall amongst the moss. They are welcoming and comforting and all we have to do is trust and follow, childlike, submissive, one foot after another – nothing simpler. There is nothing to rail against. Nothing to decide. Only ourselves to drive forward. Another of life's mysteries solved: which way? It is amazingly hard, though, to submit to the road, to accept at this point in our adulthood that little difference is made by our decisions. Our will is limited to taking step followed by step after step. As mother, career woman, feminist, survivor, fifty-seven-year-old… submission is a difficult, forgotten art. It makes you think. It makes you more forgiving, eventually.

Lucy and Alicia had planned the practicalities of our overall Camino very well and the hardest, longest walking days were now behind us at Palas del Rei at the end of Day 2 on the trail. The weather stayed wonderful into the third and fourth days – dry, sometimes with a sweat-freshening breeze and, as the shadows shortened, reached but did not exceed twenty-four degrees. The dawn air had a faint threat of autumn ice to wake us up and set our pace, but the mists skulked back to the emerald valley streams and disappeared by mid-morning. We were beyond halfway now and back in the lower lands where the road curved and the hamlets were romantic and frequent, every mile or so. In the doorways of broad yellow-stoned farmhouses, round ladies in pinnies chatted and called back '*Buen Camino*' as I called '*Hola Señora! Buenos Dias!*'

At one of our meal tables, our quiet male companion Derek and I discovered a mutual love of words and their make-up and found a thread to bring us together on the road. From then on, I would find him gently alongside me, touching my moods so lightly with a thought on etymology that I never knew if he sensed the duende threatening to overwhelm me or whether he was just coincidentally travelling that bit of the Way and had thought of something interesting to share or discuss.

Were Celtic faery folk, as my mother had told me, really just the memory of little lives and little gods suppressed and hidden in the wild woods when tall Romans and eastern saints came striding?[24] Does pixy mean Pict? Tall and grey and steady with Fiona, his small quiet wife, he reminded me of my husband Joe, back at home. He kept my feet close to the ground so I didn't drift off into the high baby-blue sky, but his company never pulled me down into the tarmac with unanswerable twenty-first-century questions.

Some crossroads, whether in villages or out in the countryside beside a giant oak, were marked by a rough and squat granite cross whose Christ figure was rather rounder and dumpier than the religious norm, reminiscent of the people in the farms nearby. Granite is not easy to carve with delicacy, but it lasts and is the abundant bedrock here.

On some crosses, there were a few little grey gnome-like figures attending to the Christ, and elsewhere in Galicia there are crosses famously covered in little figures with ladders and bundles ministering to the dying figure. These familiar scenes to meditate upon, while waiting for who-knows-who, are insignificant though beneath the spreading arms of the ancient tree beside them, its massive dividing boughs hiding dark and endless secrets with no glib answers. Until the Romans came to this peninsula, three-quarters of the flour

24. http://www.jrbooksonline.com/pob/pob_ch14.html

that Spaniards ate was made from acorns. Galicia is proud that its are the biggest.[25] The generous warm trunk ringed by a bench seat tempts a pilgrim to sit, adjust boot laces and rest a while with a swig of water and a bite of nutty flapjack.

The walking days were shorter now from Day 3 and our feet had done their bit in time for a late lunch of delicious olive-oil-fried chips, unctuous home-made chorizo sausage and sunny eggs from happy hens. By breakfast back in Palas del Rei, the penny had eventually dropped with the A-team that we at the back were not arriving late because we were sneaking a naughty stop on the journey but because we could not speed up. The risk was realised and steps taken to stop our becoming two teams. We began to ring the changes more of who walked slow and kept company with whom. We all learnt the value of walking alone for a bit of each day and each spent time enjoying the company of Stacey, who teetered on the brink of failure but kept us all laughing with her. Deedee powered on ahead with Linda and with Midge.

It isn't my normal way of life, arriving somewhere completely unknown, spending just a few hours there working out how to use the shower and what warmth you need on the bed, washing knickers, making imaginative use of a heated towel rail, emptying tiny bottles of flowery-smelling bubbles and lying with your feet throbbing as you log on to the World Wide Web, write a journal or read a poem. You rest a while, and then juggle your belongings between the pack that will go on your back and those that will be in the bag you leave at breakfast the next day to miraculously turn up 20km down the road. You wonder at the things you thought it important to bring, like poetry books, and the things you left behind, like a really truly waterproof hat. You go down to dinner then back to bed alone,

---

25. http://www.pilipalapress.com/galicia.php#people_culturess

then up and out before dawn without a look backwards at your hosts for the night.

The evening's repack of my belongings in Palas del Rei had brought forth a miracle in the shape of deep heat ointment from the depths of my bag. Despite going to sleep feeling like a broken doll, with handfuls of it massaged into the backs of my calves, I had woken on Day 3 feeling strong – stronger in fact than ever in my life. My muscles were manning up to a challenge I had dreamed of. I was drawing deep from learning I had forgotten. With every guard hound I passed, I was getting braver. I was determinedly happy in my new plan and belonging to my own self. Sometime soon the smartphone in my hand would ping with the answer to my worries – yes, let's meet before the journey's end – and my Camino would be happy and delight-filled again. I had room in my heart to think less of myself. I accepted there were those who said it would hurt to walk slowly. I lent my tube of deep heat magic. We each have our own speed and each pace is another good step down the road. My little heart-shaped pebble brought from Scotland was nowhere to be seen, deep in a pocket, and I had travelled deep into Spain. The place I call home was a long way behind me.

No message of support came through from my husband and daughter, my soul mates of previous travels. They were letting me walk alone. Some popped in though from Facebook friends spread across the planet in commentary on the pictures I posted at siesta time each day.

'I love the detail of the lichen – lichen likes pure air, must be a lovely place.'

'What's with the salamanders? Don't they live forever until they are reborn as phoenixes? Or am I confusing Spain with Hogwarts? Didn't they expect rain? Don't they live near water? I am so bemused.'

'I am thinking of you often and the photos of you laughing look like a real awakening for you.'

'Use your sticks more. Make them a bit longer for the downhills and get your upper body to take more of the load. Hang in there, there's bound to be flat coming up real soon!'

'I thought the rain fell mainly on the plain?'

'Enjoy every step! What an adventure.'

'Beautiful picture. You can see the absolute emotion in your every vein. Be very proud – having watched your face light up more every day I hope you do not cease from exploring.'

'We tend to forget we are all just passing by.'

'I'm hoping you write a book, say with a story from each of you pilgrims told nightly along the way. It might become famous.'

October 2018

'Alison, I think that EVERY person who knows you can't fail to be inspired by your grit and integrity. Highly chuffed you got to do this.'

'So pleased for you. Obviously been a fabulous trip with treasured memories made.'

'Ah, the crash after the dopamine high. Well known to seekers and retreaters of all disciplines. I hope your reintegration is gentle, my love.'

St James always provides you with what you need. We needed the miracle of a rumbustious sing-song of a party with sticky cake and a cheeky chappy Londoner for host. To bring us all together we needed it to be Stacey's party and so it was – her birthday. At the end of Day 3 we had lots of lovely sunny afternoon in the busy hilly town of Melide, when the walking was over, sitting in bars together, drinking wine, shopping and being similar.

I shared the chewy octopus with Linda in the A Garnacho restaurant and helped with a bit of vocabulary in the chemist shop stocked with what every pilgrim needs – plasters and bandages – and made sure we weren't served nuts with drinks on a corner outside the Cafeteria Chaplin which would set off Lucy's allergy.

The town was real and true and full of Gallegos going about their ordinary but lovely provincial Spanish lives. A rickety wooden cart full of hay passed by slowly, pulled by a skinny old horse. Smart senior ladies with shoulders draped in navy cardies limped proudly off to meet their girlfriends. Pharmacists in white coats with beautifully manicured hands sought confidently in mahogany and mirrored cabinets lined with bottles of cologne. Nuns scampered fretfully. Old men in from the country with clean cloth caps on their broad skulls leaned on their staffs and consoled each other in friendship or settled to backgammon under the plain trees. Handsome moustachioed fathers carried exquisitely dressed tiny princesses and sailor boys in carefully ironed cotton. Almond-eyed mothers gossiped with sisters-in-law in the neatly swept and sculptured parks under statues of pilgrims and St James, who looked down their long granite noses with gentle smiles. It felt like small-town Spain that I had lived in before, and I was comfortably contented to be at rest from the exhaustingly ecstatic and mystical Way, all around me Spanish sounds and smells and tastes and the language a delicious waterfall on my tongue.

It was fine to be one of the jokey girls alongside Deedee and Stacey at the evening hour of *paseo* when everyone comes out to walk slowly in the evening air. I could both be myself and be part of the group in comfort. Here at the table with a chilled bottle of Ribeiro or two, the paths of two different kinds of women met. I haven't actually spent a whole life deep in poetry or politics, just some key years in the 1970s. Most of it has been spent being jokey in bars, quick with the raunchiness, extravagant and thirsty and crazy and generally up for a party. I just don't normally do so while walking ancient pilgrimages. But then I don't normally walk at all.

By this stage of the journey we had eaten a good deal of nourishing pilgrims' meals. Breakfast and dinner were prearranged at our hotels. Lunches were a more flexible affair at the numerous cafes we passed. Our appetites were sharpened not just with the fresh air, exercise and good simple cooking. Our eyes had caught glimpses of our evening menus as we walked past gardens and fields of ingredients on the miles between meals. Droopy-eared sheep grazed behind high hedges of bay. Hens slipped out and scraped the yellow gravel on the tracks. Brussels sprouts grew four foot tall with plate-sized mushrooms in their shadows. Plaited onions dried, grapes glinted with raindrops, apples and acorns dropped to where piglets suckled in yards. Brown cows with cream-heavy udders waddled. Our hurting feet crushed herbs as we walked to fill the air and bless our nostrils like incense in the much-anticipated cathedral. Fertility and bounty surrounded us, and life was delicious and intoxicating.

When Wi-Fi was available at coffee stops, Miguel and I progressed our plans by secret smartphone messaging and the intimacy of it warmed me deep inside like strong purple wine. Secret shopping for Stacey in Melide was followed by surprise cake and song in a hotel filled with the army of teenagers of Day 2.

The Hotel Carlos had the traditional elegant exterior of Galicia and northern Portugal. A façade of enclosed white-framed glass terraces added on outside the bedrooms' French windows provided a lovely, sunny, sheltered place to sit a while at siesta time (and dry our laundry): a northern answer to open-railed southern balconies and a testament to Galicia's rainfall.

The Melide hotelier, a round-faced Gallego, had been brought up on the Portobello Road. He was the best of hosts and his London accent brought back to me twenty years of living in Notting Hill with my English husband and his wild, hairy brothers, and nostalgically shopping in Garcia's, the Spanish grocers, for almonds, chorizo and olives. As a little boy, our host must have passed me a hundred times as he went to and from his Spanish-language primary school. Another little thread of Gallego life twisting through my story unseen. Meanwhile I found Joe on that same London street, made a baby and was comforted by the sound of Spanish in my ears, the tastes of Spain on my lips and the smell of Spain in my nostrils.

Stacey was the queen of the night, conducting the school-kids in singing 'Happy Birthday' to her in their lovely accented English and waving the paper and plastic flags that no one had, in the end, left as litter along the way. With some jokes and racy reminiscences, my reputation for what they called sauciness grew. Better than being a drag so I played the part. All was good.

Day 5, as we had by now arranged, I would meet Miguel at the second-last stop. The assignation was my precious secret treasure that no one could spoil with question or comment or adjectives less than poetic.

Day 4 was to be short and sunny too, and I was strong and bounced out of bed and forward on the road. Feeling my strength and power, I soon found myself further ahead in the group and in different company, with sweet, quiet Grace, our youngest pilgrim, full of self-doubt and intelligence, and Fiona and Derek, who we all loved, or Linda and her envy-producing tales of camper-vanning round Spain.

Entry into every village for lunch or town for the night is over a bridge. Many other bridges – where the hills slide down to roads or rivers – likewise become meeting points where a pilgrim pauses before the road rises again and so another pilgrim catches up and conversation is prompted. Old stone bridges with their single steep arches over streams, or modern ones with slatted pavements across wide rivers, or railed ones over highways, or step-stones at ancient fords each marked another section of our journey. With these pace changes, I and our fastest walkers built new bridges between us. We were ten fellow pilgrims and, with a few wobbles and helping hands outstretched when needed, we gradually found our way to each other.

After a passport stamp at the council offices of Concello de Melide, the Camino's arrows signposted us down a high-walled alley between back gardens and allotments and followed the main road out of town. Suddenly our route took a sharp and narrow turn-off, which Deedee, Midge and Lucy, being the fastest walkers, overlooked. Following each other, not the arrows, they went astray. For one moment, by this miracle, Stacey and I were ahead of the pack! Everyone who saw it delighted in our noisy mock celebration. We grabbed the opportunity and came whooping and singing, the fastest to our passport stamp at the Church of Santa María de Melide.

By now we were well accustomed to looking out for places to stamp our, by this time, rather floppy and torn pilgrims' passports. Eve was excellent at reminding us and sometimes doing it for us. For both the most competitive and those who struggled the most, having the evidence to get their special piece of paper at the end was getting more and more important with every blister. I was blister-free and otherwise motivated. In cafes and hotels we were left to our own devices. Each establishment had their own emblem made into a stamp and had left it on a table or the end of the bar, ready for us. In town halls, churches, chapels and convents it was a far more serious and solemn affair with a man who muttered importantly as he stamped a more official mark and shared my disappointment at noisy *peregrinas* disrespectful of the meaning of the Way. Dogs that were pilgrims with us – and wore their own backpacks – waited patiently and gently outside, uninterested in me.

Here, where pilgrimage was the most serious business, was an opportunity for all to pause and learn and wonder at the story of many Caminos. By now different routes across Spain were merging together – the Way along the northern coast beyond the Picos de Europa, the English Way down from the port of A Coruña and our own Camino Francés. We stopped off in small parish churches where the carvings of scallop shells amid swags of cloth were softened by layers of aging reapplied lacquer. The wooden Virgin Mothers were dressed up as simple and sweet as dolls with painted faces, and the domed alcoves were painted with hopeful scenes of squat angels watching over us amongst the stars.

Passport stamping was free in such places but elsewhere along the route, ordinary twenty-first-century folk set up their own unique pop-up stand to raise donations for their local youth club or good cause or as buskers or exhibitors. One householder had gathered uplifting quotations from the world's great and wise and strung them out like washing along the side of his house in English and Spanish and sold bottles of water to the thirsty for inspiration.

'Travel is fatal to prejudice, bigotry and narrow-mindedness.'
— Mark Twain

'There are no foreign lands. It is the traveller only that is foreign.'
— Robert Louis Stevenson

Lifted out of the quagmire of the first part of the journey, nothing spoiled our enchantment as we made our way. Even scrawl on a litter bin at a crossroads sang out to us to '*Imagine all the People living life in Peace*'.

Across a deep flower meadow striped in purple chestnut shadow streaked a vermilion fox caught for a moment in sharp light. Not too close behind in a merry dance bounded two baying hounds, noses to the ground, struggling with the undergrowth that he slipped amongst like a sunset sunbeam. No men followed on horseback for sport. Something wilder and older was happening still here in Galicia alongside our walking. We glimpsed a life that the narrow world of pilgrimage passed through and did not bruise. But it reached out and touched us if we were open to it, and not with open fangs.

Somewhere in the still forest air a flute softly called, creeping with soft beguiling fingers around the bends in the path to where we would cross a deep brown pool. The flute player was one of the ethereal Gallegos – so thin and tall and brown and dressed in lichen green he was barely visible amongst the sky-reaching young trees. Beside him were his gentle, squat white donkey and a table by a broad old oak with a stamp for a pilgrim's passport. One of the places on the journey which felt most like a fairy story, the air was dark and thick like warm peasant wine, and the boulders made tricky stepping stones across the shining river. I teetered on a boulder as I looked back at the road I had travelled, but Linda's firm hand caught me.

October 2018

Out of a forest of pale sunbeams emerged two huge white dogs, tails high, noses low. Heralded by a glitter of midges they processed out of the shadows, one bounded down to the velvet pool at my feet where he splashed slow silver rings in the river and gulped its deep green depths. From amongst the disks of strange succulents at the water's edge, chin dripping, he leaped up the bank through the bracken, passed me without a glance and strode off across the boulders where the robin sang. Unfazed, I made it alone over the rounded stepping stones where he had led, my passing reflection in the calm chocolate pool below, my sticks jangling against the scallop shell on my back.

Camino always provides you with what you need even though sometimes you don't seem to need it. On Day 4 I gave in to the sins of gluttony and covetousness. It was no bad thing. We arrived, tummies rumbling, in the pretty village of Ribadiso de Abaixo, bordered by willow trees and a shallow ford where the sun shining through the clear water caught the emerald-weeded bed of golden shingle. Midge, Lucy and Deedee, the health and shopping freaks, were not planning on stopping for lunch but on going on into Arzúa and a very early shower. A rushed meal would produce cramp in energetic walkers. Better not to eat at all. Deedee loudly enquired of nightclubs in the town ahead. Stacey, Eve and I groaned.

But by this stage there had been some slackening of the rules about sticking together and I stuck my neck out and my feet down to stay in the gorgeous sunshine and lunch Spanish style – well and slowly. We were fundraisers not real pilgrims; the daily arrangements were modest and practical but not liberating or culturally sensitive. Something was sacrificed.

Spaniards' main meal is a long lunchtime and they aren't heated up again ready for high-standard cookery before 22.00, while we made them serve us by 20.00 at the latest. So most days we did not see the best of Spanish cuisine slow roasted, flash fried or quick chopped, for this was not the kind of gastronomic adventure I have revelled in from Andorra to Andalucía. Day 2 we had missed the pretty Palas del Rei town centre. Day 3 we had all been sad to walk without stopping through a similar village to this. The argument to stop this time and lunch Spanish style at the Mesón Ribadiso – languorously, with cultural sensitivity, round a long table in a sunny yard – was easily won and I ordered both langoustine and *calamares* which came in the hugest of portions, as sweet and garlicky and lemony and smoky from the hotplate as anyone could wish for and with the crunchiest of lettuce and onion slivers. I stuffed myself happily with the best meal of the holiday, sank into my seat, took off my boots, wiggled my liberated toes and dreamily watched a skinny kitten stalking chickens behind a barn. Builders came down from restoring a terracotta roof and took off for lunch and siesta, leaving silence beyond our chatter and the farmyard.

We walked on lazily into Arzúa and later shopped and relaxed at the café bar and home-made chocolate shop called La Esquina in pleasant camaraderie. In the town square where schoolchildren played, I went shopping with Linda and bought a leather scallop-shell necklace from an aproned leather-worker's stall in an overhung and pillared passage, and I wear it now night and day. In a pretty shop beside the church I chose a simply crafted white and blue ceramic bird 'of love' from nearby Sargadelo while the shopkeeper's chubby brown grandchild became my friend.

The 200-year-old pottery came into being when a little international difficulty affecting the Peninsula meant English pottery could not be imported.[26] While originally inspired by British china, the designs tell local stories. The bird has a little lid on its back and a motif of 'herbs of St Andrew', that we call thrift. The lady in the shop said I should gather them and store them there so that 'my love will stay alive'. Thinking of Miguel but not knowing of our secret plans to meet the following day, my fellow *peregrinas* joked, 'Which one!' Which love would be most alive by Camino end – a teenage romance thirty-eight years past or a marriage in its twentieth year?

They did not know my Joe. Only Alicia knew I was arranging to meet Miguel on the second-last night in Arca, twenty-four hours ahead. It was bound to all go well. St Andrew, who has a chapel in honour of his stay at San Andrés de Teixido on the cliffs to the north, is the patron saint of Galicia and Scotland,

---

26. http://www.spainisculture.com/en/propuestas_culturales/
   sceramica_de_sargadelos.html

who both have his saltire as their flag, and I was born on his day. My love, whichever one, would be safe.

The little bird sits now on my windowsill full of the herbs I picked on Camino and stares out at the big grey horizon where the seagulls swoop and the wild geese call in the coming of winter and my husband watches the rugby and coughs in the other room, waiting for summer when the pink thrift flowers again.

---

26 October 2018

The strange and wonderful necklace sits against my warm skin at the Inn of the White Horse. Its bright charms remember those made by the villagers of San Andrés de Teixido from bread dough and hung to keep good luck in their households. Every charm has a meaning. One figure with blond hair reminds me of my husband.

I am told I look beautiful. It only means I am healthy. The words reach the fragile places hidden beneath my flowing yellow kaftan and I welcome them with a smile and with the comfort of their unimportance.

Every sign was good. Linda urged me to indulge in a warm nut-brown shawl in a pretty boutique in Arzúa and again St James looked after me as it was wrapped.

But this that I am writing now is not a fairy story or a fantasy and the world kept turning without me knowing. Somewhere out there in the non-fiction twenty-first-century world many more important things than old romance were happening and some would make meeting me in Arca tomorrow quite impossible for Miguel. It was not to be. I didn't know. There would be no romantic get-together on the last night before I reached the Field of Stars. In blissful ignorance, I still wandered smiling through Arzúa, translating shop signs for my fellow travellers, looking for its famous cheese, comfortable that the following day my changed plans would let me have my light and happy few hours with him without it clashing with the team dynamics. With that box ticked I could go on with and be wholeheartedly part of my group and enjoy whatever else Camino had to offer. I was calmly biding my time, submitting to the road till I had walked another day to Arca to meet him. After thirty-eight years – one more sleep – then tomorrow.

As the chill autumn darkness descended on Arzúa and we travellers settled to dinner in a mediocre motel by the highway, I thought little about his message checking that I had arrived safely at our last stop before Arca – broadband connectivity on medieval pilgrimage can leave doubts.

Someone asked me to pass something down the table – it doesn't matter what. We were as a group a bit flatter in mood that evening – we didn't want to walk back into town again after dinner and our hotel bar was not filled with other English-speaking pilgrims to share laughs with. We were too near the end of the journey for some. We were still too far for others. I had been the last down to dinner after showering and changing into my favourite gypsy skirt and had taken the last seat at the long table to play listlessly with a plate full of veg. Deedee had said it would be overcooked and she was depressingly right. I was lamely waiting for tomorrow and this evening was just one to sit through beyond the limelight, feeling my tired body sag into the chair, arms at rest on the tabletop. The raunchiness was all at the other end of the table that night, the room was windowless, the décor cheap 1980s, the air was still, the day was done. And then he was there. Framed in the dark of the doorway.

'A-lee-son?'

Just loud enough to reach me. Not loud enough to reach the head of the table. A soft question searching through the years. My Miguel, of 1977. Now silver-haired, bespectacled and moustachioed. The same sparkle in his eyes that I had last seen as I went off perm-headed from his bed to miss my plane thirty-eight years ago. He had taken control and come to Arzúa to surprise me because he could not meet with me the next day. He had popped in his car and driven in fifteen minutes the distance we pilgrims would take another two days to walk.

My watch stopped at 19.15 that evening and started again when I got safely home to Scotland days and days later. Ridiculous but true. When I told my husband about this sure piece of magic he asked, 'Did he have a halo?'

CHAPTER SEVEN

CATCHING UP

What do you do after thirty-eight years, with your feet burning and your legs aching and your body flopping and your old lover in the doorway? You signal to him before the others see (it's a secret – it's a secret!). You run into the dark hall as if you were young again and a firebomb was flying and your feet and legs weren't hurting as if dragging concrete and you hug and hold and squeal and nearly strangle and say it is you, you are here, we are together, how long has it been? How long? And you breathe in the freshly showered cologne-scented Spanish man-smell of him. And you remember it well.

We are in the cold hall of an end-of-season motel with a Lycra-bummed fitness freak watching from the stairs, a cafe-bar full of truck drivers and a little dining room full of chaperones and we have, perhaps, just this one evening and I have half a pilgrimage ahead. I have a husband and he has a wife. We are strangers. His smile is the same as in the one photo I have of him in 1977 in his beige banker's trousers and navy blazer. He is, he admits out loud, and I can feel, actually shivering, shaking, with nerves. I don't remember having had a retired banker trembling in my arms very many times in my life. He volunteers that he is '*nervioso*' which means nervous and excited. I know it is not the same as '*excitado*', something quite different that is not looked for after so many years lived. That is not spoken of in a cold corridor. We had no idea what to do with each other. In a lifetime since he dropped me at that airport we hadn't thought further than this moment.

I took him by the hand like a boyfriend and introduced him to the others. I explained to the group that, after thirty-eight years, we couldn't have waited another two days. I didn't tell them that thought of a disappointing evening in Santiago playing silly games with strangers had changed our plans. Then, looking at the polite but blank smiles of my companions, I realised I had said it all in Spanish and had to translate myself back into English, and in his few clumsy words of my mother tongue he told them he was a very good friend of mine from a long time ago, as if they hadn't guessed exactly who he was. As we turned, hand in hand, hugging each other's arms close, Alicia translated for him to the group and arranged for my mediocre dinner to be brought out onto the cold terrace in the dark. I didn't eat it, being full of butterflies and lunchtime sea-food (thank St James I had ordered it). I grabbed my new warm shawl (thank St James I had bought it) and a bottle of wine and then sat with him in the secret night apart from prying eyes and ears.

We stared at each other, peering through the years to find below the surface the people we had been when neither wore glasses or had grey hair. We had not talked for a lifetime, several marriages and a handful of children. We laughed at old memories and answered each other's questions and posed many more and stretched my Spanish into the subjunctive of 'if it had been that you were this' and 'if it had been that I had done that'. His voice was luxuriously deep and softly low.

We realised that while in 1977 I had been still a teenager and a student, he was six years older with a banking career already begun and a child and a marriage behind him, nearly. We sat together now as equals in our late fifties/early sixties but I remembered that he had always been deep-voiced while I had been a squeaky girl, and I smelt the air around him and it pricked my memory and tickled my nostrils. He was sweet and wise.

Knowing that our memories have faded and filled with other living, he ever so gently – and uselessly – warned us both of mythologizing. The *meigas* cackled quietly in the bushes round the terrace. We unpicked the truths together, chastely, narrowly avoiding those that would make each other blush. We were not flirtatious but matter of fact. We talked of truths, of politics and pain and poetry and pilgrimage and all of it glorious and intimate and personal to the paths that had brought us close and not just once. We saw clearly that the special places where our lives had connected had not been just in some apparently insignificant, silly romantic summer in 1977 but at huge staging points in our lives where our finding each other had been full of meaning and import and precious to us. We noted that there had not just been one coincidence but more – in 1978 in a mysterious phone call; in 1986 when I had walked through his city with another man, now my husband; in 1995 when he had walked down my street in London, perhaps passing my young hotelier from Melide and I without ever knowing; through social media when I casually sought him out a decade later still; and now on Camino with a group who knew nothing of all that and thought it saucy and silly. There had been silly, saucy summer romances but this had not been one of them.

We were just catching up. When we spoke of perfect times and of how we remembered each other, I squeezed his arm and he, the European, drew up my hand to his lips and kissed it, and didn't let go of my eyes. My hand sank back through a lifetime and remembered where outside a fountain played in a warm Santiago night and brandy burnt with a sweet blue flame. So long after, it felt a miraculously lovely thing that we had both silently set the same rules, had the same values and were the same sort of people. It seemed to give a deep and magical truth to the belief that ours had been something special that summer long ago. We did not say or do anything to be ashamed of, crossed no dangerous lines. Doing so had never been on the menu for this meeting.

The waitress hovered, a reluctant chaperone, and I picked contentedly at my congealed chips. His life was complicated, his brother-in-law in hospital, his wife cold, his daughter younger than mine. We agreed it had been a deep thing, an overwhelming thing, a precious one-summer thing we had both treasured since, different from other romantic encounters that had been easier to let fade away. It had been the time for Spain seeping out of isolation. A time for him when he was lost and confused and failing at too much too young and feeling judged. It had, we said, been love, but Spaniards have many words for love, a subject they take more seriously than any race on earth, and it would take another book to explain their unique meanings. Knowing that honour is as vital a Hispanic concept, we trod carefully, understanding this was special territory. I told him he was better looking now than then and he groaned a deep and happy protest and again kissed my hand so that his moustache (which he hadn't had before) prickled my skin. He has become something of a silver fox. His voice was smooth and most deliciously Spanish deep, and his eyes generous river pools. We were as if seated together watching a surreal film, muted and dimly lit, playing out in the air between us, all the characters real, all the emotions recognisable, everything true and clear and comprehensible but separated from its audience by rows and rows of years of life lived differently. We were that audience now, the watchers, no longer playing out the roles.

He had told me once that in his village it had been traditional that a baby's first solid food was hot chocolate served on a *décimo* coin. If the child cried and refused it, he was seen as condemned to weakness. By refusing the tradition for fear of dirty copper, Miguel's parents had offended the community. But he was not weak.

His father, as I remember, had been a bully from the military police who had broken his young son's toe with his carbine butt for stealing the barrack's apples. The military state that laid down laws of who got education and who got employment was, as he reached adulthood, in no way separated from a church which ruled that illegitimate children were not worthy, that not divorce nor contraception nor abortion were permissible. The implications of all of these had trapped and scarred his young adulthood and career. His country had been emerging from a world hidden beyond the high Pyrenees which had kept its history different from Europe's so many times before and full of tradition and expectation. It had not quite broken loose by 1977.

That summer with me had been an exceptional, unexpected time when a Free Bird had flown in high with a fresh wind behind her, wild and rare and hiding beneath her chirpiness that she was still a bit scared of the world that she was out in. Being told thirty-eight years later what importance that summer had had for him filled me with more pride than climbing all the hills of this Camino. I trusted that feeling and did not probe for unoffered explanation. It was clear that he could still feel the places in himself where there was damaged tissue and that meeting me this night, he was retenderised. We had so little time, so little privacy, so little knowledge of who we are now. I am not his storyteller. I watched him, sensed his feeling of the years back, way back, down deep inside wherever he came from. He unpacked that evening in Arzúa only those pebbles that he chose.

We admitted with the knowing laughter of grown-ups that the language gap and the visitor's passport had made it easier to share secrets recklessly. Without fear of being trapped by their intimacies we had gone quickly from strangers to lifelong soul mates. It had been only a few months – we weren't sure how long – and a long time ago. We were strangers again now.

We talked of ourselves back then with something of a puzzled but resigned shrug of the shoulders, as if talking of our nearly adult children, for whom we are only partly responsible. To an overweight, grey-haired Scottish career woman there was a light in his smiling eyes which could have been as seductive as when I had been a second-year student. But I knew I was not that girl. I could feel that truth in my womb which doesn't lie. Now in our late middle age we were not going to be ridiculous.

We talked placidly of marriage and what our several successes and failures have taught us of the kind of love that life together means. Warm nostalgia, compromise, faithfulness, acceptance, respect and trust, comfortable cool space where once there was sticky proximity: these build up their cushions round our lives and the achievements of our children. We had told our spouses we would meet sometime on my trip but not that we were meeting this night. They were there present in our happy conversation but at a distance, like my husband in the other room as I write, where they couldn't mistake the look in our eyes. There was nothing dangerous for them there anyhow, nothing silly, only old friendship, the witchery of the Galician night and the cool coils of the serpent licking the air and offering his endless well-known temptations. Two saints, James and Andrew, were keeping watch. There was only *saudade* and the joys of surviving an already long journey.

We talked until nearly midnight and our old bones were chilled but we sat, warmed by memory, outside each other's arms, safe. We were, we knew, unknown to each other now and understood little of each other's daily realities. We were intimates who had uniquely shared secrets of each other's lives back then. We were and always had been soul mates. We were awkward with each other. We were as comfortable as a ruffled bed. We were each other's contradictions. The memories, his of me, mine of him, which we tossed back and forth were sticks of dynamite, exploding the myths and realities on which we had founded our lives since 1977. Two thoughts that he left with me burnt slowly, are still smouldering. Two burning coals I carried off with me like the other pebbles taken on my journey, but these were heavier and hot, searing into the second half of my Camino. I can feel their heat still as I sit in cold Scotland finding these words.

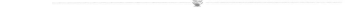

June 2019
They held on to their warmth through more than one winter and their glow lit up my steps into the precious seventh decade of my life. They no longer burn – I can pick them up and hold them if I wish or leave them safely in my hearth.

I had expected a jolly walk and a jolly last-night catch-up at the end of a jolly week. Now everything about my journey ahead, and how easy I would find it to describe, had changed because I had been made to adjust my plans and had met Miguel in Arzúa, Day 4, with two days and nights of travelling ahead. I would be walking for many hard miles onwards not towards the light, unimportant fantasy of him I had set off with in a giggle, but away from the realities he and I had unearthed. With him softly beside me I had looked back through the years and I went to sleep alone that night chilled through and shivering, disturbed, crying and very happy. I woke crying and have cried and cried since for these four days home. I have slept and slept and slept and told it all to my husband, daughter and even my mother and realised how exhausted I have been, and as I write I am not crying now but may cry again. Now I can barely see his face at that dining-room door. He is fading back into Spain and I am fading back into Scotland. And it is good that my Camino still stretched out ahead of me beyond that night and so that one night would not entirely define the Way.

We had hugged goodbye at a sensible hour (listening pilgrims checked their bedside clocks as I came up the stairs alone). He had kissed my cheek but I had held back from turning my lips to kiss his face. It was instinctive. It was sensible. Something was lurking in the silver, shining night, mesmerising me: I was so exhausted that my head spun. I had still the sense to preserve my fifty-seven-year-old self from indignity.

We Scots don't kiss so lightly as our Spanish friends. We had said '*hasta la vista*' down on the hotel terrace and it could have meant anything and we knew it. Perhaps his sick relative could be left late on Saturday night and we would see each other in Santiago but only perhaps. Perhaps I will come back to see Santiago again alone someday but only perhaps. I am a happily married, menopausal mum. Neither of us are fools. My Camino had never been supposed to be about finding Miguel, a boy I knew for a short while a long time ago. It was supposed to be about finding me, poetry and Spain.

I posted another poem, 'The Faithless Wife' by Federico García Lorca from the book in my pack onto my Facebook page before breakfast.

And I took her to the river
believing her a maid,
but she had a husband.
It was on St James' night
and almost as if in duty bound
the street lights went out
and the crickets flared up.
By the last street corners

I touched her sleeping breasts,
and they opened to me suddenly
like spikes of hyacinth.
The starch of her petticoat
sounded in my ear
like a piece of silk
rent by knives.

I meant it as a wry joke. Its title simply caught my eye. No poet writes sex better than Lorca. In my day there was never any talk of him being gay.

Miguel and I had sat with ageless eyes too close and with too much wisdom in the roundness of our bellies to talk in such poetry. There was nothing new and risky in our hearts. Our memories though were a good deal hotter than our tongues could have dared to be and Lorca's metaphors sang out from the page in a man's voice as I lay in bed without a husband near. By posting this that is not a love song I acknowledged what we had been – not just lovers but just as much lovers of poetry – and what we knew I would never be, what both knew was far behind. Somewhere in his own home, he acknowledged it all with a click.

Miguel and I had acted like the retired Celtic banker and charity fundraiser we are, not Andalucían gypsies. We might have warmly remembered smears and kisses, skin and touches from a long time ago, but we didn't speak of them and didn't do any unbridled galloping off together. We weren't swept away from our wife and husband. He was a little shorter than the man whose hugs I have become used to – he didn't lift me as high off the ground when we hugged in the hotel lobby and his looks back in the 1970s were not as striking.

I am not the pert, slight brunette he used to kiss. I doubt he thought how shell-like was my skin nor fish-like my thighs. I have no use for satin. Here in my fishing village folk ask visitors 'where do you belong?' not 'where are you from?'; 'where do you stay?' not 'where do you live?' I belong and stay in this dour, dreich, Presbyterian world. Lorca has no place in Scotland, and poetry is not the language by which we live our everyday life. Scotsmen like my father and Englishmen like my husband do not speak in warm, earthy metaphor. I return to the age-rounded sounds of these poems though, in the darkness of an autumn morning, now that I am home, as if they give me as miraculous a stone boat to sail off in as the Apostle had to reach the scalloped shores of Galicia

I was up before dawn as usual, downstairs long before breakfast was ready and out past the cheap, white plastic chairs where we had sat. As we had said goodbye after the bar lights were out, our wine glasses still sat on the table with a tinge of pink and a frosting of cold dew. The car park where Miguel had turned his back on me and disappeared was already full of morning trucks and delivery vans, and the cafe bar's percolator was busy with their drivers. I went out to the very edge of this bland piece of 2015 and sat by the road into town on a block of concrete under a small undernourished fig tree and bit down on my lip, red and wet eyed. My nostrils flooded.

Gradually breakfast was laid and Deedee, Lucy and Midge came down through the hotel and took their seats. The duendes shuffled off as the dawn threatened. I came from the other direction, sliding back the glass door from the street and with a finger to my lips, a quick shake to my head and a tight smile that squashed Deedee's joke that I was just that moment back from a dirty stop-out. Lucy asked more gently and I confirmed that the evening had been lovely, but their eyes were full of questions and of made-up answers which were not mine. I breakfasted silently.

*

Later, sweet Grace walked out of Arzúa beside me.

'So were you and Miguel just catching up last night?' she asked very carefully, her eyes intently watching the impact of her words.

'Ah yes,' I said with a tight smile, 'I suppose that is what we were doing.'

I peered out from my shawl into the low golden tunnel which called us out past another cemetery and down the lane out of town, away from the car park and dirty tables. 'But it's been thirty-eight years.'

She nodded slightly but she is twenty-five and had no concept of what thirty-eight years of catching up entails. I tried to be jokey. 'When you only have a few hours to catch up, you don't bother with "in 1978 I decided I didn't like cottage cheese" or "in 1981 I moved to a slightly larger flat and painted it magnolia".'

'No, I suppose not,' she said.

'We've done rather a lot of living to look back on, you see,' I said, looking down into the brown earth, being careful of twisty tree roots out to get me. 'And I've always looked at it from here.' I put a hand to my chest. 'Looking backwards.' I turned to her gently questioning round face.

'But he dropped me at Santiago airport in 1977 and remembers me then and wanted to know what happened after he drove away into town to start his working day. He sees me from there. We were catching up from there.'

'That's different,' she agreed.

'Yes, that's different,' I said and sank my chin into my nut-brown shawl. She let us be silent then and just walked beside me as the lane's little arrows pointed us down and down and further down, across another bridge and round another bend in the road. The low morning light shone a searchlight into our eyes as we walked due east.

'Do you mind if I walk alone a bit?' I asked and she understood and picked up pace to join the pastel ladies ahead of us.

I plodded robotically on, head upside down. My heart couldn't feel my feet.

No, after so much living you don't waste a few precious hours together talking mundane nothings. When I have looked as far back at the nineteen-year-old girl I was in Santiago I have done so as the women I have been over nearly forty years since: messed-up woman, career woman, married woman, fishing-village woman, woman who is the mother of her own nineteen-year-old girl. But that night in Arzúa, though eyeball to eyeball with me through our specs, he who had stayed looked through a different lens. He looked out from his memory at the failed teenage philosopher who had come for a brief summer then abandoned him to salvage his career in local banking. It was her, messy haired, kohl eyed, fresh from his bed that he had in his mind when he let himself be caught again in my worldwide web. It was her, pert and impertinent in two languages, that he had arranged and rearranged to meet on her Camino, not knowing how much she might have changed. It was her, that wee flibber-tigibbet that was me, his friend, that he had called from a hotel doorway just a few highway miles from home.

No, I have not been crying since Arzúa because I left Miguel in Santiago. I never looked back when I got out of his car at the airport. He did not expect me to. I had a philosophy exam to resit, a degree to finish and he was a still-married man in a country where divorce was to remain illegal for another three years. He had married because his girlfriend was pregnant, not left her to her fate. They had tried to turn romance into a life match but had failed.

I had had Spanish romances before. I had known this was not reality. There was no way that an unchanging Free Bird would think of living in Catholic Spain. It hadn't even been a place where people had trusted themselves to be democratic with each other, never mind with a Scottish-born wife or daughter-in-law. It was a place where half of the women in prison were there for having had an abortion; where 10,000 of their women had filled most of the beds in London abortion clinics; where the Pill was illegal; where divorce was illegal; where adultery was, for women, an imprisonable offence; where no women had senior positions in any field of government or industry. All this had made Spain in 1977 an interesting basis for my dissertation, and I quoted the real, career-limiting life experiences of Miguel as a source in its footnotes. But if my 2015 guide Alicia had no understanding of the difference in our countries back then, I, back then, had understood well. This had still not quite become the Europe for me. I was his friend. We had neither offered nor accepted any other promises.

I didn't walk the next days of Camino crying for one young man whose life I never belonged in. After just a few hours' sleep and with the cologne-scent of an old lover caught in a shawl, tears came again for the loss of the girl of the 1970s, toughened a bit by intimate battles with the facts of fertility – exploring all the realities of abortion and all the *Joys of Sex* book cover to bed cover by nineteen and sure of her feet on the road. That reckless rebel untied by passport or promises is the only image of me that Miguel ever knew and he made me see her still deep inside. She is sitting with me now as I write. I haven't listened to her for years.

As I walked out of Arzúa I remembered the journeys she had taken back on British soil as the giddy, hot, pre-AIDS 1970s closed and a whole brave new world opened its iron fist and beckoned us. I cried for the girl who in the early 1980s had no one and nowhere to belong to. I had been glad to stop being her in the 1990s when I married a good man who just doesn't do poetry or art or history. ('Build a bridge and get over it,' Joe says.) I was glad our daughter is living a cooler life than I did at her age.

While I had flown on, Miguel had stayed put with friends who had been mine a while too and a job and a country that had eventually made him safe. I hadn't let him know that I had misread the airplane ticket, missed the flight and been obliged to use every bit of my natural chutzpah to blag my flight home.

As I gasped myself up the hill tracks of 2015, I examined the two hot pebbles he had presented to me in Arzúa to carry onwards on my pilgrimage. One was a burning Big Question. 'Why did you not call me?'

The first to make me think though was a more tempting treasure and easier to accept and consider. As we had settled down on our plastic chairs after my manic run to him across the dining room, he had told me: 'Do you know, when you found me on Facebook I said to friends who knew you that summer, "Do you remember Alison – the Scottish girl from 1977?" and they said, "Oh yes, she made you so happy! She made us all happy!"

'And,' he said as he pulled out my chair, 'you are doing the same now,' and squeezed my plump arm.

Everything about this exquisite, enchanting, exhausting journey so far had stripped me so bare, rubbed me raw, removed all trace of normal middle-aged carapace so that, hearing his words, seeing his smile, a flush rolled up from deep inside me, as strong as the waves which roll and crash outside my window now, across some wind-whipped cold vastness, stirred up by something only small in a warm breeze years and miles ago. Sensation sprayed over me, chill and hot, fresh and sweet, sexy and clean and powerful like an Atlantic breaker. I could have been remembered – I thought I was remembered – for so many other poorer things. My heart flooded, my throat thickened, my cheeks warmed and I took his words like a generous donation and presented them to the girl I used to be who had gone on to need them like she was starving. I have been surfing on those words for all the days since. I suppose I was crying because I was very, very tired. I still am.

October 2018

The road from Arzúa is a changing road. The twenty-first century grows closer as the kilometres to Santiago grow shorter. There is more industry, more business and less hospitality. Amongst the dug-up forests and dual carriageways that the pilgrim's path crosses it is easy to miss a yellow arrow or two. And then a falling acorn smashes into the ground just past the tip of a sweaty nose and shouts out: 'You are lost!'

The dirtiest landlord of the smelliest bar in Galicia drives the hungry walker further on and further up. A bashed leg dressed with local honeycomb for the bruising stiffens and the next bedroom seems to sink further away with every one of the twenty kilometres walked in hot low October sun. A rest stop turns out to be on an ant hill and escape from it knocks and spills the last bit from a water bottle.

Some bits of the journey are just tougher than others, whatever company you keep. You make your Camino by walking. Amongst the purples and golds of the forest, a strong soft-muzzled white horse with shining sculpted jaw makes his presence felt for the first time, reminding me of St James and his battles and the wonders that await us if we can make it further up and further on.

It seems now, looking back, that I have overvalued trying to fit in and trying to be clever. Perhaps just making people happy could have been enough. I cried, as I marched, for the sunny girl in a drifty skirt who had thought she might have been a researcher of Lorca in an ivory tower, or a poetess herself, or an illustrator or children's writer, a mural painter or the owner of a small language school in the Pyrenees but instead screwed it all up, slept around, sofa-surfed a little, got into unrepayable debt, stuck more than a finger up her nostrils and kept pennies in her purse by any means necessary. I saw contempt in the eyes of landlords and bosses, nurses and flatmates, bedmates and siblings, and learnt for sure lessons worth learning, lessons I would prefer not to have had to learn.

The 1980s was a very different, less idealistic decade than the 1970s. I survived it better than many less lucky folk by dropping my own high ideals like pebbles from a hole in a pocket. Eventually I became a very inefficient and unhappy secretary to keep independent and off the dole. No one was interested in my cleverness with words or colours, in any language, only my speed on a keyboard. I progressed to buying aluminium extrusions and minuting the clever words of actuaries and stockbrokers until I lost another job, another roof over my head and expanded my mind and body in other directions. Most importantly I avoided running home to Mummy or worrying Daddy into another heart attack.

I cried, as I walked, for my oh so untragically ordinary, lucky Presbyterian life and for all the square holes I had pushed my round self into unnecessarily and tholed without poetry or paint as companion. I had submitted and stopped wandering. I had compromised and stopped wondering. I cried because although I have a husband who has given me passion, joy, adventure, security, the loveliest daughter and a life I wouldn't change now, there was a lot of life wasted, many nightmare places I travelled to on the way that would have been best avoided and there were people I lost there. Some of them were me. As my changed Camino rolled out ahead I was to meet many of them again.

I say I cried. I didn't walk along the Camino bawling like a baby. My sinuses filled. My eyes spilled. My throat thickened. My nose dribbled. I sobbed. The great chestnuts and oaks arched over my head, linking their black twisted fingers, dropping their dry leaves through the thick air. The rutted track caught at my ankles. My walking poles skited off pilgrim-smoothed rock and sank into rain-loosened gravel. Silent walkers passed. I was pathetic in the face of the second gift Miguel presented me that night in Arzúa – the biggest question I have ever been asked. 'Why did you not call me?'

When all of these choices were yet to be made, when I was at a crossroads and took a path that led from then till now but could, with a call to him, have taken an easier route, why did I not phone my friend Miguel? Why did I not hear his calm, warm voice telling me that everything was going to be OK – I had a friend, here on Spanish soil? The last days walking on from Arzúa were the core of my Camino with this question drumming like Iberian wildfire, like *meigas* dancing, like Knights Templar galloping in my head as I marched – one, two, one, two, one, two – boots scrunching into the yellow road.

---

7 November 2016

There are no atheists in the trenches, they say, and perhaps not many in oncology wards either. I empty my mind, set palms on cool sheets, close my eyes on cool pillow and ask: is there anything out there? And I am answered with total clarity and certainty. There is nothing but my life. Soon there may be nothing ahead at all. This may be the end of the road. My head may empty and stay that way. No words or pictures or ideas. These may be my last days. That is fact not dogma.

Pain will be dealt with by clinically trained others but, taking responsibility, I consider what there will be in my last look back. Realisation and regret with no time to make amends? No trace of the slightest good left on earth by my stepping on its surface? The realisation at the end that I had led an entirely useless, stupid life? That would be my definition of looking into the gates of hell.

But it is not so. I am no Apostle and I am far from being without sin, but I have total faith that it – my hell – is not to be precisely because I have walked on the yellow road beyond Arzúa. More than once.

It was 1977. Miguel had dropped me at the airport. I found my flight had left an hour ago. I had misread my ticket. I had three pesetas in my purse and a passport that ran out the next day. Direct flights were weekly. There was one leaving for Madrid in an hour and there would be more to London from there, but the Madrid flight was full with people waiting on standby. The man behind the counter was coming to the end of his shift.

'I am in trouble,' I said. 'I have a resit. I am in your hands. I am worth your effort.' I begged and cajoled. 'You are a nice man. It will make you happy to help me out.' After months with Spaniards I knew all the subtleties of language that I have forgotten since. Perhaps he just wanted to get rid of me and go on his break. He got me on the flight to Madrid, my bags transferred to the next to London and I travelled first class all the way and never paid a penny. I was still a very lucky Free Bird. I returned to Scotland with my rather inaccurate certificate of attendance at Santiago University Facultad de Filología. I resat my philosophy exam and started my last year of university in Edinburgh.

I had met a Scottish boy studying linguistics who also fell for my free mind and easy body. He wrote me sad songs and played punky basslines and toured southern Scotland with a band and wondered about his sexuality while I remained very confident in mine. I kept drawing sunny girls in hot meadows. I wrote my dissertation in Spanish and an essay in Portuguese on 'Inês de Castro – Saint or Sinner?'[27] about a medieval Gallega girl from Sarria who went on to marry a king, inspire operas, ballets and the poetry of Ezra Pound and whose tomb talks of love '*até o fim do mundo…*',[28] or 'until the end of the world…'

Our love was to be disappointing in comparison but like Inês I lost my head, not being very good at differentiating

---

27. https://en.wikipedia.org/wiki/In%C3%AAs_de_Castro
28. http://www.atlasobscura.com/places/tomb-of-ines-de-castro

legend and reality, friendship and *amor*. I had fun with his friends and thought it was with him. He wrote lyrics so I didn't write poetry. We went to concerts, played Dungeons & Dragons and cycled round Edinburgh's hidden green paths and cobbled streets through the year towards who knows what. The answer to that came in June 1978 like a slap in the face. It was a slap in the face. A boy who hated his father for hitting his mother had just revealed what I recognised as his tragic flaw. It had given me a bloody nose. It was not heroic. It was not friendly. It was not inspiring. It didn't make me happy. To slap him back, I had sat and bled down my cheesecloth shirt. I didn't run. I had refused to clean up for the taxi driver or my flatmates. I never was a victim. I carried on down my path.

Within twenty-four hours, by some strange luck and an advertisement on the noticeboard in the university travel shop, I had not only the single ticket to Spain that I had rushed off to buy – I also had a job in Catalunya for the autumn. They had interviewed and appointed me over the phone.

Still full of adrenalin and anger I bought a Euro railcard to take me right round the Peninsula in a circle for the four months in between. I needed no man trailing his daemons. I would find poets. Easy in Spain. I had twenty-first-birthday money a few months early, a head full of useful vocabulary learnt not just from academia but from summers past and a degree tucked away. A whole world had stretched out ahead of me and the misty mysteries of grey, flabby old age were very distant. There was no need to stay and actually graduate. The bit of paper didn't matter. The ceremony was an irrelevance. Democracy was arriving in Spain and I would be part of its great walk forward. Like George Orwell and Laurie Lee or perhaps just Don Quijote I would be walking bravely back to battle giants on Spanish soil. The Scottish boy with the tragic flaw was quickly far behind me and my life was full of promise.

I set off. I took the sleeper from Dundee to London and sat in an early-morning park with a liver-paste sandwich and the great warm world spread out in front of me. I rode the ferry from Dover to Calais and watched England disappear in the sunshine. I slept on a *couchette* from Paris and called it a 'courgette' by mistake and woke at Portbou to change onto the right gauge of railway for Spain. The Mediterranean was pink and gold and lime and primrose, its edges etched with pine, and the ticket collector smelt of black tobacco and cologne. I had studied for years in order that Spain could be part of my future and now it was to be.

But it was not to be.

It is Scotland not Spain that I have woken in this autumn four days after my Camino. My road went downhill and got ashaming, but I did not call Miguel back then for it was not to be. He called me but it was not to be. This, not there, is where my future lay.

Four days home I still wake early like I did every day on pilgrimage and today the sky is high and golden as it was on Camino with a light full of promises. But the wind batters round the lanes and there are no oak trees or magpies – just seagull wail to remind me I am at home. Messages are coming in from this real world where my genes belong, where they speak the only language my daughter knows. My husband needs to be reassured that I brought my heart back to him and I have. I am not a Faithless Wife. I will go and be a professional part of the humdrum challenges of real life again soon.

Perhaps it is just exhaustion talking and middle-aged hormone deficiency but my ears and nose and pores are still straining to capture something – perhaps the breath-releasing scent of eucalyptus and mint and the bloody, ecstatic cries of hunting hounds racing behind a streak of russet across the Spanish meadows. Something in any case which tingles my nostrils and makes my blood run thick and hot. I am still spellbound. How free are any of us anyhow, wherever we are when night falls, when dogs bite at our nightmares, church bells fail to toll for dead writers and men in uniforms plan Armageddon? Until I have finished writing the story of my Camino I cannot stop myself from looking back down a road full of living that I set off on – Spain set off on – so determinedly such a long time ago. Perhaps one day, when it's all on the page, I will see it all differently – Camino is a journey. The perspective, the view of the future just round the next bend, is endlessly shifting.

Galicia, in the last of the 1970s, was part of a Spain which was changing fast from when the old man died. It was a time when all of Europe, west and east, was changing. I had crossed paths many times in cafes in Spain with West Germans, shared classes with them – Heidi, Wolfgang, Kurt, Marta – in Santiago. The other kind of German and many other nationalities now my neighbours were behind an Iron Curtain we never imagined would come down.

But the world was turning and is turning still and we, small ants crawling over it to suck a bit of sweetness in the sunlight, have no idea what is coming next nor what our tiny steps contribute to its turning. I have never thought that my story of weaving threads was big to anyone but me, nor new nor important alone. This story is just one moment that doesn't matter in a never-ending saga which does. Looking back down that Camino is not entirely a self-indulgent exercise, since all human journeys are just part of the story of our planet as it turns and each brings something for us all. I have re-read my dissertation on the situation of women in Spain in 1978 and find it factual but shallow now. And how could it be much else, despite the academic – and less academic – research I put into it. Being a mother now, I realise I was barely a woman when I wrote it, submitted it and then stepped back out in submission to Spain. I see things less simply now.

As we pilgrims stoked up for another day of indulgence at the continent's extreme western edge, 2015's breakfast-room television brought us images of Armageddon from Europe's eastern gates. Now Europe's Eastern borders are crushed with terrified Middle Eastern Moslem mothers and fathers carrying their daughters through icy rivers to escape from neighbours who would make war by raping them, who would sell their bodies for sex, whose oil prices suit no one. As the pilgrims who walk by me think about saints who might save them from purgatory at the end of their lives, these living virgins, and the ordinary women and men who love them, come out of real and genuine hell. They journey to find something, anything, as the world they belong to is destroyed. Their journey is not, like ours, an indulgent break from comfortable middle-aged monotony. It throws ours into sharp contrast, requires us to make something useful of our pilgrimage.

Catching the sight of them on the screen by the hotel door as I swung my pack onto my back, I winced pathetically and kept walking on in sin: doing nothing. Though knights in shining armour knew them all, the road to Santiago de Compostela in 2015 is one thing and the roads to Damascus, Mecca and Jerusalem are quite another. Our guide talks of St James the Moor-slayer with discomfort. A young American called Mohammed asks on a web forum if he will be welcome on the Way. The Knights Templar were put to death for knowing too much about Arab magic. What understanding have we all lost on the road?

As I stepped out into the beauty, I felt the weight of these other stories on my back as only middle-aged mothers can do, not failed teenage philosophers. Back at university in 1978 I had gathered lots of shocking statistics, but I knew not much of actually being a woman. I had made many free choices but not lived with them, carried them onwards, wondered whether my daughter would do the same. With my teenage handwriting on my lap in front of me now and Camino still in my head, I see in these stories layers of human detritus like leaf mould trampled underfoot, each piece once a fact of life, mine and everybody's. They are all women's and so they are everyone's – we are all born of woman. Together, this odyssey of lives lived is a deep and overwhelming forest and I have been sinking in its shadows. I will pull myself out. But not yet. I have questions to answer.

Spain, for a generation or two, has enticed our holidaymakers with the hot passions of flashing red skirts and castanets of Andalucía and sunny bikinied Mediterranean holidays. But people on the wild British coasts have mixed with the Celtic peoples of Spain's northern extremities for much longer. Coastal people have always gone creeping round the world, harbour to harbour, and others have come by fordable river to bridgeable stream, mountain pass to valley. Seams of jet, fossilised monkey-puzzle tree, were laid down on what is now Galicia, Asturias and Whitby when our lands were perhaps still one mass and the rock we walk on hadn't drifted apart and trees were weird. The earth connects each story to the next. The earliest human remains in Europe, from 900,000 years BC, were found on the Camino Francés at Atapuerca.[29] For the first of many times this place laid down importance to our understanding of human life. Megalithic people built great cathedrals of standing stones there as here in Britain. Beaker people left traces of their pottery from my home shores all the way to Portugal 3,500 years ago.[30] European Celts came travelling the ridgeways and settled and chopped back the forests, and the villages where their women made their homes are dotted around the Camino, and gave their name, Castro, to many more modern leaders.

October 2018
At the very top of the highest hill after Portomarín, when pilgrims zigzag with dripping noses reaching out to the gravelled slope, there

29. http://whc.unesco.org/en/list/989
30. https://en.wikipedia.org/wiki/Beaker_culture

is a more ancient path. A bright blue quilt of silence sits over the grassy labyrinthine way into Castromaior, where slate houses made use of boulders of pure white quartz and nestle together in narrow streets etched with lichen. The human who takes ownership of these hills commands the landscape for hundreds of miles around where lesser hills fade into the blue and smoke rises telling valley tales. The bountiful stone keeps food dry and guarded from thieves. Safe behind their rings of circling ramparts, small folks' houses have looked out for 2,018 years and watched the fit race by, missing the point. Our failing energy feels like a tiny glowing spark in time, time which turns all the battles of the millennia to calm. In the end.

Now I am home I know I am one person a great distance from where I was at nineteen but that this still a small story. Camino is, though, a place which, if you listen, talks to you hugely about many millennia. They are spelt out not just in the Apostle's tremendous story but through the fabric of the land you walk on as lightly as a midge on a pond, through the deep dark glint of a pilgrim's jet rosary or the layers of lost sea creatures squashed into layers of sandstone, or the infinitesimal rounding of the yellow pebbles on a gentle streambed at a village ford.

Miguel had a picture on his wall in 1977 of an ancient skin and wood boat that Gallegos say their ancestors used in order to travel between Gaul and Wales (which they call *Gales*) and Scotland, the land of the Gaels. Herodotus says Greeks and Celts were trading in Spain by 630 BC.[31] Brutus fought his way to Finis Terra and found the special Druid places.[32] James the Apostle probably noticed them too. The legends of St Andrew touched both the *rías* of Spain and the firths of Scotland. Any

---

31. http://www.knowth.com/the-celts.htm
32. http://www.jrbooksonline.com/pob/pob_ch14.html

journey of Joseph of Arimathea,[33] who is said to have known, travelled with and later buried Jesus, must have come this way. Maybe he and his travelling companions anchored a while on that Spanish corner of the Atlantic and put their feet here too on the way to our green and pleasant land.

It is written that Joseph traveled through many dangerous storms,[34] from the Mediterranean to Druidic Glastonbury, past this corner of welcoming earth. Vikings raided us both, and Miguel had taken me out into the country and had showed me castles built to fend against them on the northern coast. Knights Templar fought bandits here and when no longer welcome went to the Kingdom of Fife, which I can see from here on a clear day. Remnants of the Armada straggled round to my home sea, and maybe some of its shipwrecked sailors stayed and mixed their bloods with black-haired Celts like my mother on her father's west coast.

Britain, with the help of kilted Scottish soldiers from my own north-east coast, battled with Napoleon's plans at Corunna and lost the respect of the locals when 200 became so drunk that they had to be left behind.[35] The langoustine I was eating that sunny lunchtime before Arzúa may have been caught in the common fisheries off the coast of Scotland. Now we are, as I write, all part of the same Europe and in Galicia you can see where the Euros ran out in unfinished roads ploughing down from Brussels, eating up the yellow soil and screeching to an ugly finish in the eucalyptus forest before the continent ends. It is a fact of life that all mothers, and I walked with many last week, have been sexual beings who have given birth to another chapter of human life, whether or not we see it that

33. http://d.lib.rochester.edu/camelot/text/
    history-of-that-holy-disciple-joseph-of-arimathea
34. http://d.lib.rochester.edu/camelot/text/
    history-of-that-holy-disciple-joseph-of-arimathea
35. http://www.britishbattles.com/peninsula/peninsula-coruna.htm

way, whether or not we see that as a burden or a pleasure. Each story is connected and every traveller carries another idea a few steps further down the road, just as every river is made of millions of insignificant drops and every song is formed from many beats – where centuries are mere minutes in the life of an oak or in the weathering of granite cross.

Just like the immense horizon outside my room as I write, the vastness of the world story that is told on Camino soothes the soul. One's own mistakes (some call them sins) are insignificant (some would say forgiven) in the endless dimensions of the universe (some call it the Field of Stars – Campus Stella). It would be easy for me to forget that those thirty-eight years are a very long time. It is tempting to think that decades can pass by as quickly forgotten as a shooting star. I could be no different, in the big scheme of things, from that girl full of inspiration and wide horizons who stepped off a train at the Spanish border. Couldn't I? With Camino in my mind, if I keep walking backwards, it really can seem so.

When I was a graduate of twenty (just an eye blink ago when Spain was not yet quite free) carrying few pebbles and with the gift of a couple of languages, I was to be a small part of the European invitation to Spain to change, look north. With the help of unqualified English teachers like me it could be a full part again of the rich and liberated West, turning its back on Africa, the Islamic East and its long-lost American empire.

It was still only 1978, and Europe's money and motorways had not yet crossed the Pyrenees. Expo had not yet come to Seville. The Olympics hadn't yet transformed Barcelona. Guggenheim hadn't chosen Bilbao. Guttural Catalans wanted to look out of the frilled flamenco dancing cage in which Franco,[36] his US airbases and Texan friends had kept them since

---

36. http://countrystudies.us/spain/23.htm

he brought out his Moors to suppress the revolution. Now that he was gone, Catalans, whose kingdoms, like the Basques, had never respected the Pyrenees, sent their children to the language schools popping up everywhere and looked north. The 1970s were very close to ending. The Cold War still loomed and would perhaps climax in space. Britain was shifting to the right. Society was disappearing like crumbs at the bottom of Thatcher's handbag.

Having left Scotland far behind, I was to come to live and teach amongst the *pueblo* of a small market town inland from Barcelona in the province of Lleida. I would open up new ideas for who knows which of the four- to forty-year-olds that I was to teach in a small classroom in a quiet street in a provincial town on the banks of the Riu Segre at one of the Peninsula's great gates.

First, though, it was midsummer and with my bloody nose behind me and my open tickets to freedom in my purse, I wanted my taste of the sweaty red duendes of Lorca's gypsy Spain, the trickling calligraphy of Al-Andalus's palaces, the unremembered places of Cervantes' blinding Castile and the strange extremes of the south west where Miguel was born and they serve babies chocolate on dirty coins. Maybe I would touch dusty feet on old pilgrims' roads and walk with a pack on my bag across the rainy flagstones of Santiago de Compostela again. Maybe that summer of 1978 I sent a message to Miguel that I would – I honestly don't remember. That thought has sunk far too deep into who I once was and am no longer.

I would spend as little time as possible in Barcelona which I knew too well and set off solo to all the bits of this fascinating un-European country that I had never seen, making fresh new friends along the way. I would see deserts and antelopes and eagles and barrels of sherry and the ports which had connected the great Arab poets to Spain and Spain to its vast, golden South American empire. I would walk on other old roads and see troglodyte villages of gypsies and oranges trees and black pigs in cork-oak forests and Don Quijote's windmills. I would travel through landscapes still wild enough for lynx and bear and wolf. I would complete the full circle and come to an undiscovered inland Catalunya where Christians hid their treasures from the Moors deep in the mountain ravines and the Camino crosses through the lands of Urgell, skirting the Pyrenees from the south. Then in a cosy small community with a pretty market square full of plain trees and proud gypsy vendors I would get serious about whether I could belong in Spain, live there, marry there, become a mother there. Could I, by travelling the Spanish roads, soak myself enough in the Peninsula that I could be more at home there than in a Scottish village? Could I make Spain my curriculum vitae, putting all those years of enthusiastic study to good use in the course of my life ahead?

That was the way ahead that I had written for myself in the first few days of the summer of 1978 when my nose was stopping hurting. It had been the journey across France, changing trains in Paris that worried me. My French was shaky. But now I was in Spain. As the train pulled out from Portbou and down to Barcelona, it was all within my grasp.

Sometimes, though, even for professed atheists, it is as though a great big finger of fate or witchery descends and flicks you in an unintended direction. It has for a long time seemed like that to me.

So I described it to Miguel last week at a white plastic table on a hotel terrace. In one swift, skilled piece of gypsy teamwork, my path went astray. Perhaps those fleet-foot boys from the shanty towns of Barcelona were duendes up from the south. Anyhow, I was way down the road and onto the dirtier street corners of the 1980s before I realised that it was with that one precise moment in Barcelona that I had got myself lost. Decades later I caught Miguel up with that life-changing moment in the chilly darkness outside a hotel in Arzúa wrapped in my nut-brown shawl. It led to his big question. Why had I not called him?

Sitting in the splendid Plaça Reial just off Barcelona's famous Ramblas on the eve of my journey round Spain, I told Miguel as we were catching up, I lost my purse to a well-trained swarm of broad copper-faced Romany boys. Around me under the palm trees, deals of dope were being traded, anarchists' flags were fluttering from the balconies and old men sifted endlessly through boxes of ancient coins in their white peaked caps and clip-on sunglasses. Pigeons' wings echoed round the cool colonnades and laughter swirled with the crazy swifts up high into the free blue. All was warm and happy and hopeful and my twenty-year-old heart padded gently in my chest with the rhythm of the imagined road I would set off on.

Tomorrow.

I was in love with the world, easily distracted and far too slow to stop a lightning grab by a slim copper arm. My purse and the boys were gone like a puff of gold dust in a gust of hot wind.

The swifts shrieked.

The copper feet ran.

My bag disappeared.

With it I had lost everything but just the minimum of cash stored back at my *pensión* – enough, just, for my board and lodging but not to leave any hope of a whole summer's pen-insular exploration, free as a bird, head high. The budget for that had been caught in one of two plastic cards stolen with that purse. I could not, there was no point in, going home to Scotland: I was not one for going backwards. I had a job to go to in a language school in a yet to be discovered Catalan town. I had had just a single airline ticket and now no money for another. The ability to get more was caught in the other plastic card. Crippled by my own stupidity I was to limp through a sour, oppressive Barcelona summer with my sense of adventure and self-belief leaking away into a smelly Spanish gutter. I was not a great intrepid traveller, no Orwell or Hemingway or Laurie Lee or some female discoverer of a new perspective for a new world. I was a stupid wee careless lassie with bad taste in men and handbags. I had messed up again.

I dragged my feet to the police station to report the theft because you have to. Any crumb of hope of useful support from that direction soon disappeared rather more completely than expected. As I left the hot and dirty street and, following a sign, headed up the marble stairs ahead of me, an animal grunted from the dark lobby. A pig?

There in the blackness behind the half-opened door of Barcelona's police headquarters a huge pair of hairy pink buttocks were caught for my eye in a streak of light. A rifle butt slapped slowly and rhythmically against their spot-lit nakedness. A pair of uniform trousers flopped around shiny black boots. Over broad grey shoulders curled a pair of slim brown arms ending in raspberry red fingernails catching a thin shaft of midday sun. Behind them in the dusty shadows, a pair of sharp, gypsy almond eyes caught mine and passively watched me go futilely up the steps to ask for help from whichever other Guardia Civil were fully dressed, even less emotionally engaged and on duty upstairs.

It was a reminder that Salvador Dalí's surrealism is never far below the surface in Spain. The gypsy's lunchtime client was no friendly British bobby keen to help a young lassie with a problem. I was in a place which was further from my comfy grey home than Barcelona seems to be even now. This was not post-Olympic Barcelona. Where in 2015 hotels, yachts and elegant bodies gleam, then, pre-Olympics, was Third World dereliction. Shanty-town walls were made of stolen garage doors and kitchens were fuelled by tapping into factory pipelines. Policemen were not on anyone's side but their own. As

Lorca knew, they certainly were not on the side of loose maidens and wandering travellers.

With no help in that direction I had gone on to drag myself through the grimy Barcelona summer stony broke, hungry and making feather-light day-long friendships with boys – less suspicious or bossy than girls and more likely to be travelling alone, like me. Old Spain was crumbling and there was much to see. A young Scot up for the day from Sitges and met in a cafe on the Ramblas nursing a Coke for an hour or so tapped his watch to announce the next demo parade. (Spain was cracking open. Someone was protesting every weekend). Up the boulevard marched the rainbow coloured lesbian, bisexual, gay, and transgender community of Catalunya in dungarees and leather chaps, evening dresses and beards, moustaches and crew cuts, bare golden chests and braless T shirts, pierced nipples at the ready. It was their turn. Just months before Franco's mourners were still imprisoning homosexuals.[37] Barcelona held its breath again but the Guardia Civil were perhaps too busy fighting with vice elsewhere.

The young Scot and I joined the crowd and for a while I carried a banner proclaiming that I too was a lesbian, which I clearly was not. I carried the message a step or two further up the road though, I am proud to say. In carnival mode, we reached the government square and crowded in, feeling victorious. Someone large in a shining mermaid-turquoise evening dress took advantage of a stage left from *sardana* dancing and performed an interesting strip of her doubly endowed transitional body until a different hell spurted loose.

From the darkness of a governmental archway flew a ball of fire, lobbed into the crowd. Thunderous gunfire crashing noise smashed the air and ricocheted off the walls as all the

---

37. http://www.telegraph.co.uk/news/worldnews/europe/spain/6743915/
Spain-apologises-for-jailing-homosexual-in-the-1970s.html

watchful and well-practised jewellers simultaneously brought their metal shutters immediately and securely down. I didn't stop to understand what was happening but kicked off my flip-flops and ran and never saw the Scottish boy or the shoes again. For the rest of the day the city was littered with torn-off snippets of the parade – a bearded lady and her tuxedoed beau snogging in the lamplight, a trio of baggy, saggy lesbians sulking in a park, golden boys exchanging cheerful insults with blokes in bar doorways. A fight broke out of pitched flour and water bombs across the Ramblas and soon gay and macho were indistinguishable soggy ghosts. I was living sure enough with the pavement hot and filthy beneath my shoeless feet, but it wasn't very comfortable, not what I had dreamed of when I set off to see the finery of Spain's great heritage.

Two months or more into my enforced stay in this great and bizarre city, a local boy befriended me in a sunny cafe where I was drawing and drove me in a borrowed car to helter-skelter into the secretive hills to see where the monastery of San Miquel de Fai has looked down for a thousand years from a shelf on a 300-foot cliff. Rain and wind and time had carved out just one vertical entrance-slit in the rock and many horizontal dripping grottos in the sandstone during the millennia before. Ancient Iberians found these to be safe places to hide their dead and their treasures from anyone heading up the valleys from the Costas.

Sacred places attracted holy men. Holy men were succeeded in time by Benedictine monks. The boy and I, less holy, walked behind the waterfall where the rock is smoothed and moist and peach coloured as if the mountains tucked up, and here exposed, the contours of a naked giant. Deep in one of its intimate hollows someone hid a small and perfectly geometrically patterned urn with the bones of a treasured saint, in the days when Islam gave Spaniards permission to be Christian and to share their art but not their mathematical or magical understanding of the stars.

Still under the Peninsula's magic spell the next weekend, I was easily tempted by the same boy with another free trip down the coast and out of the grime again. We had become friends, sharing thoughts as two equals. I was reluctant to be beholden, never my preferred status, but caved in to feel a bit of Costa sea and sand and superficiality. (There were no man-made Olympics-funded city beach in Barcelona in those days, only docks and warehouse sprawl). We took the train down to Sitges, a few stops down the coast and walked down the prom amongst the tourists and expats. There were plenty bright young things like us travelling up and down the Med. Thirsty to speak my own language, I got drunk with a cheery bundle of bar-room Brits and my Spanish friend and I missed the last train back to the city and scrabbled to find a bed for the night. Unfortunately, the proximity of our drink-loosened bodies – and the mounting bill he was picking up for my pleasures – made him think, in the middle of the night, that he could have me as more than just a room-mate. Being in deep drunken sleep, my consent did not seem to be required. Since he was on top of me when I awoke, it was scarily difficult to persuade him otherwise. I did though. I am not a victim. Another near miss with life.

The challenge of every Spanish day had been to tick the hours and weeks away until I had somewhere to go to. In the sticky humidity, I often locked my door and slept sixteen hours a day. Sleep is cheap, private and usually safe. I couldn't afford to pay for drinks in cafes and there was nowhere free to sit in town except on a bench opposite a brothel. I killed a few hours timing the girls as they picked up a client off the street and returned ten minutes later on the dot. We passed soulless hours that way.

Once, two men sat down on either side of me as I ate an overripe peach bought cheap. They amused themselves by describing the scene I conjured in their imagination as the juice ran down my chin. I kept my face straight, hiding that I had learnt their lewd vocabulary. I wandered aimlessly through the lovely Parque de la Cuidadela but found it a pick-up joint where I was hissed at and felt unsafe. I rounded on an old man in the Plaça Catalunya who whispered things he wanted to do to my young northern body, not realising that I understood his foul mutterings and that I was trained by *Cosmopolitan* to defend myself. I had, in any case, had enough. In fluent Catalan-accented Spanish, with deeply Scottish undertones, I broadcast his vile fantasies at the top of my voice to the crowded street till he cringed into the paving.

'So you want to ... do you, you disgusting perverted little ...? I bet you've got a good Catholic wife at home and thirteen children she never got to choose to have or not. But you think it's OK for you in your suit and watch chain to whisper to me that you want to ... to my ... because I am a foreigner and won't understand and no one will know and you can go to confession tomorrow. Well look' – I gestured, with a sweep of my hand, at the fascinated crowd I had gathered – 'just how wrong you are!' I was learning even more about the power of sex and the politics of gender. I was not a victim.

I had felt more comfortable for a week or so selling my skills to an economics lecturer from North London Polytechnic who had had a passport stolen and was, like me, washed up for a while. He spoke no Spanish, had never seen the Barcelona sights and had money to spare. I took him to the one existing façade of the Sagrada Familia and introduced him by tram to Modernism and Gaudí (who'd been killed by one) and he didn't need a guide or a booklet or a taxi. He had me: Fine Art.

I took him off the main drags and into the alleys to eat *butifarra* and *pan i tomat* and drink *cañas* and pay a quarter of tourist prices. I filled his days with intellectualisms gathered through all my explorations of Spain and art and literature and never had to put my hand in my increasingly empty pocket until his new passport came through. I suppose it was me who seduced him, being, unlike him, confident and young and slim and beyond his dreams. His company got me through a few skint weeks when I didn't know who else I could have turned to. Once, many years later, I put his name into a web search but nothing came back. Unlike Miguel he may not have remembered what happiness I had brought him.

Stuck in Barcelona, alone again, a silly wee postcard that I had dropped to the boy I left in Scotland with my nose bloodied received a reply.

I was not, as planned, already miles down the dusty track to who knows who. I was in a bed I had sensibly paid for with my few remaining pesetas when I knew I was going to be stuck a while. That meant I had to make do for food with what I had left, but at least I wouldn't actually end up in the gutter like a discarded peach stone.

The high-ceilinged empty room across from the barracks was cool and quiet. The ceiling fan danced its slow dance and the net curtains waved hypnotically in the French windows while outside Barcelona was oppressive and rambunctious and offered me no friendly face. At the end of the alley, Christopher Columbus pointed off to lands of gold and silver and barbarity and civilizations across the ocean blue, far beyond the docks, beyond Gibraltar and way out from Fisterra across the immense Atlantic.

I thought of my Scottish boy back behind me and remembered the horror in his face when he saw himself becoming his father, a beater of women. He had loved me well before. He hadn't judged me for accidental pregnancy by someone else before him nor my refusal to define myself by it. I am not a victim. He had wanted to share my philosophising, imagining, intellectualising family and loved us for the escape our picture windows offered him over the silvery Tay, away from miles of his unloved Ayrshire council estate home. He mocked his mum for opening a tin of Heinz tomato soup for guests and loved mine for her shelves of Mediterranean recipe books. That knock on the nose had sent him reeling backwards more than me and his letter gave me hope that he had taken steps to put his daemons behind him. He had done some walking while I was away.

Stuck in Barcelona with strange strangers – 'foreigners' and 'strangers' are the same word in Spanish – I had wanted to believe him, and who else was I going to share my lonely thoughts with when, in Barcelona's humidity, I couldn't sleep? Not the poor, young jackbooted conscripts I watched from behind my net curtains on the terraces of the building opposite my room at the bottom of the Ramblas. They fed them with saltpetre to keep them from sexual harm when they were allowed a break from the barracks, so I heard from their girlfriends. So there behind Columbus's back my world turned and began to twist my path away from crazy golden Spanish dreams and back to the sure grey pewter of Scotland.

I sent a letter back to Edinburgh. It opened wide a door that had been better left shut. I only sent it because I was bored and lonely and broke and stuck. No way out.

I told the skeleton of this story to Miguel that night in Arzúa last week.

'In the purse that the gypsy boys stole in the Plaça Reial,' I said, 'was not just my Eurorail card and cheque card – they stole my way forward.' When I had explained what I meant, Miguel asked me simply:

'Why didn't you call me?' His voice was full of deep generosity and warm concern. It came at me like a cannonball.

Why didn't I call him when I was so lost and he was so close, just the other side of the country – not poor, not a stranger? A banker, for Christ's sake; an always wise, tender, older lover, for pity's sake!

His question burnt a hole right through me as I walked on the next day with Grace's back going on ahead of me with the pastel ladies. Something comfortable dropped out. Spinning round and round in my memory looking for whatever it was has sent me reeling. (Concentrate on walking on; don't trip over those snaky tree roots; march on – one, two, one two).

Why hadn't I taken that chance to continue on the path across Spain that I set out on with a healing nose? (My boots hammer into the ground – heel toe, heel toe. Morning mists tease me. Air chill. March on.)

Why had it not occurred to me to do as he suggested? (scrunch, scrunch)

What would it have meant if I had? (heel toe, heel toe)

My tears as I walked on towards Santiago and since have not been to answer the simplicity of his question. They have been my catching up on thoughts of many things. (Fists grip my walking poles; beat out the rhythm of the road.)

I have, leaving him far behind me, been crying out an acknowledgement of stupid choices made in the years that separate not just me and him, but also me and me.

Who got lost back then? What got compromised? (Green light, gold light flickers and dazzles through the trees overhead. Autumn sends flashes of red from the undergrowth. Head down, my boots thump into the mud and moss. One, two, one, two.)

I was remembering lessons learnt hard, now that at decades of distance it feels safe to stop tomfooling as if I didn't care. Camino is a place for indulgences, isn't it?

I am a mother of a young woman that age. Walking on through my beloved Spain, which has taught me so much, I was crying in forgiveness of unforgivable bad judgement and of reckless abandonment of the good sense I was bred with.

I cried for a world that had felt to Anglo Saxon students to be so nearly grasped. If we escaped global thermonuclear war we would travel on across the world, from Bali to California,

Marrakech to Chelsea and everywhere would be as it was for us: hairy bra-less women's lives mattered, beautiful bi and gay and transgender lives mattered, folk who sang their own land's earth-songs mattered. Ours was a world where we imagined everybody living in peace, without religion, making coffee-coloured people by the score and enjoying every minute equally. No one body part was more important or more beautiful than another. We gathered ideas from everywhere, were our own leaders. That was our globalisation. And if anyone argued with the old hippy stuff we could spike up our hair, strap on our bondage boots, crash those bass lines and shout, and the world would listen. Wouldn't it?

I cried in frustration at my own stupid blessed sweet twenty-year-old arrogance and the compromises that, in a still imperfect world, she went on to make, that my daughter will make, that my mother made, that my sister made – for the love of imperfect men.

Why hadn't I thought to call my honourable Spanish banker friend rather than start giving in to a man I already knew was so imperfect that he hit a girl? Why do women think we can change men for the better by loving them? Why do we think they will regret it when we're gone? (Jabbing the ground with my sticks, miles go by under me – one, two, one, two, one, two.)

For Christ's sake! (Or my own.) Why hadn't I called, from lonely surreal edgy Catalunya with its bullet holes in the walls, scabby shanty town gypsies and morally redundant law enforcers to the decent Celt who might have treasured me, protected me and held me in warm brown arms a while and given me wise guidance. He might perhaps have made me a better offer – or at least a loan to get me back on my trek towards a Spanish future. (Digging in the heels, I power up the next hill – one, two, one, and two.)

Why hadn't I rung and asked for help to be safe and happy at that moment with months of freedom ahead of me when I could still have changed my life's direction back again to this passionate poetic peninsula. (Muscles stretch, joints grip, heels hit the ground hard, leaving feet behind – this is *caminar*.)

I could still have made my way safely, years later, to meet my lovely Joe in London and make our lovely daughter. Couldn't I, if fate or something more is to be believed in?

Why had I instead just stagnated in grimy Barcelona, dragged myself through familiar Catalunya to my small-town teaching job, when I had already not just lost my wallet but my illusions of poetic Spain and free me? Going about starting a new life in small-town Spain in that frame of mind, all Hispanophilia gone and months spent surviving on the city's crumbs, I was easily and quickly tempted back by vague promises from familiar grey Scotland. By Christmas 1978, I had sneaked out of Balaguer through snowy olive fields and back to my biggest mistake – marrying, not like tragic Inês de Castro, a Crown Prince, but the weakest man I had ever met. (One, two, one, two, one, two.)

I cried as I walked through the cool cathedral of Galician forest, because I saw for the first time this autumn that I had had a choice – to call for help from Barcelona and then again another choice – which had never tempted me – and then again one last choice. Before I had flown back to not put a ring on my finger (my fiancé didn't believe in them it turns out), before I had turned my back on Spain and shut the door behind me, Miguel had rung me. I had been offered one last chance.

I had already turned down a good one. A luxuriantly bearded Catalan lawyer, heir to fertile land and a townhouse overlooking the market square where I met him, had offered me many nearly perfect things, none of which I wanted enough to stay for. Above my room, round the corner from the language school in Balaguer in the foothills of the Pyrenees, he had spread out his arms for me to horizon-reaching fields of pleasure – Moscatel grapes, interspersed line by line with seed-full bushes of marijuana and ringed by fig trees from which we filled the boot of his car with moist, seductive flesh. He escorted me to a sandcastle hilltop and protected me as his windscreen was covered in slobbering hell hounds till his friend, their master, a Bourbon Marquis, trotted his stallion round from behind his castle. The purple and tangerine sunset outside our windscreen silhouetted its arching ebony neck and delicately lifting hooves.

The two perfect gentlemen held open a door cut into the granddaddy of all doors, perhaps the secret to the family's survival, and welcomed me to the Marquis's four-turreted home, his suits of armour and dressage trophies, his suites of white fur rugs, stainless steel and Picasso sketches. The handsome aristocrat himself was inevitably betrothed to some eternal European cousin, and I was a mere one-summer butterfly, her wings rather shabby in comparison. Our mutual friend, on the other hand, flattered me with an offer of legal marriage despite his mother's cardiganned, crucifixed and coiffured disapproval. He offered me status and land and ancient European friendships and exquisite glasses of thick sweet wine. He gave me whiskery kisses of greeting on my cheek and of charm on the back of my hand but he never once offered me passion or animal abandon. I had to graciously decline. I felt sure we wouldn't make each other happy.

Once more before I left the Peninsula behind, Miguel had reminded me that I had better options.

Balaguer sits at a crucial location for Spain and, it turns out, for me. One road leads up to silly, superficial, tax-free Andorra, neither French nor Spanish but an easy place to have a passport stamped in the days before Europe welcomed all its workers. With a lift from a friend I could stock up every few months on whisky and good butter to ease my homesickness.

One road leads across revolutionary Catalunya to the capital, Barcelona, with its own take on boulevards and patisseries, and out to the rest of the modern world. This is the way that Franco's army came to Catalunya from the north to squash a revolution where women fought arm in arm with men.

One road climbs immediately into the wild ridges of the Pyrenees where the stork's wheel and horses whinny and adulteresses suffer. One road heads straight across the blue woodsmoke plains studded with sandcastles and windmills, the great conquerable diagonals of Spain. One, the Cami de Sant Jaume, heads all the way to its end in Compostela.

Once, at that crossroads, right at the crucial last moment, when my pocket held an unanswered telegram from Scotland saying 'Please come home and marry me at your earliest convenience. STOP', the phone rang.

My question for Miguel in Arzúa was: 'How did you come to call me out of the blue in Catalunya days before I left to get married?'

I remembered one mid-winter evening my landlady standing with the phone that never rang for me calling, 'Alison, it is someone called Miguel del Bosque.'

I remembered my heart leaping at the name from the past.

I remembered hearing his lovely deep voice for the first time since Santiago airport a long time before. I could still have changed direction.

He didn't have an answer to my question thirty-eight years later. He remembered that when I came to the phone I did not believe it was him. I think he was hurt by that. I have a horrible feeling, now that I think of it, that he had really expected me to come to Santiago that summer once on midsummer Spanish soil, and that he had, when even Spain was cold, remembered my twenty-first birthday on St Andrew's Day (I had just passed it rather bleakly with a dinner of snails and strangers, far from home). He had cared enough to track me down. Spain had still not had the chance to vote for a democratic constitution. It was very nearly 1979.

Digging through these papers on my lap I am reminded that he and I had exchanged letters occasionally over that first year of separation after Santiago. In his, he had told me that he was beginning to find happiness again that I had first brought to him a year before. My parents had received another letter for me from him and had forwarded it to me in Catalunya. I don't remember any of them.

I remembered the suspicion of my Catalan landlady listening nearby in the cold hall, knowing about the telegram. She had become the guardian of my honour on behalf of the Scottish fiancé who she had never met. I lived with her, a widow, and her three children, and she tried to treat me like a daughter, teaching me to cook cheap meals of rice and tomato and egg and tutting around my untidiness.

I remember the telly calling out in a pompous voice, '*Día 6 de Diciembre, Día de la Constitución!*' to remind people of the importance of the coming referendum for democracy. This choice was real. My crossroads and Spain's coincided. Miguel had tracked down my number while the other boy had failed. It astonished me for years, felt like magic. No one had my number. Why would Miguel want to call me? How could Miguel have called me? Looking back, it seems prophetic. There were to be a lot of things my fiancé would give up on too easily. I was always one of those things. I would be for ever.

My astonishment at hearing his voice must have, for Miguel, had the sound of a closing door. Although he had gone to some effort to track me down, I clearly had not been waiting to welcome his call. Organising life is so much easier now in 2015 and love so much more complicated with the constant connectivity of the World Wide Web. Nothing is quite as surprising, connecting with each other so much more possible, in the twenty-first century as it was before Europe was wholeheartedly democratic and I was entirely an adult.

CHAPTER EIGHT

WORLDWIDE WEBS
AND WAYS FORWARD

I think perhaps that it is only in late middle age that you are tempted to look backwards. When I took that unexpected call, I was young, hungry for commitment and belonging, tired of six months of being *una extranjera* speaking a strange language in a stranger's house in a very surreal country. Miguel was too late. I had felt like litter in the gutter in Barcelona that summer and had given up on Spain, its duendes and gypsies and bleeding saints. I had tried to teach my class of sixteen-year-old boys useful English – for travel or work or love of Anglo Saxon girls – but they had only wanted to fuck. They would at least learn that accurately.

'The verb to fuck goes:
I fuck
You fuck
He, she or it fucks.
We fuck
You (plural) fuck
They fuck.
Stay behind and write it out 150 times.'

26 October 2018
'What would you have said if I had called you?' I ask.
    'Joder! Alison!' *Fucking brilliant! It's Alison!*
    'What did you think when I tracked you down on Facebook?'
    'Joder! Alison!' *Fucking hell! It's Alison!*
    'What did you think when you saw my paintings?'
    'Joder!' *What the fuck?'*

Catalans were so determined to become European that I was sent little girls who had, after a day of school, done an hour of piano, an hour of ballet or an hour of French before they came to me. They yawned through my class. Fat little boys stuffed into stiff shirts stank of cologne and filled the bin with the pretty shells of sunflower seeds. Pre-teens asked me to give them English names and failed to understand that we don't call girls 'Conception', 'Assumption', 'Sorrows' or 'Mercies', nor boys 'Hyacinth' or 'Joseph-Mary'. When I walked through town they called to me from beaded doorways 'Mees Al-ee-son' and their mothers and grandmothers whispered to each other I was the *'Inglesa'* which I corrected to *'Escocesa'* on every opportunity, explaining that to call a Scot English was like calling a Catalan Castilian.

Mine was not the only language school in this historic town of around fifteen hundred people and there was a little gaggle of Anglo Saxons to hang out with, but somehow none were able to reignite my Hispanophilia, all had itchy feet and something near to contempt for the wives and children of small-town professionals, farmers and shopkeepers that filled their classes, looking for Europe.

We would hitch rides on Saturday nights to Musicland, a sprawling disco village in another town, and learn to refuse dances and drinks in Catalan – or sometimes accept them, but rarely pay. One afternoon I caught a giggle of my Year 3 girls with noses pressed to the fence of the municipal outdoor swimming pool where big blond Greg from Maine was doing easy lengths. Sometimes I wandered round the edge of town, where the gypsies lived and small half-naked children with proud chests and Asian eyes played in damp gutters beneath the slimy cliff where Spain changes.

Their democratic constitution was heralded by cheery adverts on the telly and the bright cartoon pamphlets made no apologies for the past. Within days of my twenty-first birthday, *Día de la Constitución* was over and Spain was safely living in the present. My teenage road through Spain was over too.

Disillusioned and, since Barcelona, exchanging a steady flow of letters with Scotland, I gave in as my tragically flawed Scottish boy offered me the position of Muse and wife. Miguel's phone call had stirred me up and made me consider my options but I was twenty-one now – it was time for the future not the past. His offers were always gently, silently laid before me to explore. He never did, never has, dominated me with stark and simple choices – come to me and be my love. I had the clear map of real grown-up marriage to travel home for. Just like now. He was, wasn't he? Just one Spanish lover that I, a teen-ager, had left behind. It had been too late by the time his call had come through. It hadn't been with a marriage proposal as far as I know. I'm not really sure what it was. Friendship? Now there's a thought.

Now, as the one-Spanish-summer lover who did get caught in my web, he has a different status in my life. He is not the Easterhouse boy I wrote to after a school trip in 1971, nor the motorbike boy who took me up the Pyrenees in 1974 to see wild horses, nor the boy I dug escape holes in the sand with in 1976, nor the professor I stuck it out with in Barcelona, nor the child who robbed me in a square full of palm trees and antique silver, nor the boy who tried to rape me on the coast in 1978, nor the landed gentry with the cool offer of cardiganned domesticity before I flew home. Whatever Miguel was, we are still and for ever strangers. I expect.

November 2016

I didn't expect to have emergency surgery. I didn't expect to nearly die twice more that month. I didn't expect to see my fifty-ninth birthday, nor be strong enough for chemo, nor to become an exhibiting artist, nor for my cancer to disappear. I didn't expect anyone to be reading these words, especially not strangers. Life, it turns out, goes on and on and is full of the unexpected. Living is a great adventure.

Everything on Camino is a metaphor. The next morning, onwards from my meeting with him in Arzúa, my nose and eyes ran and I marched head down, deep in strange, grown-up, happy sadness and deep in his question and what it meant – not for the person I was when Spain was still on the edge of another world but for who I am.

Why hadn't I called to that other world where he was settling into a comfy life amongst old friends. I might have spent a lifetime sharing their minstrel magic in the lovely wet streets of Santiago where the fountains play love songs all night long. I might just have stopped just a while then walked on, backwards down the road from Compostela to a very different chapter. Who was I that I did not call? I cried and cried and cried for all the stupidity and bravery, innocence and instinct, passion and principles of young women who want to have it all and not feel guilty.

Strands of gossamer got caught in the snot. The rivulet running road after Arzúa snapped at my ankles. More golden leaves were falling. I stamped my heels into the ground and left my feet behind me as the A-team had by now taught me. I powered desperately, grottily up another hill with my hat pulled down, my nut-brown shawl, still faintly tinged with Miguel's cologne, wrapped around my mouth and nose. A lone Spaniard went by singing of '*triste amor*' in the loveliest of the many deep, rich tenors I had heard as I walked the pilgrim's road. Perhaps I had my bleeding heart on my back, not just on my snotty sleeve. He gave me a deep chocolate smile and I gave him a watery one. He disappeared into the forest ahead. I can still remember his sad hobgobliny face

I left the road for a call of nature. There was a much-overgrown track of four-wheeled wood-cutter's ruts sunk into the soft, sodden black earth amongst the heather and brambles. I stumbled along it for a little while then used the roots of a pine tree to pull myself up out of the quagmire and thorns and into the wet, silent mustiness. I squatted there amongst the ants and tiny silver moths and was tempted to stop longer. Much longer.

The undergrowth tucked in around me. Ivy hung down like ropes. My breathing was tight and sore with crying, and a thousand stories were clammering to be heard, jostling in from my memories and deeper in the mould of my life. I didn't want to hear them. They came from the deep, bloody, hot places where crazy women form fairy stories to explore the unexplainable. Just at that moment I wanted to hold my head in my hands and howl.

I closed my eyes, laid my head back against an old black pine with its dragon scales. I submitted. For a while there was only the thick, deep soup of leaf mould, the slow rot of bark and whistle of pine-needle breeze and then from it, into the soft steam of my slowing breaths, crept the weird witchy *meiga* and her court of hobgoblins to tell me an ancient tale.

'There was a time as you know,' I heard them whisper with a voice of rain and riverbed, 'when these woods were silent and eerie, their morality not mastered by humans. Broad-faced men travelled the barer ridgeways above or the stony riverbanks after the deer and chopped back the forest to carve out a farm. Only women snuck in amongst the bushes for berries and honeycombs and birds' eggs and found themselves in the secret places. Some lingered there even when church bells began to ring out and grew wise as scented men passed by in clean white cloaks with crosses swinging and staffs puncturing the warm, wet ground.

'The women of the woods,' the red-eyed *meiga* said, 'did fine without priests and knights and money lenders and grunting, sweaty farmers and marketplace gossip. These women instead made friends with the bears and vixens and their own wild bodies. They had all that they needed. When they came, loose wrapped, into the villages, little girls would stare at them from under eaves and see the shameless swing of their bodies and another way of being female and notice the ill humour of their own fathers till the witchy woman had gone with a still, swaddled bundle in her herb basket. And they would notice that at these times the women in the village were quiet at the washing pool. A smell of strong herbs wafted round the housewife's petticoats for a while. Sweet smoke slipped up into the hayloft mattresses where young women slept in their smooth white skin and dreamed of princes. And sometimes a little girl would whisper, "Who is that, Mama?" and sometimes her mother would answer, "Shhh, sweetheart! That's the Witch Princess. Don't let your father know she was here." And their mothers smiled as they swept their flagstones clear of ants and watched the witchy woman return to the woods. And the brown-eyed men would bolt shut the *hórreo* and the byre and check their women were headscarved by the hearth because they knew that once a young bride from this village had gone with her black curls flying into the woods and never come back.

'But,' said the meiga, 'the mothers smiled because they knew a different story and this is the one I will tell you now.'

The tree bark was warm. It must have been that I had drifted off to some kind of sleep or weird hallucination. I really don't know what.

'Once upon a time a beautiful young woman who was clever with fungi and herbs and music decided that a life of grunting, sweaty men and gossip and pumpkin patches was not for her, so she set aside her pretty headscarf and went into the forest by an ancient track full of silver moths out of sight of monasteries and classrooms. The little brown bears and the golden weasels and the red vixens welcomed her and said she was their Witch Princess and loved her and made her feel special. They built her a hut of broom and gorse and clay. My hobgoblins brought her a cauldron from the emerald riverbed and the wildcats sneaked in to lie at the hearth on a rug of river rushes. And she grew round and hot and wise and pleased herself. And the animals of the forest were grateful for her cleverness, and she was brave for them and strong for them and tireless for them because they loved her and made her feel special.

'One starry October night the Wolf Prince came courteously calling. Tall and hairy and handsome, she welcomed him and in he came. The Witch Princess returned to her hearth and his clean, dry man smell came with her.

'The Wolf Prince looked down his long nose at the beautiful Witch Princess, and with a long, low moan, asked if he could bite her.

'The Witch Princess looked at his reflection in her cauldron and stirred it with a smile.

'His fangs disappeared in the watery wrinkles. His ice blue eyes disappeared in the blood-red swirls. All she saw was freedom and forgiveness.

'The Witch Princess arched her smooth white neck to him and it shone in the moonlight. She said not a word.

'The Wolf Prince bit with precision, the marks he left with perfection, the image in her mind sublime. He wanted to lick her, howl for her, fight off the pack for her and roll over for her. He made from his guilt something archetypal, allegorical and it tasted like joy and she knew that it would,' said the *meiga*, 'because she had heard the stories women have always told at the washing pool. The Witch Princess took the pain and put it quickly in her cache beneath the oak-tree roots of her mud floor amongst her other shining treasures to keep its meaning secret from him. Now it belonged to her, not the Wolf. Looking down into her cauldron again, letting the surface smoothen again, she saw reflected the soft skin now released from his retreating fangs and knew it to be hers, not his.

'From under her tar-black curls, the Witch Princess looked up at the Wolf Prince watching over her and saw what she had done to him.

'The Wolf Prince, who had laughed through the woods with his pack of brothers and slipped past her home with its cats and cookery, was spellbound. Without a word, she had made him her slave. If she wanted blood for her cauldron, it would be hers. If she wanted beauty, he would give it to her as two garnets at her throat. If she wanted pain to conquer, great gulps of living to breathe, myths to cage and capture, marks in her skin to remember him by, he would have to give them to her just with an arch of her sweet white neck towards him. And when he went off hunting, he left her singing from her flared pink nostrils to her curling pink toes and everywhere in between,' the *meiga* said. 'The men in the village would hear him howl and think it power and him the leader of the pack and reach for their wives.'

I turned in my dream and asked the *meiga*, 'Did she never go back to washing pools, find a place amongst their happy endeavours, sing in their choirs, weave clever stories for their children?'

And the *meiga* laughed and her red eyes burned bright as she told me, 'No! Never! Why would she? She had heard the weakness of his Wolf moan and knew that it was she who had drawn him out from skulking in the purple shadows as a dog to be crowned her consort so that she could rule amongst all the beasts with his hot breath at her ear.'[38]

The fear of dog was deep enough in me that his image in my head shook me awake as every nightmare dog has done since I was a child. I started, shot open my eyes. Sat up. What on earth?

Grumbling at myself for giving in to stupefying tiredness, shaking off utterly silly, self-indulgent dreams, I pulled myself down the bank, itching with ant bites, back onto the track, leaving the Witch Princess far behind in some ancient fiction. I'm no keener on fantasy than dogma. Perhaps I should never have allowed her a place in this story, but I don't know any other way to tell you this bit of the truth that swirled in my head on that strange disturbing day. As traditional tales often end: 'Here is my story. I've told it. Now in your hands I leave it.' I shan't mention it again. Don't ask me.

I'm not sure that the hamlet called Preguntoño does mean 'Big Question (only that *preguntar* does mean to ask one and adding 'on' or 'oño' to the end of a word sometimes makes a superlative). It seemed to me as I passed through, pulling myself out of my mood, that it would be an appropriate name. Pilgrimage begins and ends with Big Questions. So many pilgrims have walked this way meditating on the hugest conundrums that birth and life and death inevitably bring. You can't, I hope, walk the Camino without empathy, without feeling small, without a realisation that your little pebbles are minute burdens compared

38. https://books.google.co.uk/books?id=84zLCQAAQBAJ&print-sec=frontcover&dq=marina+warner+beast+blonde&hl=en&sa=X-&ved=0ahUKEwii3PPO7azPAhVVF8AKHQN4CAQQ6A-EIHjAA#v=onepage&q=marina%20warner%20beast%20blonde&f=false

to the visions of hell that others have carried with them. By this stage you are nearing where you can kneel in whispering distance from St James with your sins or your wishes or your gratitude. Big Questions must have come to mind for many pilgrims through the centuries.

Beside the church in Melide which features on a thousand-Euro note and is a worthy photo stop, I had met a family whose daughter had been walking the whole Camino from the border with France. Two months beforehand her toes had been the first to emerge from a year-long coma and now she was on pilgrimage. She'd wanted to go to Jerusalem but, like many others through the centuries, had been persuaded that the Apostle's tomb would suffice and be safer. Her parents had been due to walk with her but her mother broke her own toes two days before they set off from Pennsylvania. They had come with her but while she still walked, they hired a car and could only drive to meet her at end-of-the-day stops along the way where ancient track and modern highway cross. They had watched her nearly die four times on American healthcare and now each morning for two months they had watched in faith as she walked off for twenty miles into a foreign forest and prayed. Would they meet her again at the other side?

One day, high on a lonely stretch of farm land, a Spaniard hurried past me, head down into his mobile phone telling someone that a girl was crying and crying and would not stop. His way clearly felt a long separation from where he belonged, even though this was his country. Why was she crying? Should he run to her?

We are united by the road and, in respect for the diversity of pilgrims past and present, we each are allowed to ask our own Big Questions even if they are very small compared to others. They slide past us, a sushi bar of raw flesh and emotion – some of sad love and regret but many delicious and delightful, all delicately seasoned with the clean meadow-combing wind from across the purple wooded hills. Camino is full of thankful, celebratory people for whom the scattering birch leaves are confetti. '*Jubilado*' is the Spanish word for retired. Many people have left responsibilities far behind and are open to new lives, whatever they may be. Hurrah! Jubilations! What next?

You can pick a companion for the next hill and others you can just greet and let go on. Nationalities disappear but we don't all have to be the same. We all call '*Buen Camino*', whatever our accents. Some people like me take painful little steps, others, like the old hippy I met from California with the big jaw and soppy eyes, lope along with the easy stride of a saggy big dog. He and his wife made me think of being too young to go to meet these lovely peace-loving people with flowers in their hair back in the 1960s. Are you going to San Francisco? Can I come with you?

I met Taylor and 'Swift' again, calling out to me 'Hey, Alison' from under an apple tree where they had slept the night. We criss-crossed paths many times with the fabulous South African eighty-year-old in the wide-brimmed scarlet hat and coat and lipstick. On a small arched bridge, a young Spanish school boy sang, 'I wanna walk like you, talk like you, ooooh ooooh ooooh', and I sang back about being human too-ooo-oooo and danced along the path. What does it mean to be us?

On Camino, there are so many fellow souls caught up in the current that you have to make space for your own big questions, dropping back into a place between bends where you can have the orange bracken and the brambles and the black pines to yourself. There you can sink deep between the mossy walls beneath the bright shining fields and be hugged by the cool clean dome of the forest. This is good, true ancient Spain far from the Moorish blood of the desperate stargazing deserts and far from the fascist filth of the barracks and the toreadors' arenas.

In this rich green space, there are no dust-angry black bulls and the cows are fat and brown and barely give you a stupid eyelashed blink as you walk through their yards. There are no gypsy boys with their eye on your purse. There is just you and the slowly moving sun in the heavens and the cheerful little yellow arrows silently keeping you safe. When you feel that you have carved out enough space ahead of the companionship of the slowest and way behind the fittest, you can stop and breathe and take a drink and a photo. You come home with a camera full of memories of the many beautiful places where you smiled in the sunshine. The dark duendes on the steep, dark climbs don't show in the pictures, any more than the knights and princes, saints and sinners of my thoughts, the *meigas* and wolves of my dreams. Overall, my memories of Camino will be of the ecstatic power of human relationships, not tears, though sometimes those do still prick my nostrils with harsh fingers.

Halfway through that fourth day of twisting climbs and dark mysteries between Arzúa and Arca, I reached yet another summit and paused to wipe my nose and breathe. I lifted my head.

A perfect globe of dandelion clock caught the bright light outside the dark, tunnelling track and offered to tell me how long I had been walking back to Santiago. I stopped and dropped my pack and contemplated it. With the magic of Camino, it was this delicate, dying flower which chimed out most loudly amongst all the songs and words of the week. This fragile seed head on a hilltop, not cathedral gold, is the image that is staying most unfaded in my memory of the Way of St James now my watch has started again and the hours that I have been home are tick-tocking me ahead till Monday's modern world. It is the single moment of all the Camino that was most perfect. Though the lightest, most transient of things, that dandelion told me more than any piece of paper ever could. My body was at its strongest yet. Fully alive, my survivor's lungs stretched, my aching heart pounded, my white skin glowed, adventurer's adrenalin rushed. Memories had flooded other hormones into hot places deep inside, my ecstatic head raced with words – history, poetry, music, politics, love, friendship – shared in the faculties and beds of the 1970s and 1980s and revisited on the roads this far and in that night in Arzúa.

It was time: to stop crying for a girl long gone off with the wolves.

It was time: to celebrate the woman I would return to be soon, am now in grey winter Scotland where family patiently waited in our higgledy-piggledy village. That's the only place this twisting road is heading, even if I walked there backwards.

Searching for my camera to capture that moment, my fingers found a small wave-rounded piece of stone shoved hard into a corner of my purse beneath some crushed herbs. Into my hand popped the little heart from the beach at home. My daughter's little pebble, its rediscovery perfectly timed.

It was time to understand where I was actually going. Day 5, I was walking back to where I belong.

I can see from my pilgrim's passport that after Preguntoño and before Arca (which is also O Pino), we stopped at the Lugar de Taberna Vella, where their stamp shows a Gallego *hórreo*, and at Cafeteria Andaina, where the stamp is of a painter's pallet. They are blurred memories of buying a banana to justify a toilet stop and refreshing ourselves with coffee or fruity ice lollies and not resting long. Camino goes relentlessly from one place, wherever you start, to another: Santiago. It's a one-way street. At the end, whatever way you have come, neither St James nor the more ancient spirit of the duendes can keep you there for ever. You will go home, and home for me is Scotland and the happy place I ended up because in 1978 I would not ring Miguel for help.

It is where my beautiful blonde girl who found that pebble sits waiting with Joe, who never questioned my going and who knows me right down to my creaky bones and hottest, sweatiest corners and still loves me. I have Joe to remind me of anything that I have forgotten or misremembered in most of the years since 1978. I never completely lost sight of his strong, blue-eyed tenderness and trust, nor of the daughter he gave me – their picture together at the railway station shone out from my smartphone every single time I switched it on. I was never faithless. I am glad I found this second chance of lifelong love. It is decades since we were strangers. He put me back together again after my first failed marriage in the dying days of the 1970s, made me feel special, travelled with me into the twenty-first century and gave up all of his familiar life to make one for us here because it would make me happy. I was torn litter on the edge of the gutter when he met me in 1981. He made me feel like a witch princess.

26 October 2018
Feeling like a visiting queen I allowed myself to be poured a glass of fine Albariño from the ice bucket. 'You love your husband very much don't you?' he asked, acknowledging my great good fortune. I could not deny it. There is no room in my life for another man. Not even this one.

From Barcelona in autumn 1978, I had taken my job deep in inland Catalunya. But I was already creeping back to Scotland by wintertime. Despite Miguel's unexpected call to me in Balaguer, I took the telegrammed offer to get home before Christmas and, by April, marry for the first time the boy from whom he might have saved me if I had called.

On 23 December 1978, I left the house in Balaguer at four in the morning, passed the town house of a cardiganned and crucified matriarch and her gallant son, past the closed-up language school now looking for a new English teacher for next term. A man with a stout stick and a huge, pink-bottomed hog was caught in the frozen neon gloom as I reached the bus stop across the rebuilt bridge over the Riu Segre which reconnected post-Civil War Spain and I to our futures.[39] Balaguer was dirty neon orange and yellow and black.

I slept and woke and found the coach passing through a purple predawn olive grove carpeted in lilac snow, its trees etched black talons, angry at my leaving Spain. I flew over the Pyrenees, snowy beneath me, and dozed on a freezing train-station bench somewhere in northern England, determined not to stop till I was home. I caught the milk train to Edinburgh, where no one lifted me off the ground with welcoming kisses at the station. A few months later I passed a murdered hooker's funeral on the way to my wedding in Dundee. On a Scottish honeymoon in the middle of nowhere, my groom wouldn't consummate our marriage as I had forgotten my pill and he was scared of my fertility.

Married life began on April Fool's Day but I didn't notice. He said that even if our marriage lasted a year, it would be worth it. He was wrong but I didn't hear it. He didn't want children, ever. I didn't listen. We set off to a new life in London having made vows which were meant to last for ever.

But promises made amongst broken dreams are not made safely. My new husband never lifted a hand to my snivelling nose again but set about dismantling me from head to toe by what he called honesty and then tossed me aside because domesticity was not poetic enough for him even without a pram in the hall. Marriage was unilaterally ended within nine months. I was the fallout. My husband was no Portuguese crown prince, never to be parted from his Inês de Castro, the girl who started life – like I started Camino – in Sarria. No epic tragedy for me

39. https://en.wikipedia.org/wiki/Balaguer

– head cut off before my children's eyes, corpse finely dressed
and propped up in the throne room, vassals ordered to pledge
loyalty with a mustachioed kiss to my dead hand. No, I was just
told it was over one morning in a ground-floor flat in shabby
London suburbia under the Heathrow flight path in the last
grimy throws of the Cold War. My husband generously took
time to tell me every detail of what was wrong with me, then,
as a slightly belated Christmas present, told me he had to go,
without waiting for our first anniversary.

Or actually I had to go.

I could sleep on my brother's freezing kitchen floor or come
home each day of 1980 till I found my husband gone, as was
his plan – if that is what you'd call it. My instinct as he told
me our marriage was over, non-negotiable, not worth even a
year, was of course to book a single ticket to Spain. To exit
through an airport or station into a sky full of swifts and hot
dust with a yellow road stretched out for my making, to shake
my messy head and look out through kohl-lined eyes and feel
brave enough to fight off giants – that would always be my
chosen way out.

But it was a ridiculous old dream. I had no money and not
enough confidence to put one foot in front of the other. To get
passport and rucksack I would have to walk back through my
husband's door. I chose my brother's floor.

At twenty I had had a slightly bloody but pretty nose, a full
purse and a hot, exciting Spanish road to adventure ahead of me,
to find my knight banker or crown prince or duende to inspire
a poetic future in nearly democratic Spain. Now twenty-two,
couch-surfing and in too much debt to travel, unemployed and
disassembled, all of me ugly, I staggered a bit, went crazy a bit,
got angry.

I went on marches for women's right to choose and not to
be blown apart by Cold War missiles. I hung out with bitter
lesbians, sold my soul in little bits, indulged a lot, submitted

sometimes, fought now and then, blew a few brain cells where memories of something more poetic had been stored. Strange sweet smoke swirled. My nostrils flared with something more astringent than eucalyptus. Wolves howled around me. I claimed my right to anaesthetise myself with lovers just as men do. It was something I was good at when there was nothing else. I talked my way into – and accidentally out of – brain-rotting job after mind-numbing job, refusing to sufficiently kowtow to the suits who dictated to me their letters about deals and deadlines and drudgery. I worried my old dad a little but not too much and never went back to Spain for a long, debt-ridden decade except in tormented dreams of running through Santiago's lanes.

On visits back to Scotland once a year, Dad would try to connect with me, if not through loving embrace, then through conversation about Lluís Llach or Lorca or the Tuna that we had revelled in when I was a student and traveller and he lived dusty road adventures through me or my brother. Now I just felt guilty for having forgotten what he had paid for me to study, for having nothing interesting to say anymore to a man who lived safe amongst the cover of books. My less-than-lofty life on the street corner was not a topic for gentle intellectual discussion.

I never made a call to Miguel. His world was long forgotten.

Nights in London were too polluted to see the stars and I forgot how to write sad lines. Daily life was a metaphor for nothing. I slept a lot, like in Barcelona, to save money, and face. Filthy, dangerous city days squashed me underfoot. Spain was an irrelevance to the daily grind. Yet somehow it filled my dreams.

Night after night and off and on for years, my sleeping head was filled with a desperate careering down high-walled, granite-paved alleyways.

Santiago in the Field of Stars! It was, as always, shining wet in the lamplight. I flung myself towards its centre, turning at sharp angles through sculpted squares and colonnaded walkways, past silver fountains and solemn cypress trees, welcoming inn doorways and down tunnelling steps under mossy arches. I must get there… I must be in time… if I was in time I wouldn't miss… I never knew what except it was more important than one mere boy. I ran, arms flailing, feet thumping on gleaming stone, chest heaving for air, heart racing. Headscarved old ladies were startled and stumbled as I overtook them. Dogs barked from gated gardens and ran awhile beside me under the ivied walls. Rainwater splashed as my bare feet caught the gutters full of autumn leaves. I would wake sweating in my tiny bedsit where London cabbies' brakes screeched all night and drunks dirged their way home in the predawn. I would stagger bleary-eyed into cheap market-stall clothes, damp down my hair, light a fag for breakfast, paint on a smile, add the confusion of the night to my already befuddled days and keep on pretending to know my way through London street life. And fail, always fail.

But the crazy, twisted, convoluted road that I really travelled, from which a phone call from Barcelona to Miguel in Santiago might once have diverted me, took me to meet Joe. This sweet giant of an Englishman who sits in his socks in the other room now with white in his beard, watching snooker now, gave me my power back. He rebuilt me bit by bit from my feet up with courtesy and lechery and charm which made my eyelashes flutter and eyebrows arch and nostrils flare. Joe being Catholic, we pilgrimaged to a monastery on the road to Canterbury, and me being lost he became my tender God. I was proud for a decade to sacrifice everything to him and his close-knit pack of brothers and nothing else mattered. We partied like royalty as if it was his birthright and slid between stars of stage and screen.

December 2016–18
He drives through the nightmare neon night as blood flows unclot-
ted. He cries with our daughter. He cleans the sheets again, counts

the pills, lies about his optimism. He cooks to tempt my chemo-soiled palette with protein and carbohydrate and slow cooks the one vegetable I can still digest. He counts depleted money, shops cautiously, collects good wishes. He scrubs ink off the furniture. He loads and unloads the car with paintings. He takes my hand and leads me the way to the stars as an astrologer predicted. He drills and hammers and fetches and carries. He takes happiness from my weird way of getting through. He offers to free me to emigrate to Spain should I wish to. For thirty-five years he keeps us on the road.

History and poetry and politics were a more irksome mix in Thatcher's Loads-a-Money 1980s London than in Santiago de Compostela in 1977 and were more of a bore to my new English friends than to my lost Gallego ones. I tucked away my anthologies of Lorca and Neruda, Laurie Lee and Rosalía de Castro. I met Joe and my new companions in Notting Hill bars not, as Mum had recommended, in theatres and art galleries. Conversation did not turn to Picasso's *Guernica* nor Gaudí's Barcelona nor Dalí's Catalan coast. It was the 1980s and Joe was on the property ladder in Notting Hill.

When my bedsit flooded from someone else's blocked toilet, I moved out and in with him to a nice maisonette with a handkerchief-sized garden within hearing distance of Carnival. His wardrobe was an obsessively dominated rainbow of muted pastels and pinstripes, and a crucifix hung by the door. That we were like chalk and cheese felt like adventure, which always turns me on. Jobs were there for the taking and adventure could be found in the easiest of deals. We danced dirty then cleaned ourselves off and paid the bills. We travelled and saw the world – even three nights of luxury in the Parador in Santiago to put my dreams to sleep. I could get a quick fix of Hispanophilia any time I liked just by popping down to Garcia's on Portobello Road and stocking up on Manchego cheese and tinned white asparagus. I taught him to relax, put his feet up, loll on a couch at the end of a day and not feel guilty. I made him happy. I try to still.

We partied in 1989 as if it was 1999 and once the Wall was down took democracy for granted. We played dangerous city games or sailed out to the English countryside in his beautiful cars. We saw none of it as poetic but didn't care. Poetry was a decade behind me now. If I succeeded he took pride and if I failed he didn't notice, and I adventured into a career where I could use my luck and my clever tongue and keep my integrity. I had seen more than I could have learnt from the pages of my parents' newspapers and walls of books. My wide world of ideas and my tastes of bad could do good for girls who had gone way further off the track than I who had started somewhere more comfortable. The skills I had learnt to blag my way onto a flight home from Santiago without a ticket, find a teaching job through a call to Balaguer, get my dinner paid in Barcelona, turned out eventually to make me a fine charity fundraiser. Joe helped me know I could be valuable, not like litter on the road.

One day after more than a decade of unfettered fun, Joe and I found we just wanted to trust and make a baby so we did. I never had to brew up prayers for fertility. We gave her my Catalan pen pal as godmother so she would have an open invitation to Spain. We brought her in my arms, just three months old, to visit the foothills of the Pyrenees to be blessed by Spanish sounds and smells where the wild horses race and eagles look down at valleys of pines. We packed up Joe's familiar life and came here, nineteen years ago, to the North Sea, in time for the new millennium, and she went to the village school and found a place to belong. And this is where we all belong now. My dad had the funeral of a very Presbyterian atheist. My mum still has her books and newspapers and her memory.

Once more though, years later but before my Hannah was grown, now in my forties but still capable of madness, once more before these comfortable times I live in now, Spain reached out to me and made me think again.

There was, mea culpa, one other name, seldom said now, that I found again on the web. Bass player. IT nerd. Once a student with me in Edinburgh now in Massachusetts. Once but no longer a husband. Never been to Spain or anywhere very much that didn't meet his 'it'll all turn out badly' view of the world. Didn't know a good thing when he saw it. Mementoes of that name don't lie on my lap now as I type – its secrets are burnt and buried. With one phone call to Santiago, it is a name that could have been buried deeper. But once again, Andy, the name for an ex-husband – a boy that, in 1978, I left behind as I headed for Spain and then left the Peninsula for – did recross my path. Once again, his presence in my world slapped me and sent me back down a nightmare road.

When bullies at work were telling me 'you don't belong in our team – you don't walk like us, talk like us', I had begun again to wonder who I was. I spun out a thread across the Pond and into the wide blue yonder on the World Wide Web. Frustrated with adjustment from cosmopolitan London to close-knit Scottish village life, wild-loving to decent parent-hood, city leaders to small-town business folk, I had wondered what the Free Bird had fledged into. And in contacting Andy I remembered. I thought myself healed, was tempted to pick at an old scab, where old blood had hardened to heal an old tenderness below. Looking for a sense of direction for the years ahead, I looked backwards to where he had left me.

Had I had any sense at all in loving Andy before I ran to Barcelona with his gift of a bloody nose? Had I been tempted back after *Día de la Constitución* and down a Dundonian aisle by nothing worth sacrificing my Spanish dreams for? Tripping down memory lane with Andy on the threads of the Web at the beginning of a new millennium only served to remind me that by the dawning of the 1980s, he had dismantled me piece by piece.

It occurred to me as I walked my Camino last week that he was not big enough to handle the whole of me – perhaps he had had to break me down to package me for his easy use. Unsure of his identity as man and father's son, he had to undermine my fertile, female sexuality. I can see it this way now that I have been walking backwards through my life on this Camino. He was no Galician giant shifting menhirs for fence posts. He gave me nothing but small sharp pebbles to carry. They have been working holes in my pocket as I have walked. I think I have dropped them for good now.

His words had worked their way into me when I was twenty-one like a piece of grit in a sweaty sock. I remember still. Newly married, he had taken time to tell me of a girl in his office who had impressed him with boasts of boyfriends' premature ejaculation. He had explained to me that I was not attractive enough to have the problem.

He had made me listen: 'I don't like your hair. I don't your eyebrows. I don't like your ears.'

'Don't you like my eyes?'

'No.'

They watered.

'I don't like your cheeks. I don't like your nose.' He pointed his guitarist's manicured finger at it. I had thought I had quite a pretty nose.

'But you like my lips?'

'No. I don't like your neck,' he said though I arched it towards him. 'I don't like your shoulders.'

'Not even these?' I asked pathetically, hands on my twenty-one-year-old breasts.

'Not particularly.'

That was a surprise.

Not flattish belly, not tight round bum, not short legs, not slim ankles, not neat feet, not little pink toes. He took the time. He left nothing unexamined. He left me shredded.

2017

Toenails infected, thighs punctured, belly sliced, breasts sagging, armful of intravenous piping, tooth chipped, nose bleeding, eyelashes and eyebrows gone, hair thin and still I know my body has more beauty than ugliness because from it I shine. I see it mirrored in the eyes of those who love me.

I had gone on, from Andy to a bed on my brother's floor to Joe's Notting Hill flat and at last to our higgledy-piggledy Scottish village, and under Joe's more lasting spell I had forgotten. Hearing from Andy again I remembered how he had left me.

Newly in the rocking and rolling metropolis, musical fame had not immediately dropped into his lap and it had been my fault. I was not, after all, his Muse. Just over a year after I'd left Spain for him, four days after Christmas, nine months after our wedding, he had told me I was too domesticated to belong in his life. I was nearly making him happy, which was not poetic. No more poetic, it turns out, were my brother's kitchen floor nor my dead-end jobs nor a nostril of cocaine, but they were an improvement on Andy's pathetic attempt at being my soul mate.

For a decade, what money I earned went down the plughole of one tiny bedsit after another, into the ticket machines on the London Tube or over bars and never into tickets to Spain. Meanwhile oil prices exploded and Hispania did nothing to free itself. All that mattered was the fact of democracy.[40] The ancient countryside was abandoned for the forlorn hopes of modern city living built on creaky old foundations. Hard

---

40. http://countrystudies.us/spain/52.htm

adjustments were made to what the world calls freedom.[41] From Santiago Pope John Paul II called to all of Europe to recover our ancient soul, find ourselves, and 'be yourself. Discover your origins. Give life to your roots', and because he did so from that place above the tomb of St James, travelers began coming again along the old European roads under the oak trees. At last the 1980s boomed and Europe brought its tourists, its rules, vigour, its great sweeping roads across the ridgeways and through the forests, over and under its ancient stories. Spain changed and far away I changed and forgot what it had been to me.

Twenty-five years silence, then one more time like a fool, I had let the tragedy that was Andy insinuate his weaknesses into my life. I cried on my Camino last week because for that I was to blame. An ever-reckless spirit had in my forties, by digging up his memory, sent me slipping and crashing off the road. The weight of newly being breadwinner, mother, pretending to be a normal village wife had been supportable. The bullying workplace had been bearable. But being back in touch with him awoke my daemons, my personal duendes. Guilt for my weakness tripped me up and drowned me in the gutter. Months washed by our cottage by the sea and I never saw the days flicker past through the skylight above my head, so drained was I left.

Following a map of memories, I went back down the path that Andy had beckoned me down when I had caught the bus from cold, nearly Christmas Catalunya to marry him. I was again the ghost he had made of me at twenty-one: artless, worthless, soulless, pointless. In a new millennium and in mid-life crisis, I contemplated losing everything again – job: because of the bullies; home: because of the mortgage (unpayable if I did not carry on as breadwinner); daughter: because of the bad temper (she would be taken to be cared for differently); Joe,

---

41. http://www.nytimes.com/1982/11/10/world/pope-in-spain-urges-europe-to-be-beacon-of-civilization.html

who had saved me back then (because what loyal, loving husband would want a crazy wife like me?).

The hell hounds came out of my dreams and into real life on every lovely Scottish farm track where I tried to seek gentle skies to walk under for peace. The dogs, of course just working Scottish collies, in my broken head were fear and doubt come alive and answerable only to grunting, labouring men. They chased me back into bed for months to growl at me there. I was not going in the right direction. As I walked the Camino last week I remembered the crippling fear of their farmyard drooling. All that I was when Andy had left me was traceable back to a path I took out of Spain in 1978 and could have avoided in a phone call from Barcelona to Santiago. Regrets? I have had a few.

I went on eventually, of course. I pulled myself out of bed and stepped out again into the rest of my forties and got a good job in Aberdeen and never looked back at the slithery little small-town fishes behind me, bullying each other in their little ponds. I wouldn't otherwise be here writing these words with Joe and Hannah safely downstairs. If friendless, unrespectable, mad, I wouldn't have raised the money for my Camino. I wouldn't have followed Linda out onto the yellow road and down through Santiago's alleyways last week. I got well again and the little black dogs skulked back into the farmyards and I closed the door on Andy with a firm 'Goodbye', leaving the memory of him way back in the 1980s where he belonged. Joe understood and knew he wasn't threatened. Now in a new millennium, Andy was only a ghost of a tragically flawed boy I once knew. I burnt his letters.

When I was well enough to travel, my lovely Catalana pen pal brought me and my little family to the warm familiar bosom of Spain to lick my wounds, which always heal better in the sunshine with a soundtrack supplied by the keening empathy of gypsies. They know every pain felt by humankind. My soul mates, Joe and Hannah, and I took the cheap package of a family room in a grotty hotel. Looking for real Spain, we watched the St James' Day fireworks on the beach and went hand in hand up the little alleyways less travelled off the promenade along the Costa seafront.

We found an olive-oily snake-headed gypsy with a linen-clad belly and his own bar and a guitar as much part of his body as his gold-toothed smile and his music rose from the floor tiles through his shiny-shoed feet in the warm frangipani night. My pale-skinned little daughter dressed in nylon flamenco danced with plastic castanets, my husband laughed and showed his lovely teeth and hugged me close and my heart soared again to the sounds of fingers on strings and the smell of freshly showered Spanish man.

I didn't laugh at my wee girl when she said she thought the gypsy loved her for I remembered that Spanish love is a very serious matter. I let the Iberian spirit curl up around Joe and me like a sun-gleaming snake and entwine us both, reminding him of wild Ibizan summers with his brothers before he ever came calling for me. It soothed us with its deep-licking heat. It crept into our daughter's life, leaving a shimmering path in her memory for ever. She can follow it if, one day, she wishes.

Knowing better who I belong beside, I left Andy's name far behind, this time for ever across the cold ocean trench and got on with career and marriage and middle age. But it seems I have not quite learnt to stop popping names into webs.

The nearly November rain outside keeps me still looking back down a road on which I have learnt an awful lot with Spain's help. I left my little stone heart on the waymarker there on the hill above Preguntoño near the dandelion clock between Arzúa and Arca with part of Miguel's question answered – my way had led to this warm fireside via those slim gypsy thieves in Barcelona's Plaça Reial and Andy's slaps around my pretty nose. It had not been my way – my manner of doing things – to call for help from a one-summer Spanish lover – 'Hi, remember me? I'm the girl you shagged last summer. I've been stupid and got my purse stolen. Gonna lend me some cash?'

Lost in Barcelona, I thought that was the only identity I would have had to pick up the phone with, to reintroduce myself to him. Lost in London later, that was still how I saw myself, thanks to Andy. I never knew till now, right now, that at least in Santiago I was remembered so much more happily than that. I did not think, under Andy's influence, that I was so very much more than a body. I had forgotten the difference between pleasure and happiness. I had forgotten, till now, that Miguel was my friend, which sometimes lasts longer than being my lover or my husband. I had left happiness behind in his life and gone on unseeing that I had always been someone who could have made that call. My way was not with Miguel but nevertheless he was a friend who truly cherished the knowing of me. He had not needed my feet to be on Iberian soil in order for him to find his direction. I had left enough of myself behind with him in Santiago. My destiny it turns out – my way – was waiting for me in a Rolls Royce parked on the Gloucester Road in London, with at the wheel my Joe, who turned out to be all three – lover, friend and husband, and, besides, father for my own nineteen-year-old girl. My way was not the Way of St James with its banker knights.

The dandelion clock above Preguntoño had told me it was time. I left my pebble and hurried on back down the yellow mud track to my tall Englishman, who I would run to at the airport, baggy and saggy with feet like concrete. My lover, friend, husband for thirty-three of these thirty-eight years would lift me high in the air and I would safely give him my pretty lips and he would fold me in his bigger, safer arms, put his face to my neck and make my choices clear. Everything else was behind me.

Camino does not end, however, in the hills between Arzúa and Arca and there was plenty more walking to do with all this realisation carried with me. The land was still steeply folded and it is not a gentle slope down to Santiago for anyone. The ruts in the slope down were deeply carved out by rain and feet and history. Great crags of granite jutted out, grey striped, in our way, threatening to trip us. While I was now surging onwards in the love of two good men, pebble left behind me, blister free, strong of knee and often at or near the front of the pack, others were suffering.

Stacey, in real pain, hit a wall and lost the pretence of Glaswegian bounce or any of the point of Camino at all. None of it apart from the camaraderie had been a joy to her, not physically or spiritually, nor emotionally. It had simply been a way to raise funds to help the work she did caring for others who would never know this kind of freedom to walk equally with the world. Linda was nearing the climax of her pilgrimage for Rick and was finding his tragedy and their love rising up to the surface of her Camino days however fast she walked to keep them at bay. Lucy the aspiring leader, a decade younger, was struggling to be strong for her as she learnt about what her beautiful white-haired mentor had survived. It was a strange twist in the journey at the morning coffee stop for this pack leader to burst through an unlocked toilet door in tears and for it to be speedy me who had arrived first. Strange that the next trembling person I held in my arms on this weird journey was her as she lost and then refound her very professional cool. What had been for me huge on this walk through the hills of Galicia was only huge for me.

My four hours with Miguel had only whetted my appetite to walk my nineteen-year-old steps through the city streets of Santiago. The nearer we got to the magical city which all pilgrims dream of reaching, the more my happy memories took over. It would be nice to sink lightly into happy explorations of all things Gallego. I would prefer it if the climax of my Camino were not a torture of questions.

When I set off from Scotland this autumn, I was not looking for a love affair nor any big answers, just a bit of poetry. I had dreamed of sitting happily with my back against warm granite in the Praza de las Platerías with the horse-headed fountain and hearing the Tuna play their mandolins and tambourines and sing to me about carnations and ribbons. I wanted to laugh under dripping vines and drink from white ceramic bowls and nibble at fresh sardines as big as herrings and try to translate romantic pop songs and silly jokes. I wanted to talk of when we had danced the night away in Spanish discos where spring in 1977 was always in the air, drunk Cuba libres and munched light, crisp churros and chocolate in the warm predawn when my feet were sore from dancing, not walking. I wanted to remember my romantic weekend of luxury at the five-star Parador in 1986 with Joe and to have Miguel's help to draw back all the details of 1977 that were easier for him to remember than for me because he knew the places and the times and the names and could make them come real to me again. I had wanted him to tell me how they had been and who I had been when I was nineteen and hadn't burnt out so many brain cells and I made people happy without realising. I had never meant to look backwards and analyse so much but to take the whole journey step by happy step without expectation of what would be around the next bend or over the next hilltop.

But we had made no promises back then and we had made none in Arzúa in 2015, and this was a twenty-first-century pilgrimage and not a medieval search for indulgence. Life is not about a replaying of old romances, and my Camino was not about falling into Miguel's arms outside the cathedral. He had a severely ill relative and responsibilities which outlast my visit. Just as I do. My pilgrimage end did not belong to him. My Camino was like everyone else's – about the achievement of putting one foot in front of another through the ups and downs, round the unseen bends, taking the rough with the smooth, the cliché and the unexpected. My Camino had always been about what I had lost or what I had safely treasured since, like my daughter, I had stepped out one nineteen-year-old morning. The nearer we got to journey's end, and with the happiest of my catching up with Miguel fresh in my mind, the more I thought about the details of that summer and the city that this pilgrimage was all about.

It had been a precious time, when I set off in 1977, though the year before had been the toughest in my lucky young life that far. My dad's heart attack, my abortion, another significant dead-end romance, a failed exam – they were really just a few pebbles that I carried with me through a lovely life. Otherwise I was, as I am remembered, a happy soul – born healthy, safe and able. That summer was easy for a girl who spoke the language fluently and had travelled. Santiago felt welcoming and enchanting from the start – in fact before the start.

The 1977 journal on my lap reads:

I could have been entering Edinburgh airport the landscape was so like lowland Scotland – largish fields, clumps of trees, small hills – green, grey granite, grey sky. Santiago is a town of winding streets with tall, thin flats along its narrow sides. Nearly all the houses have ornate balconies with geraniums growing on them. The roofs are red tiles. The houses are granite – either bare or sometimes whitewashed or painted green. The windows are in the Portuguese style, tall and narrow, opening out and panelled. Interspersed amongst these buildings are the enormous churches, schools, convents, law buildings in Romanesque, Plateresque or Pre-Renaissance styles, some with almost bare façades, just rows of windows and verandas along and little turret things along the top, all with enormous heavy wooden and iron doors, or covered in statuary, pillars, pilasters, towers and inscriptions.

I thought I had come across a barracks but it turned out to be a seminary. The foot soldiers of the Lord as well as the State.

> Everywhere there are statues of saints, all the clothes shops have wedding and communion dresses as their main window display and all the jewellers have rosaries and crosses and other silver and gold religious knick-knacks. There are many priests in the streets. Everywhere I am aware of religion, that this is a religious centre.

Can you hear my breathlessness, the Fine Art and Hispanic Studies student abroad?

> All over the place amongst the relief carving there are plants growing so that the grass seems to give the statues of the saints hair growing from their heads.

And my irreverence.

> There are no real suburbs but outside the main and old areas are lovely houses with gardens and painted white with red and white tiled roofs like the frills of a skirt – the tiles are red clay but painted white on the underneath and side so they look like red cloth frilled with white lace.

Spain flashes her metaphors at me even from her kitchen window.

> In one garden there were guinea pigs eating the grass and running freely on the lawn.

Spain is still a little strange even in this parochial little corner far from Europe.

There are none of the stark contrasts of the Barcelona streets here. There is no modern glamour and although there are rich and poor, the rich don't stand out as they do in Barcelona. For the one thing, the poor are agricultural not industrial poor and at least look a little healthier than the workers from the Badalona *barrios*. The old women here are fat with frowning, dirty brown faces, black stockings or socks, black boots like climbing boots, black skirt, cardigan, shirt and headscarf, long grey hair in a pigtail that looks as if it hasn't been undone in the last twenty-odd years, newspaper roll with a metal tub on top full of clothes and fruit and raw meat like some horrible stew. None of them are taller than 5'2".

The Spaniards, especially the women, do not think twice before raising their voices in argument while the Scots look on telling off a child as a reasonably private thing which reflects on their own character, especially if accusing a daughter of being 'loose' or 'forward'. Here they shout it not only at a child but to anyone who could possibly be a supporting audience.

What is and is not acceptable behaviour is very clear.

Unlike Barcelona, although inside the cathedral there is gold and silver, there is little to contrast it with – there are no beggars outside.

I was not one of the still-rare foreign pilgrims. I was coming to university, culture, language – not dogma, faith, confession.

It appears that there is more graffiti (political of course). As in Catalunya it is for freedom for the area, written in Gallego not in Castilian and much more than in Catalunya is associated with communism. There are more anti-monarchist slogans.

On the first day when I arrived at the Facultad de Filología which was in a pretty square in the old city, I had met Patty, a blonde Yank just about to leave. We went for drinks together and tapas of squid, mussels, ham, salted almonds and the best white wine I had ever drunk so she could pass on tips to me. She liked Spain but not its men, she said, who didn't take no for an answer. She'd had a knife drawn on her once, she said, when she had tried that response to a crass offer. I was surprised. It had not been my experience.

We were spotted by two blokes at the bar. I clocked and ignored them, having been taught well by Catalanas many years before. They called out compliments about her exotic white Anglo Saxon Protestant hair and hips, and she did not understand their coarse language, despite her recent Spanish lessons. She caught their eye and being free of guilt and common sense giggled straight back to them open-faced and welcoming of attention, apparently generous. Later, as she and I made our separate ways from the bar, I spotted them follow her and, fearing the worst, I turned and went back. By the time I caught them up, they were pinning her in a dark doorway. Now she had victimhood not flirtation in her eyes.

'Hello! Can I help you? My friend here doesn't understand Spanish,' I said on approach, human to human, lightly, using the language they understood.

'We only wanted to invite her to *tomar una copa*,' they replied, a little startled but still with wicked smiles.

'They say they want to ask you to go for a glass of something, a nightcap,' I translated, 'but the phrase is ambiguous.'

To be seen to be fair to both parties I left the choosing to her. 'Do you want to go with them?'

'Hell no,' she replied.

'My friend says thank you for the offer, but she doesn't know you and is tired and just wants to go to sleep. Thank you anyway.'

Treated like gentlemen, deflated, without my having shown the fear that they would, like dogs, have smelt, being unused to pretty young women who were something other than whores or Madonnas, the Spaniards lost their heat. Acting with the hurt honour which is so very Spanish, disillusioned and confused they left. Patty got on a plane the next day and took her bad experiences with her, leaving me to understand them better.

Before she left, she introduced me to Miguel. I thought him very young though he was six years my senior. I understood his world was smaller than mine, smaller than hers too. He tells me she never answered his letters from across the Pond.

The lovely old university buildings reminded me comfortably of Old Aberdeen or St Andrews or Edinburgh, and Santiago quickly put me at ease. I was put in the '*clase superior*' and found it mainly boring because I had learnt the grammar years before. I enjoyed the cultural lectures and film showings though: Luis Buñuel's *Viridiana* and Saura's surreal 1973 masterpiece *Ana y los lobos*, an allegory of Franco's Spain, heavy in man-fanged sexuality and conjuring up for its international audience the disturbance which Ana, the foreigner, brings to an orderly world of church and military.

Viridiana, though watchable elsewhere in 1961 when I was only three, had been released for the first time in Spain that very year when I was nineteen and only then because Franco was dead, his grip loosening and no longer able to fight its blasphemy. It was a privilege of that summer to be amongst the first to sit within kissing distance of St James, the state's holy patron, and watch this story of virginity and rape, crowns of thorns and last suppers, weddings and hangings, later to be recognised as one of the greatest films of all time.

I, at the time a Free Bird for whom the images had had no inbred power, reported that I found it corny and its symbolism over obvious. Nevertheless, it was with such surreal sexy metaphors of urgently releasing Spain that my head was filled that summer whether in classroom, bar room or bedroom. I slid from one space to the other freely, taking with me all that I was. Like Viridiana herself I was being educated in the realities of passion and politics and poetry all at once. Like Ana I disturbed the now too many decade-long mouldering equilibria of predatory machismo. Just a little.

The classes were full of equally confident West Germans, Swiss, Japanese, Australians and Americans who, unlike me, did not speak the language and who, also unlike me, felt the need to attend all the classes. On day one of my Santiago summer I had done a deal with Heidi, one of the Germans who had rented a room in the same *pensión* as me – '*Ja*! Good plan! We will check on each other each morning, *ja*?' – to make sure not to be unthinkably late for lessons. Whoever was up first (I wonder who that would be) would wake the other.

As it turned out, I gave up morning class and sleeping at the *pensión* and pretty quick moved in with Miguel, who completed my Gallego education. His flat had a room for his beloved photography, a closed-up room full of sad toys for the young son who stayed with his mum and a little joyless living room. Also a bedroom with a fountain outside.

We filled it with joy. We stayed in Calle Santo Domingo de la Calzada, named for the man who created the pilgrims' refuges. Both *pensión* and flat were on the steeply sloping modern streets which surround the old city on the hill.

At the end of the summer I found that Heidi had been religiously knocking on my *pensión* bedroom door to wake me up every morning, according to her programming – *ja*? It had never occurred to her to think I had thrown our sensible plans out of the window and walked off into a less sensible Spaniard-loving happiness. How surprised she would be to find that recklessness is still a force in my life so many decades after. When the lessons that I sat in on (when Miguel was at work) turned out to be boring, I stared out across the terracotta rooftops and soaring spires and wrote poems about love and revolution. I have them on my lap now, written on the back of envelopes or in the back of my jotter.

My journal from 1977 shows that I did attend a few language classes, did pick up some particularly useful phrases which caught my nineteen-year-old eyes.

A punto de caer las seis – it's about to strike six
A quemaropa – really close up
A tientas – feeling your way
A rienda suelta – free rein
No ha inventado la pólvora (he hasn't invented gunpowder)
    – he's not very intelligent
Coger alguien con las manos en la mesa – to catch
    red-handed
Estar con los brazos cruzados – twiddle your thumbs
Dares las de importancia – believe yourself very important
Vamos al grano – let's get to the point
Hasta el fondo – right in

Our teacher taught us to say '*Jesús, María y José y todos los santos sagrados y los doce apóstolos*' when someone sneezed (Jesus, Mary and Joseph and all the sacred saints and the twelve apostles). He regretted it when taking the class when he had a bad cold. The room thundered with our voices in response to each sneeze. Mainly Spaniards just say '*Jesús*' which causes less rumbustiousness.

Around the little bars of Santiago old and new town, I had soon belonged in an international gaggle that mixed with Gallegos, including Miguel and his friends. I was interpreter. The Spaniards were very dirty-mouthed for the squeaky-clean Americans. The vocabulary would hold me in good stead in Barcelona in years to come. The West Germans and Japanese complained politely about dirty glasses, squat toilets and other incomprehensible Iberian inefficiencies. The young Compostelans were more interested in the new freedom to gather and debate without having to count how many of them were there and allowed to congregate. The West Germans had no concept of growing up under fascism. The oppressed Gallegos lent much further to the left than any successful capitalist could comprehend. I could translate the words but could not fill in the gap in understanding between two nations whose dictators had been allies, whose young men and women did not know their own history. We were all young and white and secular and feeling free and looking forward and the debate was good-natured and wine-filled and stimulated our hungry minds and greedy bodies. Pleasure was equally to be had in a fat joint, a plump langoustine, a heaving orgasm, a burning liqueur or a jovial controversy – whichever came our way first. Franco was already dead and turning in his grave.

The world was also turning. The waiters were on strike and the town was jam-packed with police armed to the teeth. Everyone but them was looking forward. I was the Free Bird who sweetly tempted everyone to fly lighter and higher without Catholic guilt. I still am.

Jenny the Australian flew even further out. While her wild courage inspired me, it scared the boys – she didn't make them happy and Miguel, in Arzúa, remembered her with a shudder. While I had fixed up a nice room in a student *pensión* to store my stuff in and Miguel's modern flat to actually live in, Jenny found a stone barn in an apple orchard out in the kind of lush Gallego farmland I walked back through four days ago. It had lichen-splattered steps up one gable end and two rooms, including a basic kitchen for a farm labourer or Australian painter like Jenny. It smelt of warm hay and crumbly slate and tinkled with the sound of a dripping tap and beetles and mice in the old planks and hens amongst the fruit trees.

She unpacked the dope she'd smuggled in from Brazil in multiple Marlboro packets and the fairy Brazilian boy she was introducing to heterosexuality and the blue-dyed duckling she'd saved from a market stall and the Pyrenean mountain dog puppy. She stuck some carnations red as raspberries in a milk bottle and put them on the deep cobwebbed windowsill. She bought famously tit-shaped local cheese and fresh grey prawns from the Mercado de Abastos on the edge of the old town and fried them up just the way I ate them thirty-eight years later on the way to Arzúa. Her fingers smelling of the sea, she mooched around with thin French hippies and played guitar and never brushed her streaky Aussie hair. She was never still with anyone for more than a moment, always looking for the next adventure, the next splash of dazzling colour and twisted form that was extreme enough to paint. Coming from months in South America, Europe was too civilised for Jenny, even in this witch-ridden corner. I was awestruck. She terrified the pants off the Germans and Japanese, but not literally. For me there was, that summer, nothing on offer that could not be tried and revelled in as long as it made you smile, sounded great, tasted great – even if it was, like Jenny's kitchen, a bit grubby.

Miguel had a large coffee-table book of stunning glossy photos of the human body. Casually turning its foolscap pages one evening while he made up a terracotta cauldron of blue-flaming brandy-and-lemon *queimado*, I had found a perfect picture of an eight-week-old human foetus on a swab of cotton on an adult's hand – with fingers and toes, eyes and nose, head, shoulders, knees. Its beautifully formed truth slapped me hard. Another burden for my pocket. Ignorance of human biology had helped me with hard choices in the year just passed. I knew more of my father's heart than my own womb. Now I had lost that last shred of innocence. The baby I had sacrificed had been more than an inhuman blob spoiling my life.

Miguel and I shared modern reality in that city of medieval fantasy as the fountain in the square played out under the stars.

I still have early-morning pictures of me washing breakfast dishes in Miguel's kitchen with messy permed hair fresh from the kohl-smeared pillow and wearing one of his shirts. Beside him in his car I photographed him as we drove out into the eucalyptus forest on his days off, past emaciated men in carts with solid wheels and crones with vast piles of brushwood on their heads.

He took me to Rosalía de Castro's home and bought me her poetry and her feminism so that I could talk about her to Alicia on Camino thirty-eight years later with equal passion. We talked of how Galicia, like Ireland, was and always had been a land of tearful emigration with the brown earth's riches stored tight for the wealthy. It had fallen to Franco early in the Civil War then been ripped apart to fuel, with its dams and hydroelectricity, its eucalyptus timber,[42] the unrolling of his vision for one Spain. Then and now there are no young men in the farms along the Way.

He took me round bronze-age *castros*, the ancient hill villages Rosalía and tragic Inês are named after, and past the country villages where headscarved women scrubbed in communal laundry pools and down to the salty fishing villages where the *hórreos* are made of stone not wood. He took me up to the coast where castles still look out for Vikings and the wide rias remind me of the firths I grew up beside at home. We went down to Vigo where the smugglers' markets encrusted the shoreline with Marlboro and Rolex and transistor radios and trash from the wide Atlantic rollers. We went out to Fisterra and stared out beyond the end of the world we knew until the foaming sea spray chilled us with reality and we headed back to the cosy lanes of Santiago. Quick before the goddess of fertility caused either of us any more hassle.

---

42. http://www.pilipalapress.com/galicia.php#people_culture

24 October 2018
The pilgrims' way on from Fisterra bus-stop climbs slow and steady
to the lighthouse at the tip of the cape. The pine forest towers above
pilgrims seeking something greater than the legend of James, son
of Zebedee. Cliffs fall without respite to ever more distant depths.
No warmth of rolling pasture nor friendly oak shadow hugs tired
shoulders, but whatever the Atlantic decides we must submit to. This
is the Costa da Morte – the Coast of Death. So be it. It doesn't scare
me.

Miguel and I talked in Arzúa last week of those secrets in our
lives that make us more than strangers. He told me that he
had been drowning before we met in 1977, sucked down by
judgement. He had been lost, rejected for the career he wanted
because his marriage had failed, a sin not just to church but to
commerce in not yet democratic, far from secular, militaristic
Spain. His father had had no confidence in him, and for all
he knew his father was right. He had thought that catching a
wild, free foreigner in his bed would be a momentary anaes-
thetic. That, he said, had been the *macho* way of generations
before him. After I had gone, though, scatterbrained and messy
haired, he found I had left something behind, unseen amongst
the crumpled, kohl-stained sheets: an idea of something better.

What had begun as a summer adventure had changed.
There are two Spanish words for 'to be'. One – '*ser*' – is what
you inevitably irrevocably are. The other – '*estar*' – is for the
impermanent state in which you find yourself now. Are you
happy now? Are you a happy person? It appears I gave Miguel
happiness as a thing to be. I had walked away leaving happiness as his, owned by him to take inside himself, cultivate and

share insofar as he alone wished. I am nothing more to do with it. I came for adventure and I took it. I didn't spout guidance on how to find happiness like an Apostle's creed nor a guru's mantra nor a coach's pep talk. It wasn't from the rule book of the he-pack or the she-pack. It was just very simple, totally unspecial, healthy, lucky happiness. I had brought it from a Cold War bungalow full of art and fairy tales, noisy with atheism and democracy in a garden of wild Scottish imagination.

He said the lesson came from my ability to say 'I am' – 'I inevitably, irrevocably, permanently am'. I am a traveller. I am a sexual being. I am your equal. I am human too-ooo-oooo.

His world taught him 'you are'.

'Your father is a military man; you must go where we tell you – thirty-six times of starting again in a new town, never belonging.'

'You are a man – you must behave in this way.'

'You are a loose woman, too forward. You must be shouted at like this.'

'You are going to eat this chocolate off a *décimo* coin or you are going to be weak.'

'You are a bank employee. Your marriage has failed. Your career must fail too.'

With me he saw that he could go on his own journey, one never imagined when under the command of father soldier, father protector, father who didn't believe in his son. This wild spirit – this flibbertigibbet who flitted from Spanish summer to Spanish summer and back to her grandfather's coast – this little round Scottish brownie – me – had broken all the rules he knew. She was immune to the stinking spells lurking in the Apostle's shadow. She sprinkled disinfecting scorn upon them all:

Pert and impertinent girls don't ask pertinent questions?
Says who?
Testosterone, *machismo*, adrenalin: the fuels of leadership?
Pish!

Girls and boys cannot be friends *igualmente?*
I don't see why!
Your father's way is the only way?
I don't think so!
Only the compliant should progress? Dominators are winners?
I disagree!

Over the years that followed he had found that 'I am' spirit at all his crossroads, like a happy yellow arrow, pointing away from the duendes of dank, gossiping ditches, uphill to a sunny summit that he had thought too far and too steep. Through my sharing myself with him so naturally – asking nothing, knowing I wasn't staying, being responsible for myself, taking pleasure for myself, sure I would get to where I was going – he had found his own spirit walking beside me.

'Wherever our roads take us from now on,' he said, with force, 'I will never, ever forget that the happiness you brought that short summer carried me onwards.' He said it sang in his head, changing the rhythm of his life.

'I have realised,' he said to me aged sixty-two. 'that you can carry what you love about someone through thirty-eight years without seeing them.'

No love is less fang-filled and threatening. No such love tries to tell you who you are. Such love is friendship which builds you, not a spell which dissolves who you are.

---

26 October 2018
I listen like I never listen. Head in hand for extra concentration. Ears tuned in to only one sound amongst the chat and clatter. Eyes seeing only eyes amongst the languorous luxury of Spanish lunch. The smiles on our faces are wrinkled and lined and the pleasure is deeper than when our appetites were hungrier and satisfaction momentary, like an accidental slick of seafood on sticky fingers. Very

deliberately our roads have brought us here to pause a while again together before we go on.

❀

What I had accidentally gone and left (I didn't know) was not a faded summer snapshot to be mythologized since. It was more like my lumpy multi-pocketed backpack and has been unloaded, little by little, over all the years of our separate adult-hoods. It has kept shaping how he has reacted to opportunities, made changes of direction, loved other women in other ways. It is – I am – in the mould of his life.

Long ago, late in the night in his orange and grey bed in Santiago, I had asked him Big Question after Big Question which he had never been asked before which he could not answer.

'Are you…?'

'Why are you…?'

'Who says you are…?'

And he asked me question after question to which I replied 'I am…' with a little stamp of my foot and without hesitation.

And as I walked last week on Camino, and yesterday and today I realised that I am…

still…

… here with you – dear reader – now – whoever you are: girlfriend, husband, old lover, colleague, sister – whenever this is…

… not because you possess me but because I choose to be so – because you are… you. If I walk on away from you for a while, still you are… you. You are happy because of… you. You can choose your company. You can run with the wolves and still be yourself. You can stop racing against others if you want to go slow. You can learn to speak other people's language and be better understood. You can look after your body and make the climbs easier. You can take time to sit with your back against an old cold cross or a black, dragon-skinned pine and listen to the wind and follow its example as it thinks of changing direction. You can rummage around in your pilgrim's backpack, take things out and examine them and find your 'I am'.

2018
I am alive. I am beside you. I am overjoyed to be with you. I am greater than my fears and you are greater than yours. I am everything I ever was. I am more than I have ever been.

Don't repack what you are not. Turn it all upside down if you have to and give it a shake. Poke in the corners. Don't stop moving on – you can sort it on your way, sitting on a log by the side of the road, on a sunny hilltop, looking out into the golden green, scattering the dust and crumbs into the grit of the gutter amongst the flecks of granite and sprigs of lichen. Be careful though not to throw out by accident some healthy Galician acorn, a seed of who you are and can be. Don't drop litter. Don't be scared of going round the bend. Take your time. When ready, swing your pack onto your back, not worrying if yours is lighter or heavier than your fellow travellers'. This is your 'I am'.

October 2018
I am not dead. I am not a garden for tumours. I am not a bed num-ber or a date of birth. I am an artist, it seems. I walk beside others and tell stories of pebbles and apples and salamanders and wolves.

The dust and conkers and acorns and dropped leaves and plucked herbs that I have packed on my back don't weigh me down but create new ways through art for others to follow me on a path on which their bodies cannot take them. I can be someone who helps you be who you are.

※

I had lost much of my 'I am' by the start of the 1980s (Andy had discarded it), but my sunny Free Bird spirit, my 'I am' happiness was miraculously still safe with Miguel. It came with him when, in the early 1990s, he holidayed in London and walked down Portobello Road, my road, one unseen Spanish speaker in the crowds that I walked through too. I went there often (when Andy had emigrated across the Pond with his tail between his legs), walking through the multilingual masses. I could find a little bit of my 'I am' spirit there. It's where Joe lived and Hannah was born. I am happy that I found them there. It is a street where film-makers find *Bedknobs and Broomsticks* and *Notting Hill* for their cameras and it felt, and this all seems, a little like magic to me.

I knew as I approached that the streets of modern Santiago would have changed since 1977 and that the fountain outside our bedroom has been removed. Miguel has no doubt a grander house now that he is a retired international bank director. He has a grey moustache and I a round belly. I am who I am now and he is who he has become. But once I was the rosy-cheeked, happy-go-lucky bundle newly out of her village who gave herself to the moment carelessly. I sometimes still do. I was funny. I can be now. My dancing at our favourite 'Zum Zum' bar in the new town of Santiago was a vertical expression of a horizontal intention. I had no interest in being a cool, distant, sophisticated, sensible Northerner. I was not a Christian pilgrim. I had met no wolf princes back then, but the 1970s had already taught me a little of looking further east to find karma – I had a Hindu boyfriend for a while who took me through *The Joy of Sex* from cover to cover like a textbook – before I brought my learning to share with Gallegos. It was in confident carelessness that I brought joy to rainy Galicia which dripped with wet pleasure as we supple young Europeans shared all amongst its bulging barrels and contorted bloodied saints, their eyes averted.

To be remembered through decades by those long-lost, sad Gallegos for making people hot and happy seems to me now at menopausal fifty-seven a wonderful treasure to keep in my pocket or under my floorboards. I did not know. I wish I had. These are happy tears. I walked on towards Santiago from the hills above Preguntoño with an ever-lighter spirit and faster pace... Zoom! Zoom!

CHAPTER NINE

TREASURE

Galicia is a fertile land of green and gold. Lush, unmown meadows roll up and down and round the friendly little valleys like cosy blankets. In October, the maize stands still rich and proud but dry and waiting for harvest, silhouetted like bamboo against the lacquered, misty dawns. The voluptuous chestnuts have crowns of every kind of previous metal with feet wrapped in copper bracken. The oaks are still velvet green and the young gum trees aquamarine. Here and there we are cheered along by cottage gardens and small vegetable plots bejewelled with magenta dahlias. Baby blue and pink hydrangeas appear cut from pretty paper. Tomatoes and red peppers seem moulded from glossy plastic and, though everyday things to the villagers, are magic to our northern October eyes. We are walking through a jewellery box and it makes us smile even as we come to the end of our quest.

Maybe I would be lucky enough with the turning of the planet and would see Miguel again in 2015, sometime late after our jolly hotel supper and all-important group high jinks. Maybe I would not. All was good either way.

I bounced off round the next bend, linking arms with the jolliest of our pilgrims and feeling super powerful, my little heart-shaped pebble left behind me on the hill above

Preguntoño. I listened more to my companions, as I should have done before, and gave back more and felt happier with my years. Life is a long time, I shared with Grace and Alicia, the youngest walkers, who had shared their doubts with me as we walked. Be gentle on yourself, don't make yourself rush ahead across the next crossroads. Don't punish yourselves for being indecisive nor for being reckless; instead plan to go out walking in the world in thirty-eight years' time – like me. Don't, like me, try to experience it all too quick, too hard, too recklessly.

Remember, I wanted to say to Deedee, whatever you do, that this road was carved out by millions of feet who held St James close and vital. Respect them, hold their memory close to you even if you don't share their beliefs. Don't misunderstand that there is a magic in arriving this way on tired feet, pack on back, eyes shining from the fresh air and exertion, bewitched by the *meigas*, seeing for the first time or half remembering the cathedral square. It's not the same as flying in and out and staying in a Parador as I did with Joe or with your husband's friends as Deedee had done. Don't stick your finger up St James' nose. Don't wind up the village builders like a silly Anglo Saxon teenager by wiggling your muscle-hard bum at them and gig-gling back at invitations you can't translate and wouldn't accept if you could.

Saudade is a word unique to Portuguese and Gallego for a uniquely northwest Hispanic feeling. My university tutor told me it was something like homesickness or nostalgia, an attach-ment to land and the spirits of it which are well understood here and part of life. More than most of us can appreciate, it is attached to a more particular place and is more all-pervasive a mood. It is a slow emotion and you can understand it here if you walk slow so the green duendes can reach out and touch your heart. Look up and out with the viewpoint of a mouse. Breathe big gulps of the sweet meadow air, open yourself up, know less, be led by the unfamiliar, look backwards to see where you have come from and how long it has taken and how steeply you have climbed and you can feel all the magic that is there for you on Camino.

At lunch of crisp, delicious salads and salty, meaty morsels under a shaded awning at the Casa Calzada, the fastest and the slowest of us discussed that night's arranged hotel, the last before Santiago. This one was to be far from the sort of small-town shops and bars we'd enjoyed the last two evenings. We were in commuter-reach of the city. Was it possible Deedee asked Alicia – and yes it was – to catch a bus fifteen minutes into Santiago and back to go shopping? Stacey's face lit up. I shrieked out loud. Just the idea of such a prosaic entrance into the glorious city we had struggled every day to reach the right way… The words for that are… are… are… This may be your Camino but…

'You can't do that!'

The 'Why not?' might have been shouted over the Bay of Biscay given the gulf that I again felt between me and some of my fellow walkers. I went to the loo rather than reply.

I would have to stuff my ears and blind my eyes when you returned from your shopping trip so that you could not tell me what you saw there at the end of my Camino.

I could not be near you if you bussed into town and back to walk with the group the next day in case you spoilt one step of the arrival I have seen in my dreams so many times.

I have waited thirty-eight years and conquered my phobias and left my soul mates behind and faced my daemons so as to see its magic, fresh and sparkling for myself (as a million walking, hurting, crying pilgrims have), not to have it described by someone to whom it means so little.

In fact – like the littering merchandise, dog attacks, broken ankles, week-long sickness, taxi trips and faithless, dirty stop-outs – the shopping trip into Santiago didn't happen. Linda, so much wiser than I, had said it never would. I apologized to

Deedee for my shrieking and tried unsuccessfully to explain. We didn't share the same language but she said it was OK, she hadn't noticed. That got up my nose too.

October 2018
In fact, it turns out that there is very little I cannot bear for myself. The weight on my back seems to swing up there by itself these days. Tell me more of your story, my darling. There is nothing of what you have carried through your life that you cannot ask me to take on board. There is nothing too grimy for me to kick around with you on the road. There's only one way ahead and it is often going to be uphill for both of us. Life's litter and disillusionments are very light in the big scheme of things. Let's walk on calmly together.

We passed yet another bend in the road without mishap and arrived at our last hotel, O Pino, at Arca, one we had seen from the road from the minibus to Sarria. It lay on the edge of the last sleepy hamlet before the city. There was a lovely covered lounging area at the front with banks of squishy-soft couches and low coffee tables, and I sank there a while with a glass of cool white wine and my journal and Wi-Fi and watched the other pilgrims limping in.

Later, refreshed, and while others rested, I once again arranged and photographed my little red felt hearts, caught in the iron handle of a barn door, up on a tiny narrow window ledge, tucked into the lines of creamy yellow stone. The last squat, warm buildings sang with a chorus of swallows and starlings, happy sparrows and sizzling flies. Just over that last forested hill lay the spires of the city I had dreamed of walking into with a pack on my back and my eyes sparkling with the magic of the road. Though rested I could hardly breathe. We were particularly early to bed that night so as to be ready for tomorrow, and though I can remember the old-fashioned wooden stairs and carpeted corridors with their dressers and vases of flowers, I have no recall of the room in which I crashed into the best sleep of the journey so far.

We left even earlier than usual the next day so as to reach the cathedral well in time for the Pilgrims' Mass for those who wanted it. It was still pitch black as we took advantage of yet another great photo opportunity and conga-ed from hotel car park to waiting farmland. Stepping from hamlet to forest, Linda needed an arm to find her way where no streetlight had ever shone. The pilgrims who passed us – the fittest, tallest, thinnest, malest, fastest, well-equipped type – were like will-o-the-wisps with the blue light of their head or bike lights just catching a faint outline and a pool on the rough track.

The nearer we came to modern life, the less ancient pollarded oaks and the more slim, straight gum trees surrounded us, soaring, mimicking the pillars of the cathedral ahead. Everyone on the road was nearing the end, whether they had walked from the Pyrenees or any of the other starting points on the Way. Like millions before them, they grew contemplative. There was a quiet on Camino that morning unlike any other silence I can think of. Voices spoke more gently, more rapturously, more mindfully and the air was full of the stillness of secretly beating hearts. Where greedy eucalyptus has eradicated all nurturing scrub below, no acorn-loving beetle rustles, no bee buzzes, no waking pigeon flaps, no snail-hunting thrush sings. No witch or wolf waited. Whatever company we walked in, whatever our stories, it was our own quiet selves – belonging to no one – that were sensing journey's end and whatever this great achievement would mean in the noise of life going on across the world.

My spirit soared amongst them. Late in the morning, I marched up the steepest of all the hills, the last, to Santiago de Compostela. I had breath to whistle the theme tune to *The Great Escape* and felt like a hero. I had conquered my body, conquered the miles, conquered the dogs, conquered the past and walked my own Camino.

We stopped only briefly to have our passports stamped at the Hermitage by the Pope's monument on the Mount of Joy because it didn't live up to its name and there were rain clouds galloping in like a grey invading army from the estuaries to the west. It drizzled as we treated ourselves to pizza at the Ristorante Italiano L'Incontro at the start of the modern town and I did not object to its unSpanishness now that we were beyond the city boundary. Even Stacey had made it to the end and the threatened downpours stayed off us for one last day.

I was glad that Joe and I had visited as tourists in the 1980s. I had taken him back forgetting that there is a modern city round the old one and that Santiago leads Galicia comfortably through the millennia and is not a pocket of medieval dreaming. You don't walk from countryside straight into the flagstoned alleys of the fairy-tale old town. This time I remembered and was not disappointed that we walked through industry and retail and regional HQs and knew the twenty-first century was waiting for us just one day ahead. Some hurried faster towards it. Some slowed our pace.

---

24 October 2018

I had stumbled with a stabbing pain across my chest just in sight of the motorway bridges which divide Galicia's spirits from their capital. Were my achievements of the last week to end here on the edge of this ugliness?

A rest, a breath and a smiling face restored my faith.

His round, flat face under his cap beamed with contentment. Behind his short, broad back I spied through the open door of his yard shelf after shelf of gleaming gold – not Incan or Mayan but Galician, Spanish. He welcomed us in to admire it. His harvest was in. Because of his maize, his livestock would grow fat and so would his wife and baby granddaughter. Because of his maize, he would have surplus to sell. Because of his maize, his son and daughter would follow their studies and prosper in business.

Beyond him the steeples of the greatest cathedral in all of Spain soared and St James looked down at him and smiled – because of his maize now stacked and gleaming in golden beauty. He, and we, had so much to treasure from the lands we had walked.

The call of '*Buen Camino*' from every stranger encountered on the Way means more than 'have a good walk'. It means 'have a good life'; 'make as much as possible of this experience'; 'you are doing a good thing'; 'you are doing well'; 'we understand, we are with you, walk it well'.

Sometimes it is said with a touch of irony – when the hills are particularly steep, the flesh weak, the rain cold or the distance thirsty. It says 'we know', 'be strong', 'you can do it', 'we don't find it easy either'. Each step is being affirmed by a cascade of every kind of human – women as old as your mother, men like your husband, the most handsome, the well-travelled, people who are the age you were once a long time ago. It is as if they are incanting a spell, a mantra, a prayer which, after a few days, converts you. You become more at home on the Way of St James than anywhere where there are divides between human beings – those who vote one way or another, those who worship one way or another, those who have one kind of body or another, one kind of tongue or another. *Buen Camino* becomes your norm; you belong here on the road – here which is no one place except the piece of earth under your foot just now for this second...

… till you lift your foot and go on another step. Here you are free to be yourself, free to go in one direction. Here you can conquer pain and make it pleasure. Here you are a supreme being who can achieve any impossible thing.

Anything…

… just by putting one blistered foot in front of another: one, two; one, two; one two.

It rained a bit as we entered the old town and the flagstones gleamed like mirrors and the old inns beckoned us in amongst their barrels, just as I had known they would. My heart was racing. I remembered my recurring dreams as I echoed them. My sore, tired feet felt like they were flying. Ahead of us a young man helped a tiny old lady in black unpack from a country bus huge bundles of juicy greens to sell in the city. Her life was behind us. We had walked through it.

I glanced in pretty shop windows at lacy children's clothes and students' books and hanging hams. I remembered to look up at glass-fronted balconies overhanging us and down through pillared pavements, past wrought iron lamp stands and pollarded plane trees. I gathered the city round me as I marched. My walking poles clicked on the paving. One, two. One, two.

The pilgrim masses were coming together now in the crowded streets. The doors had fancy, hand-shaped brass handles. Cockle shells were everywhere, carved and inlaid, in stone and wood and shining metal. The singing from the pilgrims was even louder as it bounced off the alley walls. Voices rose and rose in song sweet and rich, up past the shuttered windows and terracotta tiles to the ribbon of blue and puff of cloud high above us. Black faces, brown faces, yellow faces, tanned white faces, puffing pink faces, white faces under hats, all smiling whether from relief or rapture. We were near, we were near, we were nearly there.

We tumbled through the streets together like leaves in a stream. It seemed impossible that we would ever stop. It was truly and unforgettably intoxicating. I will carry the memory with me forever. It was just like my dreams.

Carved in the paving stones read the words, in many languages, 'Europe was made on the Way of St James.' On this road, because of this road, the skills and ideas of men and women great and small had been practised and shared to build the great medieval cathedrals and monasteries that dot the route from France. Such buildings had to be filled with works of art worthy of their purpose and sculptors, goldsmiths and silversmiths worked to create reliquaries to hold the bones of minor saints as well as Magi, Madonna and Apostles. Beautiful jewellery was made to hold tiny pieces of bone or cross and even vials of Madonna's milk to be carried by pilgrims. Great works of art were created commemorating occasions when processions of the venerated objects moved from place to place.

With the wealth of the Holy Roman church and the spreading of the great Latin words travelled the skill and beauty and creativity and invention of working hands from one corner of the Christian world to another, enriching our world and feeding the families of artisans and labourers.[43] They took their love of their own daughters, mothers, sons and imagined them, immortal and faultless, and shaped their likeness into the faces of altarpieces and frescoes and plaster pieta – their eyebrows, chocolate eyes, pretty noses, kissable lips, round breasts, strong arms, tear-wet cheeks.

So when you look at Santiago himself, whose face do you really see smiling down at you, in village square, country chapel or grand cathedral, familiar and comforting? Another human worth your respect, if not your faith?

Smaller more guttural words spread too, not in Latin texts but word for changing word between those ordinary, brown-clad folk with clever hands who travelled from Brittany and

43. https://www.youtube.com/watch?v=blK3IF51B0M

Normandy, Holland and Germany with ideas spawned in the dark woods or salty shores and caught in songs round snug hearths and washing pools where plump priests couldn't overhear but teenagers could. Catchy songs, great legends and little stories of lovers lost and left behind all intertwined, one impossible without the other. Not just faithful Catholic pilgrims came home from Santiago to northern villages like this one where I sit typing.

---

24 October 2018

Stop a while in Santiago de Compostela. Shower and rest and change. Go back to the Camino gateway into the old city. Watch the faces of those with packs and sticks as they leave the open roads and the last diesel-ridden crossing and step again into human-sized ways through cosy streets. If you want to see humans at their best you will see them here, squeezed in together into this shaded lane, still mesmerised from the great wide forests and mountaintops, not yet thinking of their small singularities back home.

Here is the group of blind people and their guides joined together, holding the edges of their flag, filling the lane. Here is the first friend on the road at Morgade. Here is the last friend who lied about his age, deceiving no one at dinner in Fisterra. Here is Señora Mariposa, old enough to be my mother, who taught us all about a jewel-laden caterpillar. Here are Americans who got off the coach an hour ago and the French woman who has walked from Mont Saint-Michel on the English Channel. Here is Superdad with his bike and his three-year-old, brown as a berry. Here are two women, Robin and I, from different hemispheres and different worlds who have become sisters from other mothers.

Soon we would reach the end of that great coming together and go back to our own small front doors and shut them behind us and unpack our bags and hug our spouses. What of this great labour would have smuggled its way into our living rooms?

Before the last archway, I caught up with Linda. We had spent happy times sharing fantasies of buying a crumbling Gallego cottage and exchanging tales of the Spain we loved. But I had lingered, nourishing and indulging myself, and she had powered on through her duty to her lost Catholic soul mate. She had found more common cause and new friendship with the A-team than had been my experience. On the snivelly hill out of Preguntoño she had come alongside me and I had shooed her off, scared that my tears would infect her ability to hold hers back and that she would mistake mine for faithlessness. Now my Way came back alongside her Way.

At the same moment, we both recognised where we were – just a few yards from journey's end. Our hearts leaped with memory. The others, ignorant of how few paces remained of our great adventure, were distracted by the encrusted grandeur of our hotel, the Hospedería San Martín Pinario, a sixteenth-century monastery. At one end of the street past a side door of the cathedral, a simple pale wall was pierced through by a small round tunnel half hidden deep down steep, foot-softened steps. Cyclists dismounted and the most exhausted pilgrims clutched at a handrail. In the darkness, high-pitched bagpipes played a special welcome for pilgrims from the Celtic lands and a surprise for those who had not read their Gallego history.

Tightly arm in arm with its lament the only sound, Linda and I came through the damp darkness and out into the vast and joyously sunlit stone-flagged Praza do Obradoiro, high above the wooded farmland and surrounded by cathedral, five-star Parador, university and colonnaded town hall.

Without dropping our packs, we wrapped our arms around each other in joy and hugged tight beneath the cathedral's watching saints, and at last she let the grief out. Tears rolled down her face and we wept together for lost love, and I knew that hers was the tragedy and the greater love lost and I was the one with a warm man ahead of me at home in Scotland. She said, 'Enough now,' to me, herself and the universe and we found the others for more hugs and congratulations and were asked to recreate our embrace in branded T-shirts for the cameras and Annual Report.

Others waved their plastic flags, safely carried all this distance for this moment. All across the immense Praza, other pilgrims also dumped their bags and stared up at the façade of the largest Romanesque cathedral in the world and St James looking down at us, from amongst scaffolding and blue plastic netting. We had not arrived in Paradise. Pilgrimage tells a more complicated tale than that. Neither pigeons nor swifts nor tourists cared. The air seemed to sing in one great swirling chorus.

---

24 October 2018

I dropped my sticks, dropped my rucksack and dropped my body to the paving stones. Up from my belly came heaving sobs. They shrugged off the very last loops of rope which had dragged me through the last three years and, floating lighter than ever, I lifted my head to look beyond the spires (newly cleaned and cleared of 1977's weeds and 2015's plastic veil and scaffolding) like the masts of a giant sailing ship.

I break the surface, gulp in the air and from all sides of the Praza do Obradoiro come waves of memory truer to my life than any cancer – memories of reaching the cathedral with Linda, of luxuriating in the Parador with Joe, of teenage exploring with Miguel and friends and now with sweet Robin by my side – innocent of Spain's magic till just a week ago and now bewitched. I am all of it and ahead of me is whatever I, afloat in it, will become.

For those for whom it had been a fundraising walk, it was over, in a grand hotel, with great shops and a flight home tomorrow. The converted monastery's palatial front entirely filled one side of a square and its reception was arrived at through cool glass-enclosed cloisters with fountains and trimmed hedges of bay. Our rooms were well-furnished cells with white walls and little desks looking out through deep shuttered windows to quiet gardens. The dining halls and bars were massively vaulted and full of stained glass light. For my fellow walkers, this was the end. They would go to Mass, get their pilgrim's Compostela from the cathedral office to put on the wall and its jokey equivalent from our leader and have a nice wee wander before hitting the sack.

Santiago was majestic and towering and sculpted where the hamlets of the Camino had been simple and squat and plain. It was a fantastic reward at the end of our pilgrimage. There were jolly bars with cheery waiters in starched white aprons in pretty squares and colonnaded streets. There were chocolate shops and biscuit shops and markets of scarves. The silver and jet shops sparkled like little jewels, tempting pilgrims as they had done for centuries. Round every corner was another church or monastery, seminary or convent, faculty or town hall.

Buskers sang 'Ave Maria' or Leonard Cohen's 'Hallelujah' in echoing passageways. Cripples begged unaided by political correctness. A horrid little white tourist train chugged round the streets. Though showered and dressed for the city, we could recognise our fellow recent pilgrims by the fact that they hobbled still. We whispered *'Buen Camino'* to each other in recognition and solidarity. I took a few enthusiasts from our group out into the lanes and markets to buy souvenir soaps and trinkets but lost them in a tiny music shop. I told the wizardly cravatted man there that I was looking for something to evoke the Gallego concert I had been at thirty-eight years ago when the songs of the Celts were forbidden. He looked down his long sharp nose and smiled.

'I was there,' he told me.

He had been there too on that momentous day. I caught my startled breath. That one day had seemed through the years to be another one of my Compostelan dreams. He and I stood in utter stillness in his shop and shared a long, wet look back into air full of bagpipes and flutes and fiddles while he let the strong keening voices of Luar na Lubre fill the air and float out into the darkening city. He was more interested in sharing the mood than selling and my friends drifted off and I stood breathlessly happy, my still-sore feet floating off the ground.

Now the event that started that day that he and I had been part of has become the four-day Festival de Ortigueira. I had gone with Australian Jenny in her VW van and we had been the only non-Gallegos there amongst the hundreds. We queued up outside the scruffy fence and bought our tickets and ate huge sardines fresh from the griddle, caught in delicious crusty, chewy rolls piled on a rickety trestle table. We had met up with Miguel and his friends and drunk warm purple wine from stacks of wooden barrels and sat on a hard mud-village football pitch and heard songs about the brown-earth living of the Gallego people. Until that day in 1977 they had not been sung to a crowd since the Spanish Civil War, which Franco had won. Had my generation sung them or even spoken their mother tongue in public or at school, they would have been beaten hard. The memory of that singing is one I have cherished ever since, though I didn't know the words.

At one stage of the afternoon a wave of anger passed through the seated crowd and group after group rose to their feet in fear but with fight and determination. My blood pumped and I wondered where to hide in the hard-packed yellow ground. The men with guns had indeed come again as we feared, but the times were a-changing and no one was running away this time. The Caudillo was long dead. We had all had enough of being treated like rats obliged to dig escape holes in the dirt. This time my friends were heading to the fight.

The world had, however, turned more than we had had the confidence to believe. It turned out the anger at the far side of the ground was directed at some scallywags trying to get into the concert without a ticket to cover the cost of fish, bread and wine, without respect for what this day was. At last police and *pueblo* were on the same side.

This sign of a truly changed reality had a further intoxicating effect on the already delirious occasion. The adrenalin had rushed, solidarity displayed itself as a reality, fear turned to hope fulfilled. Relief made us laugh, the fiddles soared, the knucklebones danced on the drums, hands clapped. To be with a people who are not your own, to be welcome in such a moment of their history is a privilege, a treasure in the great adventure that is the turning of our planet. It is these huge shared outpourings of unstoppable, unforgotten and archetypal truths in poetry and song and myth and story which truly builds civilisation. Here, if you listen, is the art of living together while walking your own way. Those chords wire us backwards, through and with the generations who travelled those rhythms and melodies and metaphors from cold north to wave-crashing west, from one side of our planet across the vast wastes to other people's dreaming lands.

The enormous rawness of the emotion, the fragility of hope, the force of individual human will that hung in the air that long-gone afternoon wove its threads through the person I came to be in the years that followed. The emotional energy that has fuelled this Camino half a lifetime later came from that day. The bonds between the members of that audience which I was amongst were true and strong enough to last a lifetime. Whether deep down we are wizards or heroes or demons or witches, Gallego or Scottish or Australian, that day in that music tied everyone present together, even if the knots are hidden inside. We were spellbound. Its magic would stretch for thirty-eight years ahead till I walked into that music shop in Santiago and it is knotted still inside me now.

This foot-tapping audience – whose trembling breath, whose wet eyes, whose embracing arms I had felt as the fiddles tuned up and the drums began to beat – was the team I belonged to still, not those of a six-day group challenge. The skin-drummed music I had heard there in Ortigueira had enchanted me with its keening for the Galician forest, the misty valleys and wolf-guarding hounds, the tight little hamlets. In the high pipes and flutes, played out again in the music shop, I heard the rain-glazed alleys of the city and the clouds racing in from the great Atlantic coast and through the decades to whip round a statue of an Apostle in a village square and a silly woman in a pastel fleece. It was not the sound of Lorca's southern duende nor of Franco's bloody Catholic Spain. It had a spirit I, a village Scot, could accept and absorb and it had wrapped around that wild student summer of loving and debating with a cold Celtic fire like the blue light of a bowl of brandy-burning *queimado* flickering on bare flesh, throbbing. It was true not legend. It was far more important than silly, saucy summer romance.

Standing in that shop at the end of my Camino, thirty-eight years later in 2015, listening to the Luar na Lubre CD chosen by that proud Gallego musician, the spirit of that concert hugged me again like a warm shawl on a cold evening in Arzúa and was at least as vital to my journey. I will drive back to work on Monday with it playing in my car and I have it ringing in my ears now from the music centre on the shelf beside me. As I have spent these four days recovering and writing these words, its fiddles and accordions have been playing out in my living room, weaving in and around my memories. It has been a thread of sound so perfectly matched to the sensations of my Camino it is as if by some magic its music was with me, around me in the green-scented, sun-scoured air of the road, unheard by others who didn't listen hard enough. In the voices, strings and pipes I swear I hear the plain trees in Portomarín before dawn, the dancing pilgrim statues of Palas del Rei, the children of Melide and the voices in the dark at Arzúa.

꽃

October 2018

There is a Luar na Lubre version of a traditional song which talks of a place called Camariñas, a pretty seaside town some way up the coast from Fisterra. The bus service between one and the other is legendary – in fact mythical or non-existent. I know. I made Robin try with me to reach this place-that-I-heard-of-once-in-a-song, but we never got to Camariñas. It was a step too far. It remains in my imagination to tempt me back one day.

꽃

One last task on Camino. I had left pebbles from my backpack along the way and now it was nearly full to bursting with things to take home – a bird of love, a handful of crushed leaves and chestnuts, a warm shawl, a leather scallop, a phone full of happy photos, shell-shaped soap and pebble-shaped biscuits, acorns and chestnuts and music, water-of-hope perfume made from shells and herbs, a purple meiga doll and memories old and new. Out from amongst them I took my faithfully carried bag of felt hearts, each a reminder of a lovely friend somewhere in the wide world who, here in middle age, had backed me, only knowing how fat and lazy and old and unaccustomed to being vertical I am and nothing of my Camino – the story I have been telling. Few of them are folk impressed by all I have learnt and forgotten about the history of Spain and the situation of its women in the last thirty-eight years and the hundreds of years before. Maybe each has enjoyed something of me in the years since.

Remembering my promise to take a heart for them to Santiago and also back again, I walked back to my favourite horse-headed fountain in the Praza de las Platerías and took my last photographs there. I remember sitting on the steps there in 1977 with a warm Spanish-man scent beside me to turn my lips to and being told by the singers not to fall in love as the minstrels pass by and failing to take the warning to heart.

I found the Praza de Fonseca with its pretty flower beds and benches and the little bars we used to go to with the minstrels when they stopped playing. The deep stone taverns had been excitable in 1977 with their dashing cloaks and shining shoe buckles, their tambourine rhythms. Their beautiful deep voices and big smiles had filled the little rooms and caught me up as if they were pop stars and I was a groupie. Passion was easily aroused with fantasies of Knights Templar racing down the stone streets, white horses' nostrils high like the stone fountain. Deep amongst the poetry of Spain, such fantasies spun like golden threads through Santiago's quiet lanes. No wonder my dreams were troubled for decades after and full of running to get back to this shining heart of Galicia.

As a student, I never saw a pilgrim walk into Santiago, for so very few did back then. My ambitions to do so were fed here, though, in the romantic inns of the old city which had been built for them as well as for students like myself. Now in 2015, I was an invisible stranger, looking back through tavern windows, one of hundreds of thousands passing through each year. The Spaniards of a new generation were just getting on with their normal lives on any ordinary Saturday with no more chivalry than any EU citizen. My self was finding its way back into the twenty-first century.

I bought a little jet *figa* – a clenched fist catching one finger – set in silver from a sparkling shop in the colonnades behind the cathedral and tucked it in my purse for my girl Hannah to keep the *meigas* and duendes out of her life.

I wandered till dinner when we gathered for silly celebration of what our team had achieved and was happy. The team activities were not, of course, so bad or so long as I had dreaded. Lucy gave us all a certificate – mine was for being a 'Saucy

Señorita'. It felt petty to disagree that I was either. Nor would it have been a sin to miss the disappointing last-night feast but I had no better offers. Midge had received news that her father-in-law had died that day. Real life was searching us out again and we all knew it.

I was, though, unsubmissive to its pull. The hospitality of the *hostal* was surprisingly sullen, the football in the bar noisy and so the silhouetted and shining fountains drew me back out into the lamplight, though I have never been so tired in my life. No one was up for a drink. It wasn't for the banter of the bars or the casually catching of music rising up from it, for freshly cooked sardines slid across a counter, nor admiring the beautiful long faces of ethereal Gallegos that my party of ten had walked all this way. They were done. Wi-Fi brought me no invitations. My Camino was mine and mine alone.

Dragging feet like blocks of granite I went out again, out beyond the Wi-Fi and unreachable by Miguel or Joe, belonging to no one, and proud of it. I would not have it any other way. At nearly midnight, still propped up by adrenalin, a magic sound of mandolins and baritones curled and coiled through the tunnel to the square and whipped me up once more. The minstrels of the Tuna were throwing a rope of sparkling sound to net me and pulled me deliriously back to meet them. No voices could have been more welcome.

My heart leaped to them, dragging my feet after it. I ran. I could have flown. Tradition has it that they play according to their own timetable, where they wish, not to be pinned down. There had been no guarantee that they would be waiting for me before tomorrow's flight home. I ran to them as surely as I had run through the streets in my dreams or across that dining room in Arzúa.

Under the arches, their black cloaks and bright ribbons swinging, their deep, delicious voices booming, they sang to me that it was not for lack of love that they no longer brought me carnations, that I should not give my heart to a Compostelano who serenaded many foreign girls who came on summer courses from America or Scotland.

They sang to me the other music of Santiago de Compostela – the music not of land and peasants, sea and sailors, sung by Luar na Lubre but of sixteenth-century learning, of courtliness and culture, romance and collegiate comradeship, seduction and silliness.

Under the arches opposite the cathedral, in wonderful acoustics, I was amongst a small crowd of Tuna fans, endless romantics. We were students and true lovers of historic Spain. I loved its language, its desperate poetry, its proud and barbarous twisted history, its brutal courtiers, scented men and heroic women, its innate surrealism, its sad and saintly princesses, its copper gypsies, its honourable seducers, its raw ripeness, its forgiving, forgetful distance from Brussels and Scotland, the highs and lows of its music, the knowledge that its wild places hid wild beasts, its duendes northern and southern. More than anything else, more than anywhere else on the days of Camino, it was love of Spain itself, not comradeship or hill-climbing achievement that filled me and made me happy. I sang quietly with them, very flat but remembering the words through the years.

The Tuna had been at the high points of my love of Santiago not only in 1977 but in 1986 too when I had brought Joe to the Parador. On my earlier trip, I had been banished from the forecourt of the hotel for being a scruffy student and had vowed to return one day as a wealthy paying guest. When my Hispanophile Uncle Mac died, leaving me a little cash and we had been to his funeral, full of the family of Robert Graves, his neighbour in Majorca, Joe and I had flown in for a quick luxurious break, no time for walking.

We had played at being prince and princess each night in our marble and mahogany bedroom, reached through bat-squeaking, cloistered squares of orange and lemon trees, in the Hospital de los Reyes Católicos, built for pilgrims by all-conquering King Ferdinand and Queen Isabella. We had breakfasted from heaped, five-star buffets in the grandeur of the huge pilgrims' hall, but in the days had taken a train out to small-town, coastal Galicia for fishermen's fare and returned to dine on simple ham and turnip tops in comfy inns.

It is old city bars and the cheery entertainment of street corners, harbour sides and under arches that we enjoy most together whether in Spain or London, Paris or Venice, Hong Kong or Sydney. It was to find Santiago's wandering Tuna and their schmaltzy love songs and flashing tambourines that I had come back again with Joe... and again now. Like the drums and fiddles of Ortigueira, the mandolins and tambourines of the Tuna were for me the essence that rose from the paving stones of the field of stars.

---

24 October 2018

Robin says she hears music. Mandolins. Tambourines. Utterly astonished, she sees me run, though she knows how our legs are aching, across the moonlit vastness of the square back to where they played three years ago.

These days the cognoscenti and sophisticates of the old Spanish university towns turn their fine noses up at the aging Tuna and their pretence of being impoverished students, just as we Scots might do at much of the supposed folk culture sold to our visitors. But joy is joy and that is what the Tuna bring to the largely Spanish crowds around them with their perfect voices, half-understood bawdiness and the catchy tunes that their aging audience remember from their youth. No one else could get the feet of exhausted pilgrims dancing late into the night.

Late in this last October night I told my tale of long-ago mutual
bewitchment with a local boy to a big bald minstrel with a
Roman nose and flat Gallego cheeks and, unasked and ready
to go home, he knocked something off the price of their CD
'for love's sake'. When his troupe eventually stopped playing, I
found myself following one of their wandering number back
through the archway before our hotel, his black cloak swaying,
coloured ribbons streaming from his broad shoulders as he
strode homewards and sank into the wet, black night and I felt
my Camino perfectly ended. Like a bad friend of Heidi's from
1977, I had to ring the hotel bell to get in. I had wrung every
drop from the Santiago night and from my fifty-seven-year-
old self and had walked with the Tuna to my door.

---

24 October 2018
A big bald minstrel with a Roman nose and flat Gallego cheeks kissed
my hand and had the crowd applaud me for being a Scot who knew
the Tuna, but he did not remember my face from 2015 amongst the
thousands that he had charmed in three intervening years. A silver
salver of a full moon adorned the sky and poured white light on the
cathedral's clean stonework. Everything was perfection. Next day
the same minstrel sat in civvies with his wife in the bus station café
and watched us travel on down to Fisterra.

One more twenty-first-century morning in Santiago. The minibus would not collect us till 12.30. The square was the setting
for a half marathon and crowded with sponsors signs, high-vis
stewards and crash barriers which divided the city and limited
where we could go. I never got to visit Joe's favourite bar and
have a drink there for him. I couldn't cross into the beautiful

park where the palatial university is laid out and trees collected from around the world tower above pretty promenaders. I couldn't find my abandoned *pensión* or the street whose fountain had played all night outside Miguel's flat.

As stringy young men with unimaginably stronger feet than mine streamed by in numbered tabards, I had only hours left to walk the colonnades below elegant overhanging rooms and windowed terraces. All around me was the bustle of a modern sporting event and, walking through the crowds, a very familiar aroma pricked my nostrils and sent reaction racing round my body. I laughed out loud that this oh-so-special freshly showered Spaniard smell that I had secretly carried with me from 1977, through one night in Arzúa and on to the end of Camino wrapped in my nut-brown shawl was around me now in vast heady swathes. Every sporty body had been splashed with it. All Spaniards love their cologne and do not stint. It filled the square in invisible clouds for me to walk through, nostrils a-tingle. Though practically orgasmic for me, one limping, frumpy nostalgic Scot in a crowd of Spanish athletes, it was a scent ordinary, everyday, unpoetic for them. It had nothing to do with me at all. I was back in 2015 and Santiago was not all about my Camino. The fast folk didn't notice my whelps and tears of ecstatic laughter.

I found Linda looking for how to arrange Mass for Rick and offered my help to find a way round the crowds through a pretty lane that I remembered. We were full of mutual love of the city and in pleasant camaraderie. She was worried she wouldn't have the language for the task and I reassured her with my offer of help. I was very unsure actually that I, brought up an anti-papist, would have the appropriate vocabulary for the task. But here the words 'My friend is a widow' were all that were required for Linda to be given the service she needed.

We searched out the sacristy where the bishop swept in amongst flustering nuns and altar boys and the mysteries of

St James soared around us in incense-reeking encrustations of gold. The squat purple priest, round-bellied from Gallego farms and *hórreos*, swept through in a crowd like a star from the silver screen. A giant door opened to a glowing backroom with an endless, soaring ceiling flooding the birdy little Sisters with a heavenly golden light. A small form existed to make Linda's Camino complete with bureaucratic ease. This place has been a factory for answering prayers through more than a thousand years.

It was the morning after the Pilgrims' Mass and the cathedral was relatively quiet. I, the girl who had railed against the Catholic imposition on the life of women in the 1970s, went with my friend up the softly foot-moulded marble steps behind the altar and hugged the Apostle as is tradition. We went down to see where he lies, safe from pirates and infidels and Presbyterians in his gleaming, encrusted silver casket near the end of his world. It was just a thing to do now that it was all over. Then we, still unbelievers, sat outside the congregation at Mass. Gold was all around us again – not in the soft light of Galician dawns or midday hay meadows but real and ripped from another barbaric continent in the days when the sun never set on the Spanish Empire. The foot soldiers of Ferdinand and Isabella's conquistadores were largely Gallego, men used to adventuring out into the wild Atlantic wastes. The word *'camino'* flicked out from the pulpit in perfectly poetic imperial Castilian and whipped more exhausted spell-bound tears to our eyes. The Way, the Light undoubtedly shone all around us, but we did not belong to it.

When I got on the train from Montrose to begin my Camino, I wondered whether I would, at the end, want to go to the cathedral office, taking my pilgrim's passport with its stamps from all the stops along the Way and give the Holy Mother Church the final say on what it all meant. That girl in 1977 who I was remembering had felt under attack from that

Church for her quick loving of Spanish boys, her pagan ear for poetry and music, her siding with the Catalan *guerrers* and most of all for her decision to abort a baby that would have changed her life before she ever came to Santiago.

Returning from three months au-pairing in Llavaneras in 1976, I had been met off the train by the cannonball love of my kid sister tearing down the platform, too young to have sealed up her affection. Winded by her head in my stomach, I was wrapped in mother hugs, reliably available for welcomes, making up and other big moments, though never gushing otherwise.

Over her shoulder, sister-arms around my knees, I saw my dad's stiff fingers twitching by his sides as he stood by the exit, too Scottish to embrace me without a wee dram. Days later, his heart attacked him for keeping too tightly screwed shut all his life. Days later still, I drowned worry in drink and unprotected sex. The morning after, knowing for sure that a less than miraculous spark of a bad idea had been conceived inside me, I decided on what seemed a fair exchange. I dismissed the possibility of worrying my father into the grave with my exposed truths. Instead I would have a father alive to hear my poems and music and stories of Spain and in return my own little bundle of guilt to last a lifetime. He would never know the price had been an unborn child. I would carry my own pebbles until he was dead.

Carrying my part in the bargain to Santiago into 1977, by when the spark of that unwanted life had been abruptly snuffed, I had hated the great lump of cathedral but been jealous of those who felt comforted by it. I had ridiculed the authorities who had been troubled that St Daniel's painted eyes stared towards the ample bosom of a lady saint across the aisle. Rather than a touch of paint to divert his gaze, the Church authorities had ordered her tits sawn off, planed down and her lacy neckline painted on higher over a less appealing chest. I had gone and sat apart from these stupid shrines, to where I could only see stone simply carved with peasants' shapes by simple people from somewhere in Europe's villages. I had turned my back on the gold and had cried there wordlessly for the baby I had never let myself love, dispatched one cold Edinburgh's morning in the winter just passed. And I went and found the same cold stone and cried again there in 2015 for that almost child I had been back then. It was a strange, exhausted thing for an unbeliever to do. But who is to judge me?

Somehow, the walking gives the pilgrim ownership of this great space and it is more ours now than Rome's. The pillars soar no higher than the trees we have walked amongst and they are carved no deeper than oak bark. Marble is only stone and jewels are only pebbles. Priests are only men and nuns are just women, and the words of both are only air moved by pink lips and tongues and their books just wood pulp. Incense is not a stronger perfume than foot-stamped roadside herbs and cathedral gold is not as bright as morning sunlight. Pain is not the privilege of martyred celibates. Our tired feet, which took us along the greatest of European roads, surely give us the right equally to tap into the immense human energy stored in this cathedral and use it to soothe ourselves in our own way. Or so it seems to me now I've got the stamps on my passport.

I don't know what my fellow *peregrinas* chose to say to the man in the cathedral office about the Camino they had just completed – 'religious?', 'spiritual?', 'fitness and leisure?' – or whether in the end we had all, all along, been on a real pilgrimage of a sort. Miguel had guessed I would not take the Compostelan certificate. But he was wrong. In the end, I could not be one of those for whom it had just been a fundraising, sporting challenge. I couldn't be mistaken for a Catholic sinner nor for someone who could have ever abused someone else's Apostle, leave litter or could go shopping before the last walk into the square. In the end, I wanted testimony that I had experienced the spirit of Camino, evidence that I had been searching for something, whether or not I found it.

October 2018

I am unmistakably alive. My heart beats. My breath comes in through my nostrils cold and goes out warm. That is the non-miracle that is me. There is no other than the power inside us, each of us – microbe or elephant, foetus or president. There is absolutely nothing in the universe which is supernatural, beyond nature. I am one hundred percent certain.

I have been to the end of the Cape of Fisterra and looked out at the immense, incomprehensible ocean depths of the Atlantic, and at the Pacific and Indian oceans from other capes and I have seen how very small I – and my sins – have been. No bit of paper, nor the lack of it, has any meaning at all when faced with time and tide. Thirty thousand people received their certificate from the cathedral office in Santiago in October 2018. But not everyone who was entitled to felt the need of one. Neither you nor I have anything to prove to anyone. My certificate of 2015 sits alone on the wall beside my bed.

In order to avoid the marathon runners, the minibus at 12.30 took a more circular route from hotel to airport than was expected. From its window, I spotted the sign for the bar 'O Pozo' which I had searched for with Joe in 1986 and failed to find. I had gone to this dark inn down a dark alley with Miguel in 1977 – a little piece of Middle Earth in a twentieth-century city with a well in the middle of the room, an open charcoal fire and hunks of meat hanging from the rafters. The wafting herby, smoky juiciness was the richest I have ever smelt in a lifetime of foody exploration. Its little wooden stools wobbled on its stone-slabbed floor and voices boomed up to lose themselves in the spidery heights of sooty ceiling. Its wine was purple and warm and its corners intimate and seductive. Its landlord was a wizard and his customers handsome knights, packs of long-nosed wolves, snake-headed witch queens and smooth-skinned Gallega girls who dreamed of marrying well. Like the Tuna, this little place had been for ever at the end of my dreams and once again I had failed to reach it.

In the end, I was glad Miguel got me wrong. We had been strangers all my adult life. He doesn't know me. I flew out this time without a kiss at the airport. I left my walking poles behind because I am not planning on going up or down any more steep hills for a while. I took my bag of felt hearts back with me because I had promises to keep. I know my Achilles heel is to easily be made to wonder whether there is a group I belong to. But wherever my feet want to take me, my blood belongs here, in Scotland, where I am known and loved, not there in Galicia. I am still bewitched by the *meiga*, under the spell of the duendes but I reach my hand up to my white throat today and find that I forgot, this morning, Day 4 since my return, to put on my scallop necklace, bought in Arzúa, my mark of a pilgrim, my nod to Venus, the southern goddess of love. My daughter, though, wears her little jet *figa* on a silver chain to keep her safe from *meigas* as she steps out towards her nineteenth birthday and beyond.

I will sing the songs, silly and sad, that came out to find me on the Way and remember the prickle of a kiss on my hand. I will play my CDs of Tuna and Lorca and Gallego bagpipes in the car as I commute. I will treasure my little ceramic love bird and my leather scallop-shell necklace and all the felted hearts that marked the detail of my days through Spanish villages. I will feel *saudade* though I am not Gallega and keep my eyes open for any duende that lurk in my own wet green woods. I will know that I belong here and ask Joe to frame my Latin

Compostela as proof for others that I went (though they won't understand) and I will hang it on my Scottish cottage wall near my bed, where it will look out at every morning that I step out into from now on. I will close my eyes and bring back the smiling faces of fellow pilgrims met along the way, minstrel faces in lamp-lit cloisters and one face in a doorway in a mediocre Spanish motel, the faces of two soul mates that saw me off at Montrose station and one who lifted me high in his arms at the airport on my return and kissed me on the lips. He may be sixty-two and very mortal but he's the nearest I will find to a prince in twenty-first-century Scotland. And that is fine because I am no princess either.

I will write this for someone to leave under a pillow somewhere on their own Camino. I will stay part of the worldwide human web, not sink into the moss and mud underfoot. I will stay Free as a Bird. I will forgive myself for my non-existent sins. I will be happy and know I can make other people happy, and I will be whole and I will pick no more old scabs where tenderness lies below. I will soak myself in poetry and indulge my love of Spain like I have soaked my aching limbs in steaming bubble baths for the last four days. I will try to work out what I have learnt about the self and bring it back into ordinary, lovely Scottish life. I will try to just submit to step after step.

Someone (I am sorry, I don't remember who) said: 'Poetry is the voice of a man – or a woman – who had God to prompt him.' And I am prompted to find again my woman's voice now that I have once again unlocked its passion. I will listen more carefully to hear my daughter's cooler, gentler rhythms and my mother-writer in her last days. I won't let the splatting of raindrops on my grey head stop me walking, and I will try to walk more beside others on their journeys because I may have missed many other journey tales. I will think about indulgence, nurture and self. I will consider the difference between group, team, family and community and what leadership of thought and action means in each. I will meet with friends who knew me back then and know me now and we will walk beside each other again.

I will dance in my husband's arms and look up high into his blue eyes and tell him in Leonard Cohen's words that my love goes with him as his love stays with me, and Joe will smile and know that I am not saying goodbye. We both had many loves before, long ago. We were never new when we set off together thirty-five years ago. We will love each other till we are old and no longer walking.

But I will go back – one day in the next thirty-eight years – on the Camino to Santiago and hear the Tuna and the bagpipes and the flutes and the crows and the hounds and the robins and the guitars. I will remember the soft yellow-brown tracks deepened by millions of pilgrims' feet and leaving my eyes at mouse height to a dandelion. I will remember the golden mists over the maize fields and the impenetrable indigo space between the tree trunks. Maybe I will find O Pozo again – if it hasn't dissolved again into myth – and sit in a dark corner on a bottom-smoothed stool with a plate of oak-smoked meat and a thick warm wine and write poetry or paint. Who knows who might come and sit beside me and start a new adventure?

---

24 October 2018

The white horse sign looks down on the square as I sip my chamomile tea in order for calm to reach my digestive system over lunch. He arrives early, a very strange kind of Spaniard, he says. He orders with a flick of his wrist over his shoulder and chooses delicacies for me. My Spanish wasn't up to explaining the concept of walking backwards in words alone and I had, in the middle of the Praza de la Pescadería Vella, to push back my seat and demonstrate what I meant in the title of the book I have been writing. Smiles all round the square at this odd woman dressed in gold, stepping backwards away from a smiling, retired bank director.

We talk about our expectations and concerns – are we stuck in 1977? Do either of us think the other is in love? Would the essential me he knew have been eaten away by cancer? Would I throw away the story I wrote in 2015, my perspective being so altered as to make a nonsense of the words you have been reading?

And the answers are calmly 'no'.

The love we talk of is of our fathers', daughters', spouses' – the reading and speaking of such love being the centre of our lives. We talk of the expectations of the wider world, the philosophy of endeavour: those who believe that if they strive to speed along the road, sparks flying, then it must be good; if we find beauty in stuff that we fall upon too easily it cannot be gold. We talk of Spain's place in my life – at all my many crossroads. He had no concept that his big questions to me in Arzúa three years ago had turned my world around.

We talked of who we are and why we are and how we are, and we listened with gentleness and respect and restraint and tenderness and honesty, knowing that it is the untouchable four-times-in-forty-years nature of our relationship which keeps it magical. Knowing that we listen harder, explain more carefully because we don't share a mother tongue. There is and always will be a sea of words dividing him from me, just as I am separated from everyone but my husband.

Only Joe heard the clinician's words and saw how they trapped me when I could not walk – 'suspicious', 'preventative', 'therapy', 'inoperable', 'stage', 'chance', 'curative'. Joe has seen me bleed and vomit, give birth and mourn, aspire and fail, reach more than orgasm. Miguel who called me 'guapa' though he knew parts of me are not, is a reward, a special gift, a treat, a soul mate not a life's mate.

He takes me to lunch in a grand old building with fine food and attentive team and to meet a dainty friend in her delicate lingerie shop. Her name means wolf killer. He takes me to places we once knew and we take each other's photographs.

Our time together plays out just as I wanted it to three years ago when instead we snatched a cold hour or two on plastic seats outside a motel and filled it with momentous questions and trembling.

The journey is over. There is nothing for me to be afraid of anymore.

O Pozo is closed now, taken over by squatters. Kisses at the airport are soon washed off. The past is where it belongs. It is not for living in. Neither is the road. We walk on, arm in arm, two old, grey-haired friends who cherish each other with a respect which is as unfathomable to others as the deep, wet places where the sweet sea-tastingly delicious percebes *cling, buffeted by the great outlandish Atlantic spread. Our nostrils keep drawing in clean, cool air and that is the beautiful be all and end all of it.*

The sea and the rain and the wind are roaring outside now and it is November in Scotland and nearly my daughter's birthday and mine. Soon I will be fifty-eight and never again nineteen. My hair is grey and not permed and Joe doesn't let me miss planes. No one wears authentic kohl eyeliner anymore. I have a pretty nose and pretty lips and pretty eyes and a pretty neck and lots more besides. I have lots of important bits of paper. These are some of them.

I will let Camino fade and soon, now that four days have passed, I will stop crying and see things differently. I am packaging up the little felt hearts that I brought home. Tiny strands of moss, minute grains of granite have to be picked out of the threads of some with a stubby fingernail. I have posted pictures of them on Facebook.

'Awws such a beautiful thing to do, Alison, thank you so much. We were thinking of you,' came back one reply.

I posted one for Linda. 'This little heart is for you. I think it was lost somewhere on the Camino by someone speeding ahead of me but I picked it up,' and she replied that she was touched and would treasure it.

The real rushes of adrenalin, dopamine, serotonin, oxytocin and maybe some stirred up oestrogen and testosterone fade along with the spirits and imaginings of the Way of St James and I will look backwards, as if from a high, breezy summit, resting with a refreshing swig from my bottle and a sun-beaming, slightly wrinkly brown smile. I will be looking to see just how far we have all come and what we have dropped along the way. When walking backwards up a hill, you are still going in the right direction.

I went into work in Aberdeen today. Out of my home by the grey sea. Out into the grey world. I carry the shining smiles of pilgrims with me and know I always will. On the train, I closed my eyes a moment and felt, as I know I can anytime, the rough, cold stone of a granite cross in Portomarín against my back, under my buttocks, against my thighs and instead of the sound of chattering commuters and metal mechanisms moving, I heard the sound of the wind in the trees above the great Minho rustle the drying leaves as the weather, and I, thought of changing – for the better.

Past the harbour. Past where excavations beneath the granite and the Mither Kirk have revealed fifteenth-century pilgrim skeletons clutching treasured scallop shells and women tortured for witchery, wombs and wisdom. Past the statue to the Gordon Highlanders who fought across Galicia to escape the Peninsula at Corunna, just like me. Past the windy mercat cross, round which the witchy women danced in the middle of the shining flagstoned square.

There was a homeless guitarist busking badly. There was a neon-haired couple there in each other's arms under a rainy archway. There was a wee lassie, unsupervised, extracting some-thing juicy from a nostril. There's a plaque on the wall for some forgotten revolutionary. There was a group of performance artists capturing sound and word and walking miraculously slowly to better take in the world – step, step and step. I walked an inch or so with them outside my office door and took a while to do so. Back to getting up people's noses. I have a red felt heart and a large shiny acorn in my suit pocket and there are many treasures hidden at home.

---

20 October 2018
On this day two years ago I finished writing this book of treasures…
I thought.

One week later they finished operating on me to save my life.

Two weeks later they opened me up again to save my life.

Three weeks later they cauterized my nostril and stopped me from bleeding out.

One month later they gave me a fifty per cent chance of living out 2021. If I was operable. If I had chemotherapy. If I was strong enough to take the poison.

I went home and waited and while I waited I painted. I painted because:

I couldn't do anything else but sit and think and I couldn't let myself think.

Because I have always painted to fill my time and now time was long and slow and started in darkness not sunny meadows.

Because I wanted images to focus on and control but I don't have any to worship. I had to create my own icons. Painting them became my ritual.

I painted wolves because dogs were my nightmares.

I painted salamanders because they are magic survivors of fire and I found them on Camino.

I painted apples because my mum said I had a strong core.

I painted wild cherries from the gean tree my mother sits under, skin as fragile as a butterfly, visceral love for her children her strength in her ninetieth summer. I painted out my response to that love: my wish to live beyond her.

I painted Little Red Riding Hood as Madonna because her cloak is a symbol not of virgin fragility but of the power of an ordinary, plucky girl to beat the wolf. If we believe that we must turn to saints or angels, gurus or messiahs, the reincarnated or supernatural, we are telling ourselves that we are incapable without them – and so that is what we become. I believe in absolutely nothing but the power of human beings and with their brilliance, love and generosity I painted myself brave. I can do anything I want. So can you.

I painted female bodies because I have a scar that runs from saggy breast to balding pubis by way of squint belly button, I wear a leaky bag of hot shit on my tummy, my cunt is dry and nothing of me is toned and honed, yet for all that I know that I am beautiful – without any man telling me so (though they do, in several languages).

I painted inexpertly in styles inspired by Aborigines and Mexicans, Islamic calligraphers and early Renaissance men, Spanish surrealists and fairy-tale illustrators because I was looking for a language of words bigger than my own since mine felt pathetic.

I painted because I wanted to scream but I didn't have words I could trust.

I painted astounding ideas in astonishing colours because that came easily to me and I saw no value in it because it met no one's expectations.

I painted golden yellow roads because Camino had taught me how to go on living.

Because of Camino 2015 I took one step at a time and didn't try to see over the next summit. Because of Camino 2015 I knew that I could overcome challenges that had previously been unknown to me. Because of Camino 2015 I knew how lucky I have been to have had so few misguided moments and to have faith in my own strong core. Because Camino 2015 was the way it was, not the way I hoped it would be, I faced whatever came round the next bend with calm.

All my regrets had been trodden out and into the gravel of the Way to Santiago.

One month after starting chemo I postponed Camino from 2017 and started sixteen fortnightly cycles of intravenous chemotherapy.

    One month after that I dismissed a friend who said I should exhibit my paintings – then another, then another. Ignoring them, I kept on painting – a picture every one to three days for a year without stopping – whether I was in hospital plugged into chemo or sitting in my living room in my jim-jams. And I am still painting – captured images from Camino: the white dog in the river, the gentle white horse, the lady with the butterflies walking in the forest, the dandelion and the salamanders, the red fish from the market and restaurant.

    Six months ago, The Way Through Project opened. A dozen people invented it and with the help of dozens more raised the funds which initiated it and, as I got stronger, created it with me. Now they and hundreds of others from all over the world can join me on this journey through life – by way of touring exhibition and poetry and music and installation and photography and street art.

    A man who looked like a wolf wearing a lamb's fleece waistcoat came to my winter village with his crew and filmed me with the waves around me as my ileostomy bag leaked and my legs wobbled. He made an award-winning elegy of my story, magic of my wolf paintings projected against the lobster shed and tears in the eyes of my neighbours. A bright, sweet South African stranger bought a painting, made me a dress and became 'Robin', my fellow pilgrim. My paintings became tools for speech therapy and youth work, bereavement counselling and palliative care, child psychotherapy and creative writing.

I met a cancer survivor in Lavacolla two days out of Santiago on Camino 2018 who will take my Way Through book to his hospital in Birmingham. I wrote my Way Through website into the sands at

Fisterra and in a book in a barn on the hills above Portomarín. At Santiago airport, it went off to Miami with a lady we had met in the Tuna's audience and it went off to Finland with a pilgrim at the dinner table in Morgade. Way Through books and paintings and prints have gone to Shetland and Sheffield, Dundee and Dunoon and Sydney, Australia. The experience of Camino – with all its pilgrims walking with their pebble burdens, the experience of being one of those surviving cancer, of painting myself brave and sharing my artistic output as a story of value for others – all of these are steps on one continuous journey.

In 2015 as I walked from Arzúa I cried for the creative girl who had taken a different path and never found the courage to go public with her self-expression. It is not cancer that changed my life but this whole story.

On this day in 2017 I was told that I have no trace of cancer and my ileostomy is irreversible. I started planning Camino 2018.

I sold paintings of the golden road, the apples which decorate it and the duendes and wolves that haunt it. I was commissioned to paint a Way Through on a wall in the city and collaborated with others so that local people could make and leave a pebble there. Painting kept me and they looking straight ahead to where we want to go. With the proceeds, I headed off again onto the Camino road exactly three years after I set off the last time. One year after I came off chemo I walked the same miles but this time on my own terms.

I am not the woman I was. I took it slower and with more respect. I walked with Robin, a sweet soul with legs nearly as short as mine and a mind as wide open, who searched amongst the trees just as I did and sensed the presence of the duende. The wolf hounds were silent as we walked by. Robin told me what they were thinking and I learnt to speak dog.

And once I reached Santiago this time we went on, down to the sea. I had carried a pebble with me – a special pebble I made from fused glass. It represents my wish to walk better beside my siblings in these last years of our mother's life and had been a focus of this Camino. I had thought to leave it on the hill above Preguntoño but I never found that place again this time.

A blaring sermon from across the fields had broken my mood and focussed my mind on who my siblings are and what it is they need of me if I am to walk calmly down this last terrible road, as I have been doing on this Camino. I had considered throwing the pebble off the cliff by Fisterra's lighthouse, shedding any silly sibling issues from my life with finality, but it felt too brutal an act.

With the end of my pilgrimage so evident at my feet, I considered taking my pebble home to the North Sea. At the last moment, I saw that the colours I had mixed in a workshop in Scotland mirrored the colours of the rock pool on the Costa del Morte. I thought of our childhoods finding treasure in pools like these.

I left our pebble there to be brushed by the tide and made to fall as shelter for a hermit crab or anchor point for an anemone. I left it with a determination to concentrate more on the common ground between my siblings and I and went off to wash my tired feet in the vastness of the Atlantic and was done. I have walked backwards. I have found my way through with no Apostle to guide me and I am now walking above and beyond. Leave me under your pillow on the road if you like. I will be just round the bend.

---

28 October 2018

Steel blue sliced through the incensed darkness of the chapel of San Pelayo and the organ wept. Snow came to the hills of Spain and its chill beneath the monastery door scissored my skin. November approached. Time to go home. Ever-present belly ache responded to the unseen musician's expert fingers – I know the true meaning of gut-wrenching. I left the memory there for ever in the dusty darkness.

Later that morning, granite glistened wet under the thrumming wheels of the suitcase on Santiago's paving stones and the minstrels' chocolate eyes smiled as I passed, lifting their glasses to wish me well, waiting for another evening. The little jet shop was closing down for ever and in the seafood stalls, the red fishes stared unblinking from their boxes, their eyes, like the jet-seller's, imperceptibly clouding.

I waited for him on the corner of the market, near the university where it had all begun forty years before. Only when the plane lifted above the deep green forest where pilgrims crawled in ant lines did my tears come. Not for him but for the more exquisite and bewitching tumbledown villages, the crack of acorns falling, the song of robins in apple trees, the soft purr of a fishing boat, the deep voices singing, the wagging of white dog tails, the delicious red fish, the prickle of cologne in my nostrils. The space ahead of me where my true self walks with yours.

ACKNOWLEDGEMENTS

Well here it is. And it wouldn't exist out here beyond the drawer under my bed without first of all Emma Myatt who sent me along to Mearns Writers where Alistair Lawrie worked his magic on my first stabs. Thanks too to Jakki Shylan, Katie Berker and April Bofill Shanly, who read and fed back on the first version of the whole manuscript, and Zoe Ross and Karelia Wright who helped so much with the final structure. Thanks to Guillermo Caldera for translating Gallego words. Thanks to Angela Joss, Maggie Hepburn, Charlotte Tuesday Rochford and Gerard Rochford for their encouragement too. Thanks to Laura Kincaid for proofreading services and more and to Chris Hegharty of Random Ninja Productions for the photography, patience with the IT and all of the Way Through Project including its website https://www.waythroughart.com.

As always, my endless love and gratitude for my inspiring daughter and patient husband who does everything around me as I sit here tap-tap-tapping on my laptop (when I am not covering the house with paint). Right at the foundation of it all though, beyond my sister and my big brother who set the bar so high, my thanks go to my wonderful mother, Enid Elizabeth Gauldie, and my late father, William Sinclair Gauldie CBE, who filled our beginnings with the written word and painted image, as well as with love.

GLOSSARY

Castilian is the language most know as 'Spanish'. It is the language of Castile, including the Spanish capital, Madrid.

Gallego is the language of Galicia, the region of North West Spain in which Santiago de Compostela lies.

Catalan is the language of Catalunya, or Cataluña in Castilian.

Al-Andalus	Arabic	Moslem Spain which gave its name to the region of Andalucía
amigo	Castilian	friend
Ana y los Lobos	Castilian	Ana and the Wolves
bisabuela	Castilian	great-grandmother
bota	Catalan	portable wine pourer made from goat's stomach, for sharing straight to throat
buen	Castilian	good
butifarra	Catalan	white Catalan sausage
cami	Catalan	way, path, road
camino	Castilian	way, path, road
Camino Francés	Castilian	the pilgrimage road from French border
capilla	Castilian	chapel
castro	Gallego	a pre-Roman fortified village
chutzpah	Yiddish	nerve, audacity

clase superior	Castilian	top class
conquistadores	Castilian	Conquerors (specifically in Americas)
Convento de la Merced	Castilian	Convent of Mercy
Corunna	English	the Anglicisation of La Coruña (Castilian)/A Coruña (Gallego); famous for battle in Peninsular War/Spanish War of Independence
costa	Castilian	coast as in Costa Brava (wild coast)
couchette	French	a railway carriage with non/semi-private sleeping accommodation
Cuba libre	Castilian	free Cuba; a drink of rum and Coke
décimo	Castilian	ten cent coin in pre-Euro Spain
Día 6 de Diciembre, Día de La Constitución	Castilian	6th Day of December, Day of the Constitution
duende	Castilian	spirit, elf, hobgoblin
El pueblo unido jamás será Vencido	Castilian	the people united will never be defeated
Escocesa	Castilian	Scottish (female)
excitado	Castilian	aroused, excited (sexual connotations)
Facultad de Filologia	Castilian	Faculty of Philology
Finis Terrae	Latin	end of the land/earth
Finisterre	Castilian	end of the land/earth
Fisterra	Gallego	end of the land/earth
flibbertigibbet	Scottish	a silly flighty person
gean	Scottish	wild cherry tree

guapa	Castilian	gorgeous, pretty (adj. or noun) (female)
hasta la vista	Castilian	until we see each other again
haugh	Scottish	low flat land beside sea or river
hola	Castilian	hello
hórreo	Gallego	a traditional produce store
Hospital de los Reyes Católicos	Castilian	Hostel of the Catholic Monarchs
huerta	Castilian	a garden for fruit, vegetables etc. amongst others in fertile land; similar to an allotment; often walled
igualmente	Castilian	equally; the same to you
Inglesa	Castilian	English (used to mean British) (female)
Jaume	Catalan	James
Jo també soc adultera	Catalan	I also am an adulteress
joder	Castilian	to fuck
Manchego	Castilian	from La Mancha, an area of Castile; a cheese
mariposa	Castilian	butterfly
me encanta	Castilian	it enchants me
meiga	Gallego	a red-eyed witch or wise woman
meseta	Castilian	flat tableland of central Spain
Mither Kirk	Scottish	Mother Church; main church
nervioso	Castilian	nervous, excited
O Pozo	Gallego	the well
paella	Castilian	technically the dish in which rice dishes are cooked; complex saffron rice dish, the most famous version being Valencian with seafood

pain perdu	French	French toast; fried egg-soaked bread
pan i tomat	Catalan	bread and tomato (bread or toast is rubbed with beef tomato, salt and olive oil)
Parador	Castilian	a luxury hotel in a historic building
paseo	Castilian	a short walk, a turn-around-the-block; at *la hora del paseo* (*paseo* time) Spaniards of all ages and types go walking round the village square catching up with friends and neighbours, being seen and often stopping for a pre-dinner drink
pensión	Castilian	accommodation with basic facilities
peregrina	Castilian	pilgrim (female)
pesetas	Castilian	pre-Euro Spanish currency
Picos de Europa	Castilian	Peaks of Europe (first sight of continent)
preguntar	Castilian	to ask
pueblo	Castilian	people; village
queimado	Gallego	an alcoholic drink of burning spirit
ria	Gallego	firth; broad estuary
Sagrada Familia	Castilian	Holy Family; Antoni Gaudí's famous Basilica in Barcelona
Santa Compaña	Gallego	Holy Company; procession of undead
saudade	Gallego/ Portuguese	nostalgia; homesickness; longing
Señora	Castilian	Madam, Mrs

tomar una copa	Castilian	to have a glass (of brandy or similar); to enjoy a social drink with someone
tortilla de patatas	Castilian	Spanish potato omelette
tostados	Castilian	toast
triste amor	Castilian	sad love
Ultreia et Suseia	Latin	Further up and further on
Weegie	Scottish	Glaswegian, person from Glasgow

BIBLIOGRAPHY AND
FURTHER READING

Hopper, Sarah C., 2006, *Mothers, Mystics and Merrymakers: Medieval Women Pilgrims* (Stroud: The History Press)

Lorca, Federico García, 1967, *Lorca*, selected and translated by J. L. Gill (London: Penguin Books)

Neruda, Pablo, 1995, *Love: Poems from 'Il Postino'* (London: Harvill Press)

www.csj.org.uk/the-present-day-pilgrimage/thoughts-and-essays/2000-years-of-the-pilgrimage/

https://albertosolana.wordpress.com/la-aportacion-de-la-arqueologia/

http://www.metmuseum.org/toah/hd/pilg/hd_pilg.htm

https://albertosolana.wordpress.com/santiago-zebedeo-entre-la-historia-y-la-leyenda/

https://en.wikipedia.org/wiki/1976_Spanish_political_reform_referendum

https://en.wikipedia.org/wiki/Camino_de_Santiago

http://www.everyculture.com/Sa-Th/Spain.html

https://en.wikipedia.org/wiki/Dominic_de_la_Calzada

http://www.bing.com/videos/search?q=Garcia+Lorca+video&view=-detail&&&mid=19AE388C867F30BB828719AE-388C867F30BB8287&rvsmid=5CB6E8833112071EE4B-25CB6E8833112071EE4B2&fsscr=0

http://www.poetryintranslation.com/PITBR/English/CanterburyTalesVI.htm#_Toc163145570

https://en.wikipedia.org/wiki/To_Be_a_Pilgrim

http://www.poemhunter.com/poem/caminante-no-hay-camino/

http://lyricstranslate.com/en/lestaca-stake.html

http://www.duendeart.org/

http://d.lib.rochester.edu/camelot/text/history-of-that-holy-disciple-joseph-of-arimathea

http://www.mcfarlandpub.com/excerpts/0-7864-1953-9.Chapter2.pdf

https://www.theosophical.org/publications/1555

http://www.studiocleo.com/librarie/jung/essaymain.html

http://www.iberianature.com/material/wild_nature_sites/wild_galicia/galicia_nature.htm

https://www.youtube.com/watch?v=blK3IF51B0M

https://artsymbol.wordpress.com/tag/charlemagne/

http://countrystudies.us/spain/23.htm

http://www.galiciaguide.com/Culture-gallego.html

http://www.wsws.org/en/articles/2003/10/lorc-o11.html

http://www.nabasque.org/old_nabo/Pages/gernika_tree.htm

https://en.wikipedia.org/wiki/In%C3%AAs_de_Castro

http://www.atlasobscura.com/places/tomb-of-ines-de-castro

http://www.pilipalapress.com/galicia.php#people_culture

http://www.telegraph.co.uk/news/worldnews/europe/spain/6743915/Spain-apologises-for-jailing-homosexual-in-the-1970s.html

https://www.youtube.com/watch?v=ee_iLexM55E

https://en.wikipedia.org/wiki/Trasgu

https://en.wikipedia.org/wiki/Santa_Compa%C3%B1a

http://www.ccel.org/g/gibbon/decline/volume1/chap2.htm

http://www.iep.utm.edu/greekphi/

http://www.english.illinois.edu/maps/scw/farewell.htm

http://spartacus-educational.com/SPibarruri.htm

https://en.wikipedia.org/wiki/Beaker_culture

https://en.wikipedia.org/wiki/Maria_Pita

Printed in Great
Britain
by Amazon